So Spoke the Uncle

So Spoke the Uncle

Ainsi Parla l'Oncle

by

Dr. Jean Price-Mars

Translation and Introduction

by Magdaline W. Shannon

Three Continents Press
Washington, D.C.

ISBN 0-89410-389-X
ISBN 0-89410-390-3 (paperback)

LC No: 82-74251

Cover Design by Lyle W. Shannon

Three Continents Press, Inc.
1346 Connecticut Avenue, N.W. Washington, D.C. 20036
3*6*P

First Edition in French: Copyright, Imprimerie de Compiègne, France, 1928.

Second Edition in French: Copyright, Parapsychology Foundation, New York, 1954.

Third Edition in French: Copyright, Editions Lémeac, Quebec, Canada, 1973, (with introduction by Robert Cornevin, Secrétaire perpétual de l'Académie des Sciences d'Outre-Mer).

Table Of Contents

Preface

Price Mars was a versatile man. Trained as a physician, he served his country in many capacities. In the political realm, he was Minister of Foreign Affairs, Minister to France, Ambassador to the Dominican Republic, and a diplomatic representative to other countries. As an intellectual, he was the author of many books, articles, pamphlets, and other publications, and he served as president of the Congress of Black Writers and Artists. In innumerable discussions in Haiti and elsewhere, he stimulated the thinking of those who shared his intellectual and scientific interests.

As Magdaline Shannon points out in introducing her translation of *Ainsi Parla l'Oncle,* one of Price Mars' continuing interests was the dual heritage of Haiti — French and African. In the 1920s and 1930s, this question was of great interest to many Haitian scholars, journalists, artists, and political leaders. Price Mars helped substantially in clarifying the thinking of Haitian intellectuals concerning the nature of Haitian culture. In the long discussions that I had in Plaisance and Cap Haitien with J.B. Cinéas, lawyer, writer, and, later, Justice on the highest court of the land, this subject came up again and again. In his novels, *Le Drame de la Terre,* *L'Héritage Sacré,* and *La Vengeance de la Terre,* Cinéas examined the character of peasant life, and other Haitian writers dwelt on the same theme. In almost endless debates on "the Haitian reality," and on Haitian "identity" ("Who are we — Frenchmen or Africans?"), Price Mars' views were influential. Incidentally, Cinéas came from the North of Haiti, as did Price Mars, whom he greatly admired and always spoke of in superlatives. There was no doubt in Cinéas' mind that Price Mars was the leading intellectual that Haiti had produced.

In 1937, I attended a number of informal discussion sessions in Port au Prince, as well as meetings of the Société d'Etudes Scientifiques. Price Mars was the central figure among the Haitian writers, physicians, lawyers, journalists, office holders (and former office holders), and others — and a few Americans, visitors or persons residing in Haiti, present on these occasions. Among the Haitian intellectuals whom I met through Price Mars were Dantès Bellegarde, former Minister to France and to the United States; Dr. J.C. Dorsainvil, physician and author of *Manuel d'Histoire d'Haiti, Vodou et Nevrose,* and other publications; Dr. Louis Mars, psychiatrist and son of Price Mars; Maurice Dartigue, former Director of Rural Education, and, later, Minister of Industry and Labor; and Dr. Camille Lherisson, physician. Because of his keen intellect, his great store of knowledge, and his delight in discussing a wide range of interests with his colleagues and friends, it was always a pleasure to be in his company.

Price Mars was one of the first to see clearly the nature and significance of the syncretism of African religions and Catholicism in the New World. Like many others who have a strong interest in African cultures and in the Afro-American experience, I have benefited from reading Price Mars' publications, especially *Ainsi Parla l'Oncle,* but also such studies as *Formation Ethnique, Folk-Lore et Culture du Peuple Haitien,* and *Une Etape de l'Evolution Haitienne.* Many colleagues, Haitian, American, and European, found that Price Mars was generous in counseling them in their studies of Haitian history and culture.

In reading *Ainsi Parla l'Oncle* in the original or in this translation, one should keep in mind that the book is based on Price Mars' observations of Haitian life in the first quarter of this century. It would be difficult, if not impossible, to try to supply new anthropological, sociological, and psychological interpretations for all of the topics that he discussed. In her translation, Magdaline Shannon comments on some of the concepts that have undergone changes since the 1920s, for example, new views on magic, animism, "prelogical mentality," and possession trance.

Price Mars was a man of great intelligence, learning, integrity, charm, and achievement. During his lifetime he received many honors, but his work remains relatively unknown. The publication of this splendid translation of *Ainsi Parla l'Oncle* will stimulate interest in the work of a distinguished pioneer in the fields of Caribbean and Afro-American studies. It is truly an event of great importance.

George E. Simpson
Oberlin College

Introduction

Jean Price-Mars

Jean Price-Mars (1876-1969) is considered by contemporary Haitians to have had the most creative influence in Haitian social thought during the first half of the present century. Many white as well as black French and Caribbean scholars regard him as the greatest of Haitian intellectuals because he played a significant role in shaping the new histories and concepts of African culture and racial ideology which were developing in place of the stereotypes prevalent in Western Civilization at the turn of the century. Later, when different interpretations of *negritude* were being discussed many French-speaking black writers would refer to him as the father of this movement, although in no way did Price-Mars ever consider this concept as differentiating the Negro from the rest of mankind. It is, nevertheless, extremely doubtful that many persons in the English-speaking United States, outside of a few social scientists, historians, and scholars of French literature, have ever heard of him much less recognized his intellectual stature despite the fact that the *Académie Française* awarded him special honor for the whole of his work in June 1959.

Part of the reason for this lack of knowledge of Price-Mars and his works stems from our historically racist attitude toward Haitians. The new black nation of Haiti (1804) received little recognition from the United States, its white counterpart in successful rebellion in the Western Hemisphere. Although there was some assistance from President Adams in the early days, Haiti was largely regarded during the first half of the nineteenth century as either a suitable area for the colonization of free American Negroes [1] or much more significantly as a stimulus to rebellion

---

[1] Loring D. Dewey, *Correspondence Relative to the Emigration to Hayti of the Free People of Colour in the United States*, 1824; James Theodore Holly, *A Vindication of the Capacity of the Negro Race for Self-Governemnt* . . . , 1857; James Redpath, *A Guide to Hayti*, 1860; Charles H. Wesley, "Lincoln's Plan for Colonizing the Eman-

amongst black slaves in the United States. Such potential uprisings could upset the Southern plantation economy and social system and quite possibly bring about the disruption of the newly formed republic. During the Civil War it became politically expedient for the North to recognize the small black nation (1862),[2] but concurrent expressions of cultural racism which continued to dominate white Anglo-Saxon society into the twentieth century prevented any acknowledgment of black social and cultural accomplishments or political abilities. In 1915, imbued with strong sentiments of nationalism and of the need for law and order to protect democratic ideology as well as political and economic interests in the Caribbean area, the United States arbitrarily occupied Haiti, assumed control of its financial structure, and virtually rewrote its political framework at will. The Haitian elites, divided in reaction to these events, accepted what they termed a hopeless situation.

Price-Mars had foreseen the crisis which might befall the Haitian elites. He perceived that they had become entrenched in the belief of their intellectual superiority as "colored Frenchmen," especially since the French historian Jules Michelet had referred to 19th Century Haiti as "Black France." As a group the elites believed that Haitian greatness lay in considering their nation as a "spiritual province of France" and in denying their African-Haitian background.[3] Nevertheless, though they felt themselves superior to the illiterate Haitian peasant they were proudly aware that the political heritage of all Haitians surpassed that of American blacks. Price-Mars, as the head of the Haitian mission to the St. Louis World's Fair in 1904 and in a trip through the Deep South to Tuskegee Institute, had himself experienced the treatment accorded to Negroes in the United States.[4] Such racist attitudes had only strengthened his primary resolve to refute the widely accepted theories of the French scholar Gustave Le Bon, who posited the inferiority of the black man and condemned any hybridization with the superior white.[5]

cipated Negroes," *Journal of Negro History*, IV, January 1919, pp. 7-21; *Annual Report of the Secretary of Interior, 1863*, p. XVIII.

[2] Rayford W. Logan, *The Diplomatic Relations of the United States with Haiti, 1776-1891*, 1941, p. 303.

[3] Jean Price-Mars, *Ainsi parla l'Oncle*, 1928, (*So Spoke the Uncle*, p. 8) and *Lettre ouverte au Dr. René Piquion: le préjugé de couleur est-il la question sociale?*, 1967, p. 6.

[4] Jean Price-Mars, *La vocation de l'élite*, 1919, (Reprint, 1976, pp. 179, 198-200). See also Dantes Bellegarde, "Hommage à Price-Mars," *Témoignages sur la vie et l'oeuvre du Dr. Jean Price Mars*, 1956, pp. 6-10, hereafter noted as *Témoignages*.

[5] Gustave Le Bon, *Les lois psychologiques de l'évolution des peuples*, 1894.

Just prior to the occupation of Haiti in July 1915, Price-Mars had been appointed as Haitian minister to Paris. Upon his return home in late 1916 he sought to reactivate the morale of the immobilized elites. With the assistance of close friends who were aware of his ability to persuade through the spoken word, he organized a series of conferences in which he reminded the elites of their duty as leaders and guides in safeguarding the historical and legal basis of Haiti and chastized them for conceiving of themselves as "colored Frenchmen." In attempting to ignore the existence of Haitian Voodoo as beneath their intellectual dignity, he told them they were like ostriches hiding their heads in the sand. He applied to such actions the term of "collective bovaryism" because they were envisioning their society as other than it was. He appealed to them instead to act "as Haitians" who should appraise the values of their historical traditions and societal heritage realistically and who as elites should instruct all of their countrymen to be proud of their indigenous culture. In 1919 he published these lectures in collective form in *La vocation de l'élite.*[6] In December of 1920 he held his historic conference on "Haitian Folk-lore" at the Cercle Port-au-Princien and introduced the subject of Voodoo at length for the first time in public. From that moment, according to critics, he won the respect of the intellectual milieu at home and in France.[7]

By this time Price-Mars was also committed to studies that would reveal the fallacies in prevailing racial theories. It was his contention that scientific objectivity and historical fact would upset the racial hypotheses of Le Bon. Through an ethnological and historical examination of African origins and of the factors influencing cultural growth and change in the New World environment he believed it would be possible to demonstrate that the development of a socio-cultural system that was uniquely Haitian and of a political community governed by Negroes was merely a process of growth that occurred in any societal group. By elevating the pride of Haitians in their folkloric past and racial competence, Price-Mars hoped to encourage a national spirit that would weld intellectual elites and illiterate peasants together and to inspire Haitians as a whole to resist oppression of any kind. Any occupation by a foreign power, in this case the United States, symbolized subjection and was regarded

6   Price-Mars, *op. cit., Préface,* pp. I-IV, and the specific conference, *La vocation de l'élite* held at Port-au-Prince, Saint Marc, and Cap Haitien in December of 1917, pp. 55-90.

7   Jean Fouchard, "L'ecole nationaliste Price-Mars," *Témoignages,* pp. 177-181.

as a barrier to the development of a people and a race.[8] His comprehension of cultural dynamism, derived from Durkeim,[9] enabled him to conceptualize Haitian Voodoo as a syncretized religion of African animism and of Roman Catholic beliefs, rather than as the generally accepted manifestation of fetishism, magic, and sorcery. In such context, he contended, Haitian Voodoo became an expression of the total community rather than of a particular class and ought to unite rather than separate elite and peasant. Price-Mars also favored the establishment of night schools and centers of arts and trades including experimental agricultural plots in order to reduce illiteracy, to form good work habits, and to develop the potentiality of the peasants. Using the pedagogical precept of Pestalozzi,[10] "from the known to the unknown," he pushed for the use of Creole in the elementary schools as a transition to French in the higher courses of instruction. Again, he blamed the elites for perpetuating a dual language system which deprived the lower classes of the benefits of communication media — the press, cinema, and radio. Thus the direction of the systematic argumentation by Price-Mars was toward ending internal divisiveness. He sought to raise the national morale through the recreation of pride in indigenous cultural and political achievement and thus to unite Haitians in their efforts to cope with the problems of a nation in adjusting to the modern industrial world. To emphasize and demonstrate the efficacy of the integrative cooperation of all social classes in order to reach these desired goals, he pointed (as he himself had witnessed) to the success of collective associations — religious groups, trade corporations, and mutual aid societies — of Negroes in the United States and to the example of Tuskegee as a partial solution to the educational problems of Haiti.

Price-Mars devoted his own energies toward attaining these ends. From 1912-1915 he served as Inspector-General of Public Instruction. He cooperated with Catts Pressoir, Pauleus Sannon, and J.C. Dorsainvil in founding the Haitian Historical and Geographic Society in 1922 and was its president from 1932 through 1947 as well as one of the principal editors of its bulletin.[11] As Professor of History and Geography in the

[8]   *Ibid.*
[9]   Emile Durkheim, *Les formes élémentaires de la vie religieuse,* 1912.
[10] Johann Heinrich Pestalozzi, *Wie Gertrud ihre Kinder lehrt,* 1801, and *Schwanengesang,* 1826. Price-Mars is referring to the fundamental Pestalozzi doctrine known as *Anschauung.* Please see Annotated Bibliography.
[11] Maurice A. Lubin, "A Giant Dies — Leader of the Haitian Thought," *Negro History Bulletin,* 32, October 1969, pp. 16-18.

reputable Lycée Alexander Pétion from 1918 to 1930, he endeavored to give inspirational direction to Haitian youth on the secondary level. He would accept no other position under President Borno (1922-1930) whom he opposed.[12] Meanwhile he began daily explorative excursions on horse among the peasants in the surrounding countryside, administering to their medical needs regardless of remuneration and questioning them about their customs, beliefs, and practices.[13] From daily notes, absorption of new social scientific theories, reactions to the conferences, and discussions with fellow-intellectuals came his classic effort — *Ainsi parla l'Oncle* or *So Spoke the Uncle* — in 1928. It was his evaluation of the Haitian folkloric past and contemporary customs (early 1900's) based upon ten years of contemplative thought and the accumulation of factual evidence. This was followed in 1929 by *Une etape de l'évolution haitienne*, an inventory of Haitian literary, scientific, and historic glories, intended to fortify national and racial pride, and an essay, *La renaissance nègre aux Etats-Unis*,[14] emphasizing the success of American Negroes in lifting themselves from the condition of "slave days" to grudging admiration by the larger American society of their scholarly, literary, and artistic abilities by the 1920's. Price-Mars advised the Haitians, especially the elites, to do the same, to "Plonges vos baquets!" ("Cast down your buckets!") into the rich resources of the Haitian community. These initial efforts of Price-Mars were partly a response to the injunction of Le Bon to write a book about Haiti. When the Haitian intellectual had confronted the French scholar in Paris in 1915 as to the inconsistencies of his racial theories he had argued that it was preposterous to hypothesize that only the defects between two races of dissimilar character were inheritable or capable of being transmitted and it was inconceivable to engage in a theorizing that attempted to explain "the psychological mechanism of the behavior of part of mankind . . . by illusory and fanciful data." It only revealed in that scholar "a frivolity incompatible with the seriousness of the subject and the strictness of scientific methods."[15] The studies of French scholars, as Arnold van Gennep and Roger Bastide, would affirm in particular the timelessness of the Price-Mars study of

[12]   *Ibid.*
[13]   Price-Mars had received his doctorate in medicine in July, 1923. See Emile Paultre, *Essai sur M. Price-Mars*, 1966, p. 38.
[14]   *Negro Renaissance in the United States — An Appreciation* also appeared in August-September, 1929, in the English section of the Haitian daily newspaper, *La Presse*.
[15]   Leon G. Damas, "Price-Mars: The Father of Haitianism," in Albert H. Berrian and Richard A. Long, eds., *Negritude: Essays and Studies*, 1967, pp. 24-38, (quote, p. 29).

Voodoo and confirm its religious character while the German scholar Janheinz Jahn would refute the popular idea of Voodoo as "mass madness" and corroborate the belief and teaching of Price-Mars that Haitians had developed an independent culture which had some African survivals but was a continuously living one of which Haitians could be proud.

The efforts of Price-Mars did reawaken Haitian self-confidence and pride in themselves. In 1927 the *Revue Indigène* began systematically to renounce slavish literary imitation. The newly formed *Griot* group, led by Louis Diaquoi, Lorimer Denis, and François Duvalier, espoused a "return to African roots" to discover their ethnic and historical origins and thus understand Haitian realities. A Haitian literary renaissance slowly emerged. The works of the "Three D's" as well as those of Carl Brouard, J.B. Cineas, the Marcellin brothers, and Jacques Roumain recreated, according to Price-Mars, "the picturesque and dramatic life" as well as the mystic faith of the Haitian peasant which was a blend of African animism and Christian beliefs bringing "charm and honor" to his life but also leading to "passive submission" to the inevitable and inexorable misfortunes that befell him.[16] Many students were encouraged in another direction to undertake a scientific exploration of African civilization and its residuals in Haitian folklore in the new Bureau of Ethnology founded in 1941 by Jacques Roumain. Price-Mars, founder of the Institute of Ethnology in the same year, was its president until 1947 and occupied the Chair of Africology and Sociology. Meanwhile, aspects of the message of Price-Mars were spreading elsewhere in the Caribbean and in the larger world. In Paris in 1932 the West Indian Etienne Léro edited the *Légitime Défense*, short-lived because of its subversive character. In 1934 the Martinican Aimé Cesaire and the French Guianan Léon Damas joined hands with the French-speaking African writers led by the future President of Senegal, Leopold Senghor, to launch the more moderate *L'Etudiant Noir*. Both journals reminded the elite of their proper vocation of cultivating the values of their race and of being one with the people by instructing them in their traditions. They believed, in their interpretation of the spirit of Price-Mars, that their new-found pride in *Mother Earth* (Africa) would not foment racism but bring closer cooperation with the progressive-minded West to attain a "universal consciousness."[17] Thus began the movement which Cesaire termed

[16] Jean Price-Mars, *Préface* to *La montagne ensorcelée* by Jacques Roumain, 1931, pp. 9-13.

[17] Damas, *op. cit.*; Abiola Irele, "Negritude or Black Cultural Nationalism," *Journal*

negritude. Price-Mars was unanimously chosen President of the First Congress of Black Writers and Artists held in Paris in 1956 and again at the Second Congress in Rome in 1959, and became the first president of the African Society of Culture, the permanent organ issuing from these meetings. At the age of ninety, in 1966, he was brought to the African Guinée to be acclaimed once more by President Ahmed Touré at Conakry and by President Senghor at Dakar as "the imcomparable Master."

In the political arena, Price-Mars was elected senator from the Department of the North after the Haitian National Legislature was restored in 1930. He was one of the candidates for both the provisional and the permanent presidency of the re-established Republic as the United States prepared to withdraw from Haiti according to the Forbes plan, but was defeated.[18] In 1935 he and ten other Senators were ousted from the legislature because they opposed the policies of President Stenio Vincent. But in 1941 Price-Mars was returned to the Senate through presidential appointment by Elie Lescot. He served as Ambassador Extraordinary and Plenipotentiary to the Dominican Republic from 1947 to 1949. In the latter year he was delegated Ambassador of the Haitian representation to the Organization of the United Nations in San Francisco and was president of the Haitian group in 1950-51 and again in 1955-56. Throughout his active public career he was a leader of many diplomatic missions: to Prague, Geneva, and Paris in 1932, to Havana in 1942, to Washington, Chicago, Baltimore, Boston, and New York in 1943, to Honduras and Mexico in 1946, to Washington in 1947, and to Sao Paulo in 1953. He was installed as Rector of the University of Haiti in 1956, made Minister of Foreign Affairs in 1956-57, and served as Ambassador Extraordinary and Plenipotentiary to Paris from 1957 to 1959. Upon his return he retired from public service and was awarded a pension for life, equivalent to that of a Chief of State, by President Duvalier.

As Price-Mars approached his eightieth birthday in 1956 he was showered with honors and affectionately regarded as the *Uncle* portrayed in his classic work. Price-Mars was now himself the old man to whom all listened, the Father of all those who lived around him. On the occasion of his birthday an impressive number of testimonials to his ac-

of *Modern African Studies*, 3, October 1965, pp. 321-348; Donald E. Herdeck et al, eds., *Caribbean Writers*, 1979, pp. 323-324, 349, 427.

[18] Magdaline W. Shannon, "President's Commission for the Study and Review of Conditions in Haiti and its Relationship to Hoover's Foreign Policy," *Caribbean Studies*, XV, January 1976.

complishments came from renowned scholars in Europe, Africa, and the Americas.[19] Price-Mars continued to speak out and publish. By his death in early 1969 he was the author of a dozen major books or pamphlets and innumerable articles, biographies, critical essays, and reports. His two-volume *La République d'Haiti et la République Dominicaine* (1954) is still regarded by critics as an excellent intellectual analysis of Haitian-Dominican relationships. While his literary critiques of studies of national institutions and the social structure of Haiti by American social scientists such as Ludwell Montague, James G. Leyburn, and Melville Herskovits were generally praiseworthy in tone, he did not hesitate to point out certain fallacies in their interpretations with a persuasive reasoning.[20]

Lettre ouverte au Dr. Piquion (1967), his last major effort before his death, is essentially a summation of his thoughts on the social question of color in Haiti. Particularly he resented the intimation of Dr. Piquion that he, Price-Mars, had lost his chance for the presidency because of his failure to exploit the color question to his advantage. Not only, he answered incisively, was his whole lifestyle predicated on disparaging the use of color for personal benefit but most of all he was deeply indignant at being considered as one of those individuals who would do so. In fact he perceived his presidential defeat as a blessing, for the Haitian political period which followed the American Occupation had convinced him that no Haitian, including himself, was prepared to lead the Haitian republic in a practical and democratic demonstration of justice, liberty, and social progress. Thenceforth he had devoted his capacities to the development and the implementation of that cause. His last book, *Antenor Firmin*, appeared posthumously in 1978.

The public efforts and literary contributions of Price-Mars brought strong repercussions in Haitian political and social life. Correspondingly in Haitian-American relationships he was instrumental in the formation of a group which opposed foreign occupation. Both Haitian and American resistance organizations succeeded in convincing governmental agencies of the United States that forceful occupation was not an advisable or necessarily fruitful type of foreign policy to adopt toward weaker and smaller nations. Although the stronger and more developed countries

[19]   *Témoignages*, 1956. See also *Bulletin de l'Académie des Sciences Humaines et Sociales d'Haiti*, No. 4, 1977. It is dedicated to the centenary of the birth of Dr. Jean Price-Mars.

[20]   See, for example, Jean Price-Mars, "Caste ou classe?," a study of *The Haitian People* by James G. Leyburn, 1941, *Revue* de la Société d' *Histoire et de Géographie d'Haiti*, XIII, July 1942, pp. 1-50.

continued thereafter to relegate Haiti to a minor role in world affairs, the disposition of the Western world to stratify cultures by race and color was slowly and gradually being modified and transformed. Price-Mars lent the effective energies of his long productive life to help bring about this change of opinion. Primarily, he had demonstrated that history is a continuous societal process based on the accommodation of folkloric past to changing behavioral patterns, irrespective of color, and that therefore the role of the black man is an integral and consequential part of the history of civilization. Though perhaps Haiti was not yet ready for his reform measures, his persistent voice stirred black men to hope in themselves, to strive for an identity, and to achieve realistic maturity of thought in the process. One begins to realize the enormity of his effort when one considers that his concepts had developed and matured in a country concerned historically with the liberty and dignity of the black man but which, from the moment of its independence, had been ill-loved, ignored, and worst of all judged as of little human consequence by her fellowmen in either the Old or the New World.

So Spoke The Uncle

I

The opening sentence of the book is "What is folk-lore?" It was a term just coming into use in the intellectual world around the turn of the century.[21] Price-Mars seeks to familiarize his readers with the word so as to popularize its use. His ambition is to rehabilitate Haitian folklore in the hope, as he states in the preface, "of restoring the value of Haitian folk-lore in the eyes of the people."[22]

Through this framework Price-Mars methodically refutes the racial theories of Le Bon historically, ethnologically, and biologically. His argumentation is sustained by personal research and reference to the current literature. He emphasizes the contribution of the African past to the contemporary Haitian social structure. He concentrates on the evolution of Voodoo, emphasizing its religious nature throughout, from the animism of prehistoric Africa to a synthesis with Christianity in modern Haiti so as to demonstrate the strength of folkloric custom in the gradual development of the culture of a society.

[21] See William J. Thoms, in the *Annotated Bibliography* following the translation.
[22] *Preface, So Spoke the Uncle*, p. 7.

Introduction

As the reader progresses through *So Spoke the Uncle,* he becomes aware that the author's perspective of society is quite broad. He is not narrowly absorbed with Haitian problems and difficulties but is attuned to the larger world attitudes toward racial and societal capacities. The annotated bibliography which follows the translation is intended to reveal the breadth of sources used by the author, many of which he did not include in his bibliography. Price-Mars was quite familiar with concurrent theoretical sources in ethnology, anthropology, and sociology and with the new detailed studies describing and analyzing the geography of Africa and the diversity of its peoples with their corresponding mores and customs. The authors in these different fields of inquiry were instrumental in disproving or challenging prevailing notions of society and its physical world, particularly in what was so popularly known as the "Dark Continent." Price-Mars makes us aware of the new framework of thought amongst social, medical, and physical scientists as he progressively explains not only the historical glories and the problems of modern Haiti in the hope of encouraging his fellow-elites to regroup and to join as well as lead their more unfortunate countrymen in a national effort, but more importantly he is emphasizing how folkloric patterns of Haitian experience fit into the schema of societal behavior. The resultant Haitian cultural design is but one of the many different but viable and integrative parts of the whole historical process of human development.

As one can readily see, Price-Mars leans heavily on the works of French authors since they were the leaders at the time in social-scientific theory and exploration. He selects Marcellin Boule because he links geological, archaeological, and paleontological phenomena. To develop his conception of Voodoo as a religion he relies on Alexander Le Roy's explanation of popular beliefs, Salomon Reinach's thorough history of religions, cults, and myths, and Emile Durkheim's recognition of religion as being closely integrated with the structure of society especially in "collective representation" or "symbolic systems." In dealing with the history and culture of ancient Africa, Maurice Delafosse, Joseph Deniker, and the American historio-sociologist W.E.B. Du Bois emphasize the social phenomena of the different types of man bringing about ethnic groupings based upon community of language, religion, and social institutions regardless of specie, race, or variety. Though Price-Mars did not accept Levy-Bruhl's concept of the "prelogical" nature of primitive men it is clear that he is in agreement with both Levy-Bruhl and Durkeim in that to understand the processes by which institutions are established man cannot study the "adult civilized white man" merely as an individual but must base his conclusions upon the collective representations which are common to the members of a given social group and are transmitted from one generation to another.[23] Through the meticulous study of the mind in different types of human societies, through the comparative approach to the study of human social institutions, and through the consideration of primitive thought as part of a single body of human tradition (Sir James Frazier) there would be shown to exist a similarity of institutions among peoples. Sir Harry Johnston's studies, for example, stressed the similarity of tales not only amongst African countries but among European groups, especially the Low Germans and Walloons.

Price-Mars does not accept the popularly used term "Dark Continent," as accurately describing the African scene. Rather, various African regions differ in degree of cultural development because of the extreme variance of astronomical, geographical, biological, and orographical conditions not only within Africa but in relation to exterior areas. He believes that there was "a close relationship between the habitat of races and the stage of their civilization."[24] Physical environment, economic possibilities, and religious inspiration became principal factors in the development of material and moral prosperity and were conducive to the creation of highly organized political and cultural entities. Furthermore he emphasizes the dissimilarity of African types which developed, rather than their homogeneity. Some, he says, produced high civilizations and these were usually in more temperate zones. Amongst the so-called primitive peoples he believed that adaptation to environment was molded more by physical forces which established an "equilibrium of action and reaction between man and nature," rather than by the degree of intelligence. These physical forces were more pronounced for example along the extreme southern borders of the Sahara in the densely forested areas and tended to block intercourse with other peoples in Europe, Northern Africa, and Western Asia, thus restricting the flow of new ideas and stimulation of the intellect.[25] Amongst the diverse groups of Africans who became slaves in Saint Domingue those with highly cohesive political, religious, and familial systems, as in Dahomey (Benin), were apt to be the leaders in

[23] Lucien Levy-Bruhl, *How Natives Think,* Translation by Lilian A. Clare, 1926, pp. 13-14.
[24] See *So Spoke the Uncle,* p. 55.
[25] *Ibid.,* pp. 74-78, (quote, p. 74).

syncretizing the old African world with the new life in America.

In explaining the evolutionary process of Haitian culture Price-Mars stresses the special language of Creole developed between slaves and masters of colonial Saint Domingue, the stirring legends built upon the deeds of martial heroes in their struggle for liberty and political independence, and the development of a syncretized religion. Because, he explains, the greater number of Negroes imported to Saint Domingue as slaves belonged to the linguistic family of Bantus it was possible for those of different tribes and regions to communicate with one another. Forced to accept Christianity, forced to adapt to the white man's tongue, forced to economic livelihood under subhuman conditions, they drew closer to one another and developed a common language and a syncretism of beliefs which permitted religious meetings in which leaders wielded religious and political power simultaneously, much as they had done in their African tribes, particularly in Dahomey. It is interesting to note here that Price-Mars is in agreement with the English-speaking Africologists of the time, including W.E.B. Du Bois, that Voodoo is a New-World phenomenon rather than an African survival.

After assessing Haitian folklore and literature, Price-Mars adds a final chapter which is actually an address given in 1922 to the young women of the exclusive Primavera Club in Port-au-Prince. It is already clear in this lecture, as Jacques Antoine states, that Price-Mars no longer sees the black man as just Haitian, but rather as African. "The black man of the United States and the black natives of Africa are no longer his brothers. They have become his very self."[26] Likewise he wants his works to be larger than the Haitian world itself. They are intended "to go into the mainstream of civilization for the benefit of the Black Race and the general progress of mankind as a whole."[27] It is evident that the author wishes not only to leave us with a specific picture of Haitian peasant life as it occurred in the early twentieth century but also to re-emphasize clearly in this concluding chapter the division in Haitian classes, the imbecility of French imitation by Haitian intellectuals, and their shame of an African past disparaged by Western Civilization. He is directing

[26] Jacques C. Antoine, *Jean Price-Mars and Haiti*, Washington, D.C., 1981, p. 140. This is the first book in the English language about Price-Mars. The author is Haitian, a personal friend of Price-Mars and who often worked in close association with him. In recent years Antoine was Professor of Literature at Howard University. He believed that Price-Mars had the unique ability to analyze the national problems of Haiti and to suggest the appropriate remedies for them.

[27] *Ibid.*

his plea to the elite Haitian youth that they may take heed, gain pride in themselves as equal to all other members of the human genre, and he hopes that this generation of the American Occupation will remedy these enervating conditions through a rejuvenation of Haitian nationalism based on pride in their folkloric past.

While earlier publications of Price-Mars had served to arouse the elites at crucial moments in the American occupation of Haiti, the response to *So Spoke the Uncle* was even more startling and intense. There were many esteemed and erudite Haitian scholars, particularly J.C. Dorsainvil and Arthur Holly in the field of Voodoo and Dantes Bellegarde and Pauleus Sannon in Haitian history. But no one of them had attached their beliefs "to a cultural nationalism" and presented it "as a base of resistance against the American oppressor" as Price-Mars had done.[28] Even after Haiti again became politically independent the controversy over the cultural theories presented by this classic would continue.

Those Haitian intellectuals who felt that Price-Mars was reproaching them personally immediately defended themselves as being genuine Haitians while others, quite validly, attacked the loose wording or generality of his concepts. Arthur Holly reproached him for his inattention to Protestant viewpoints and Catts Pressoir pointed out his propensity to moralize though he claimed to present a scientific approach.[29] Somewhat later the Abbé R.P. Foisset, typically representative of the Catholic theological viewpoint at the time, objected vigorously to the stress upon an ethnological-religious thesis rather than the traditional Christian explanation.[30] In his three-volume work on Haiti, J. Verschueren identified Price-Mars as a sympathizer and admirer of the cult of Voodoo and therefore was skeptical of his ability to treat the subject impartially.[31] Dantes Bellegarde, a lifelong respected friend of Price-Mars

[28] Emmanuel C. Paul, "Taches et responsabilitiés de l'ethnologie," *Revue de la Faculté d'Ethnologie*, Series III, December 1958-Jan/Mar 1959, pp. 11-19.

[29] Arthur Holly (pseud. Her-Ra-Ma-ël) was respected for his esoteric knowledge on the subject of Voodoo. He was the author of *Les daimens du culte Voudo*, 1918. Catts Pressoir, "Ainsi parla l'Oncle," *Le Nouvelliste*, October 20, 22, 23, 1928.

[30] R.P. Foisset, "Ainsi parla l'Oncle," *La Phalange*, May 26-30, 1945, and "Le folklore," *La Phalange*, December 30, 1948. The reply of Price-Mars is in "Ma réponse à l'attaque de M. l'Abbé Foisset," *Haiti Journal*, June 18-21, 1945.

[31] J. Verschueren (pseud. for Op-Hey, Henri), *La République d'Haiti*, 3 vol., 1948, (Vol. III, pp. 379-381). See also Henock Trouillot, "La pensée du Docteur Jean Price-Mars," *Revue de la Société Haitienne d'Histoire, de Géographie et de Géologie*, 29, July-October 1956, pp. 59-60; Jean Price-Mars, "Sociologie religieuse, Essai critique," *Revue*

but a staunch partisan of the French rather than the African heritage, questioned him on the concepts of culture and civilization as defined by Latin and Anglo-Saxon societies and called for a more detailed and specific explanation of how he would establish a Haitian culture which would blend the crude traits of four-fifths of the Haitian population with those of a minute but more advanced intellectual group.[32] Though Emile Paultre faulted Price-Mars for his generalization, he was quick to add that it was precisely the patriotic and critical spirit of Price-Mars which had rejuvenated Haitian literary efforts and had succeeded in reviving the national conscience by denouncing the collective bovaryism of those intellectuals lost in extravagant hypotheses and denial of ethnic origins. Through the Institute of Ethnology he was also continuing to produce evidence of an indigenous culture.[33]

Rémy Bastien, Haitian anthropologist and recognized authority on modern Haitian society, believed that Price-Mars tended to show the life of the peasant as an idyllic, gentle one and ignored the precarious nature of his day-by-day struggle for survival and his proclivity to depend upon the power of magic as a panacea. Price-Mars and his disciples were inclined to simplify the basic societal problems of Haiti by holding up the elite as the scapegoat. They neglected to formulate a feasible economic program that would take the place of "archaic structures or agricultural practices," one that would stimulate peasant production and eliminate the battle of privileged versus non-privileged classes of whatever color. The Price-Mars school had not really served national development. Too late, says Bastien, did Price-Mars, in his *Lettre ouverte au Dr. Piquion* (1967), urge his compatriots to unite and forget their own political and social sin of color prejudice. Nonetheless he concedes, "If today we find weaknesses in *Ainsi parla l'Oncle*, it was nevertheless a gallant attempt at objectivity, an objectivity tainted, of course, with legitimate nationalism and a will to rehabilitate Haitian culture and its African heritage."[34]

de la Société Haitienne d'Histoire et de Géographie, 19, October 1948, pp. 1-21.

[32] Paultre, *op. cit.*, pp. 63-64; Trouillot, *op. cit.*, p. 49; Lorimer Denis and François Duvalier, "La civilisation haitienne (Notre mentalité, est-elle africaine ou gallo-latine?)," *Revue Anthropologique*, 46, October-December 1936, pp. 353-373, (Paris).

[33] Paultre, *op. cit.*, pp. 72-73, 128. See also Antoine, *op. cit.*, pp. 85, 112-113, 170-174.

[34] Rémy Bastien, "The Role of the Intellectual in Haitian Plural Society," *Annals of the New York Academy of Sciences*, 83, January 1960, pp. 843-849. See also the following articles by Bastien: "Ideologie, recherche et développement," in Emerson Douyon, ed., *Culture et développement en Haiti*, 1972, pp. 121-130, and "Social Anthropology: Recent Research and Recent Needs," in Vera Rubin and Richard P.

But Price-Mars had a particular faculty for assessing and evaluating the Haitian situation of his era in both a local and a world-wide context which most of his confreres would admit made him the unique incomparable Master. He had the disposition of placing himself "au carrefour" as the Haitians say, ("at the crossroads") where ideas, beliefs, or cultures converge, enabling him "to study the evidence and to seize the psychological and sociological significance of Voodoo." He had the ability "to observe things and men, to penetrate their most intimate thoughts and their collective inclinations."[35] Above all, Price-Mars was a thinker and one who was able to project an innovative idea in such a compelling manner that people listened, thought, and responded whether negatively or in complete accord. Although he had no advanced degrees in the social sciences, he presented an original concept, that of a national folklore which would instil pride of cultural and racial achievement in Haitians. He succeeded in arousing his fellow intellectuals to self introspection and to action regarding Haitian nationalism and he gave the youth during the American Occupation a new hope — the development of Haitianism. As Leon Laleau says, *Ainsi parla l'Oncle* became ". . .à la fois arme et bastion. L'arme ultime et le dernier bastion du dernier assaut" against the foreign invader.[36] The word "folklore" had stimulated a national pride in Creole and Voodoo. *Ainsi* was "the first attempt to explain the Haitian religion and customs through African origins."[37] *Ainsi* must be regarded as epochal, as an extraordinary book for its time not only because of its "valorization of Haitian folklore, but because it presented the past grandeur of Black Africa."[38] This was a viewpoint that differed entirely from the popular notion of a primitive Africa and one that has been authenticated by contemporary writers of the western world, including African, to the present day. Yet, as Auguste Viatte notes, Price-Mars did not adopt a wholly African perspective that excluded classic and Christian contributions but rather sought a synthesis of these approaches which would be enriched by the acumen of the common genius.[39]

Schaedel, eds., *The Haitian Potential*, 1975, pp. 11-16. In answer to Bastien please refer to the quoted words of Price-Mars, p. xiv and footnote 16 of this introduction.

[35] Trouillot, *op. cit.*, p. 23.

[36] ". . . both weapon and bastion. The ultimate weapon and the strongest bastion of the final assault," Leon Laleau, "Ainsi parle un neveu . . .," *Témoignages*, p. 15.

[37] Robert Cornevin, "Jean Price-Mars (1876-1969)," *Introduction*, Third edition of *Ainsi parla l'Oncle*, Montreal, 1973, p. 41.

[38] *Ibid.*, p. 37.

[39] Auguste Viatte, *Anthologie littéraire de l'Amérique francophone*, Sherbrooke,

Price-Mars regarded the concept of race as a myth,[40] and perceived Voodoo as a religion. His attack upon racism and his defense of Voodoo as a folkloric pattern served not only to unite Haitians but to affect the rigid condemnatory attitudes of much of Western Civilization. Though Haitians experienced American racism and imperialism first-hand, Price-Mars was attentive in pointing out to them the practical and technological aspects of the American and British systems. Haitians in response did not completely reject the humanistic tendencies of the French culture and institutions but instead turned to their own African past, more specifically to the folk culture of the Haitian peasant. Price-Mars was their intellectual leader and guide. American social scientists who became interested in Haitian society in the 1930's, as Herskovits, Simpson, Leyburn, and Ludwell L. Montague, relied upon this encompassing study of Price-Mars to make precise and knowledgeable statements about the Haitian people to the English-speaking world. In the ensuing decades however American blacks were interested in winning their own battle for human rights. It was not until the late 1970's that the United States populace really became aware of the island of Haiti. It is for this specific reason that the remarkable book by Price-Mars written in 1928 is being introduced in an English version to the American public in the hope that it will erase the old stereotypic notions of the Haitian world. As Coulthard has noted, "Writers like Antenor Firmin, Hannibal Price, Claude McKay, George Padmore, Jean Price-Mars were in the vanguard of the revaluation of African culture long before the nationalist awakening in Africa and before the concept of *négritude* was developed in the Caribbean."[41]

And finally, Roger Bastide stresses that Price-Mars is a pioneer of the most contemporary research. Though Price-Mars is ambiguous at times he has true scientific objectivity. While he was not the first to utilize the idea of syncretism he saw its different aspects clearly through cultural dynamism. He envisioned the possibility of fusion of color or class differences through social dialectics — in the case of Haiti a national conscience or community. Because he viewed Voodoo, the religious expression of the rural masses, as cultural instead of pathological, his descrip-

Quebec, 1971, p. 429; "L'oeuvre de Price-Mars dans son cadre mondial," *Témoignages*, pp. 66-67.

[40] Jean Price-Mars, *Préface* of Lorimer Denis, François Duvalier, and Arthur Bonhomme, *Les tendances d'une génération,* Port-au-Prince, 1934, pp. I-X.

[41] G.R. Coulthard, *Race and Colour in Caribbean Literature,* London, 1962, p. 117.

tions of its vitality in community life are of undeniable historic value.[42]

II

I have endeavored to follow the literary style of Dr. Jean Price-Mars, not just because *Ainsi* was written in the early years of the twentieth century but also to portray as faithfully as possible the distinctiveness of the flow of words and phrases which characterize his writing. No attempt has been made to translate freely and loosely into the present-day vernacular, to employ current terminology, or to utilize modern social science or medical phraseology. The word *Negro* is retained because it was in use during the era in which *Ainsi* was written. The footnotes have been preserved in their original form except where a printing error or misspelling of an author's name had occurred or in an attempt to follow a consistent structural pattern. Wherever clarification or additional information seemed prudent, in either the text or the footnotes, the explanation or correction is included in brackets at the appropriate place or in additional bracketed notes.

In *Ainsi parla l'Oncle* there are several French words for which I have chosen a particular meaning. For example, *l'âme* could refer to *mind, soul, spirit, sentiment*, but "mind" seems to represent the context of thought most accurately. In like manner the italicized English word was selected for the following French terms:

le culte — *cult*, religion, worship

la maladie — *malady*, disorder, sickness, disease

le Vaudou — *Voodoo*, Vodû, Vodou, Vodoun, Vodûn

Because the world "cult" may raise visions of such modern traumatic occurrences as the Jonestown episode in Guyana, I ask the reader to refer to the lucid explanation of the meaning of "cult" presented by Simpson in *Black Religions in the New World* (1978) on pages 12-13. In the case of *la maladie*, I would have personally preferred "disorder" but believe *malady* is of such broad nature as to be less likely to provoke debate.[43] After much deliberation and thought, I chose to translate *le Vaudou* as *Voodoo*, though this English word seems to be objectionable to Professor

[42] Roger Bastide, "Le Dr. J. Price-Mars et le Voudou," *Témoignages*, pp. 196-202; and "Price-Mars et le Vaudou haitien," *Présence Africaine*, 71, 3rd Quarterly 1969, pp. 19-23.

[43] For all intrinsically medical terms used throughout the text I consulted *Dorland's Illustrated Medical Dictionary*, 1975.

Simpson and most probably is to all of his colleagues who have completed extensive research in this field.[44] While I respect their concern I am taking the liberty of differing with them, and in the following paragraphs I offer my explanation for doing so.

In his preface to *Life in A Haitian Valley* (1937), anthropologist Melville J. Herskovits expressed the hope that the use of the term Vodûn (meaning "gods" in ancient Dahomey) to describe the religious beliefs of the Haitian peasants would replace the word *Voodoo* used by popular American writers in the first part of the twentieth century. Although the English author Sir Spenser St. John had employed *Vaudoux* in his work in 1880, he emphasized the sensational aspects of these Haitian beliefs and distorted the facts just as did the later American writers such as Seabrook, Wirkus, Craige, and Taft. The American sociologist James G. Leyburn followed the example of Herskovits in *The Haitian People* (1941), while other anthropologists used various spellings as Vodû, Vodou, Vaudou, Vodoun, and Vodûn.

Dr. Price-Mars uses *Vaudou*, I believe, because he wishes to distinguish the Haitian variant from similar African beliefs and practices. He quotes from Moreau de St. Méry, one of the most reliable early sources (1797), who states that *Vaudoux* as it exists in Saint Domingue is not just a dance but is a religious cult. Other Haitian writers however do employ the other terms, while French authors seem to prefer *Vaudou*. The English translation of the term as in Alfred Metraux's *Le Vaudou Haitien* (1959) is *Voodoo in Haiti*; Roger Bastide's *African Civilizations in the New World*, translated from the French (1971), uses the spelling *Voodoo*. The social psychiatrist Dr. Louis Mars, son of Price-Mars, has an English translation (1977) of his study on "possession" entitled *The Crisis of Possession in Voodoo*. American historians, such as George Tyson, Jr., *Toussaint L'Ouverture* (1973), and Thomas O. Ott, *The Haitian Revolution* (1973), use *Voodoo* as does also the British political scientist David Nicholls in his articles and in *From Dessalines to Duvalier* (1979). Similarly the Haitian-American scholar Michel Laguerre chooses *Voodoo* and unlike the assessment of the Belgian priest J. Verschueren in 1948 seems to have had no compunction in assigning Voodoo to an important role in the Haitian social and political state in his recent works. The English translation of Janheinz Jahn's *Muntu* (1961) from the German language refers to Haitian *Voodoo*. Finally, the Library of Congress in its National Union Catalog employs *Voodoo* to identify the

[44] See *So Spoke the Uncle*, Footnote 14, p. 36.

subject in reference to foreign works.

Thus, one of the most compelling reasons for selecting *Voodoo* for the French word *Vaudou* in this translation of *Ainsi parla l'Oncle*, the classic study so long unrecognized in the English-speaking world, is that it is the word that Americans seem to have adopted for better or for worse despite efforts to eradicate its pejorative meaning by using the original variants of the term. Hopefully those who read *So Spoke the Uncle* will be persuaded by Price-Mars that *Voodoo* is the viable English word to describe a religion that evolved over centuries from African derivatives syncretized with Catholic beliefs to serve the needs of Haitians, as slaves and as citizens, in the New World.

As has been noted earlier, little is known presently in the United States about Jean Price-Mars and his activities to kindle a national pride in Haitian elites and peasants in an effort to regain political independence. He appealed to the intellectual class to appreciate and glory in their African historical as well as their French cultural past. Both had affected and shaped societal experiences in the New World forming an indigenous or Haitian culture. He insisted that it was the duty of the more fortunate elites to act as the leaders of Haiti and to assist the peasants in enjoying the benefits of the society. Together they would prove that the predominantly black Haitian nation could be as capable as any other, even an American one. It is for this reason that the *Académie Française* gave special honor to Price-Mars, as Leon Damas says, "not only as a writer but also as a man, especially for his courage, his mettle, and for that intellectual honesty which he has never ceased to display in the interest of the triumph of ideas not long since regarded as subversive."[45] It is hoped that this English translation of *Ainsi parla l'Oncle* will accurately portray his approach to undermining cultural racism and will support his central belief that "all men are man."[46]

All of the photographs which appear in this translation have been reproduced from the original edition of 1928.

I would like to extend my grateful appreciation to George E. Simpson for his meticulous reading of the translation and his valuable suggestions for its improvement — especially the addition of notes identifying the changing theories and interpretations of contemporary anthropological research. His prompt and lengthy replies to my queries were a source of tremendous inspiration to me. I am most honored that

[45] Damas, *op. cit.*, p. 30. See also Maurice Lubin, *Haiti et Culture*, 1974, pp. 44-54.
[46] Victor Hugo. See Jean Price-Mars, *Lettre ouverte* . . . , p. 6.

he has consented to write an introduction to *So Spoke the Uncle,* as he was one of the very few American scholars who knew Price-Mars personally and who recognized that *Ainsi* was indeed a classic.[47]

It is with equal gratitude that I thank Jean Fouchard, dean of Haitian historians and intimate friend of Price-Mars, for his contribution to understanding the argumentation of Price-Mars and for a frank appraisal of Haitian sentiment toward him during and after his long and varied lifetime.

I owe much of course to the family of Price-Mars, to his daughter Mme. Marie Madeleine Price-Mars and to his son Dr. Louis Mars[48] and his wife Madeleine for their sincere hospitality, for their invitation to do research in their homes and the private library of their father, and without whose unfailing courtesy, patience, and assistance I could not possibly have understood the nuances of the writing of Price-Mars.

Throughout our visits to Haiti since 1968 Dr. J.B. Romain, Dean of the Faculty of Ethnology and Director of CRESHS has graciously made us feel most welcome and has extended himself to support and aid us in our search for the pertinent data.[49] Likewise, Brother Lucien and Brother Constant have always endeavored to locate primary sources and information in the library of St. Louis Gonzagues in Port-au-Prince, data which are for the most part unavailable in the United States.

I appreciate the assistance of Nancy Turner in the first stages of translation of the French work into English. And not only do I wish to thank my husband Lyle for his invaluable and timely sociological suggestions which have lent depth to my evaluation and analysis of *So Spoke the Uncle* but most of all for his continuous support of my efforts and his unflagging faith in my abilities to accomplish this task.

Magdaline W. Shannon
Iowa City, Iowa
April, 1983

---

[47] George E. Simpson, "Au Dr. Price-Mars," *Témoignages,* 1956, p. 48.

[48] Louis Mars, *The Crisis of Possession in Voodoo,* 1977, translated by Kathleen Collins from the French, originally published in 1946; "Une nouvelle étape dans la réflexion sur les théolepsies en Haiti," *Cahiers des Religions,* X, July 1976, pp. 203-210. Please see also footnote [15] in *So Spoke the Uncle,* pp. 134-135.

[49] Jean Baptiste Romain, *Quelques moeurs et coutumes des paysans haitiens,* 1959; "Jean Price-Mars ethnologue," *Conjonction,* 110, 1969, pp. 3-7; "Introduction au Vodou haitien," *Conjonction,* 112, 1970, pp. 3-17. CRESHS is *Le Centre de Recherches en Sciences Humaines et Sociales.*

So Spoke the Uncle

Ethnographic Essays

A Mademoiselle Marguerite Brunot,
Homages Respectueux
P.M.

Table Of Contents

the Habbès. The Mossi of the Sudanese plateau and among the Dahomeans on the coast of Guinea.

The great majority of the Haitian people are a rural community. The religious sentiment of this rural mass. The importance of the African contribution in the formation of its religious thought. Colonial Voodoo. Its evolution. Contemporary Voodoo and its principal manifestations: the dance, the trance or ecstacy ("les lois"). Scientific study of the phenomenon. The Voodooistic sacrifice and the sacrifice in other religions. Voodoo and Catholicism. Voodooistic syncretism. Ville Bonheur and its miracles. Comparisons drawn from ancient Christianity and the death-struggle of paganism from the third to the fourth century.

Folk-lore and literature. Is there a Haitian literature? Folk-loric matter and the work of art. Poetry, Fiction, Music. The Haitian writers and folk-lore.

The peasant family. Local mores and African survivals. Establishment of a family in a rural community: Kenscoff. Peasant mores relative to marriage. Marriage in Greco-Roman antiquity. Types of marriage in Africa. Conclusion.

Preface

We have nourished for a long time the ambition of restoring the value of Haitian folk-lore in the eyes of the people. This entire book is an endeavor to integrate the popular Haitian thought into the discipline of traditional ethnography.

Through a disconcerting paradox, these people who have had, if not the finest, at least the most binding, the most moving history of the world — that of the transplantation of a human race to a foreign soil under the worst biological conditions — these people feel an embarrassment barely concealed, indeed shame, in hearing of their distant past. It is those who during four centuries were the architects of black slavery because they had force and science at their service that magnified the enterprise by spreading the idea that Negroes were the scum of society, without history, without morality, without religion, who had to be infused by any manner whatsoever with new moral values, to be humanized anew. And when under the protection of the crises of transmutation given birth in the French Revolution, the slave community of Saint Domingue rebelled whilst reclaiming the status which no one thus far had recognized, the success of its demands became all at once a difficulty and a surprise for it — the difficulty, unacknowledged moreover, of the choice of a social order and the surprise of adaptation by a heterogeneous mass to the stable life of free work. Evidently the simplest choice for the revolutionaries badly in need of national cohesion was to copy the only model that they comprehended. Thus, for better or for worse, they inserted the new grouping into the dislocated framework of the dispersed white society and this was how the Negro community of Haiti donned the old frock of western civilization shortly after 1804. From that moment with a constancy that no defeat, no sarcasm, no perturbation has been able to weaken, she tried her utmost to realize what she believed to be her superior destiny in shaping her thought and sentiments, by drawing closer to her former mother country, by copying her, and by identifying with her. What an absurd and grandiose task! A difficult task, if ever there was one!

But it is this curious approach that the metaphysics of [Jules] de Gaultier[1] calls collective bovaryism, meaning the faculty of a society of seeing itself as other than it is. Is this not a strangely productive attitude if this society finds within itself the incentive to a creative activity that elevates it beyond itself because then does not the faculty of conceiving itself as other than it is become a stimulus, a powerful motor which urges it to overthrow obstacles in its aggressive upward path. Is this not a singularly dangerous course if this society, dulled by impedimenta, blunders in the ruts of dull and slavish imitations, because then it does not appear to bring any tribute to the complex play of human progress and will serve sooner or later as the surest pretext for nations impatient for territorial expansion, ambitious for hegemony, to erase the society from the map of the world. Despite spurts of recovery and flashes of clairvoyance, it is by the use of the inferior approach to the dilemma that Haiti sought a place among peoples. The chances were that her experiment would be considered as devoid of interest and originality. But, by an implacable logic, as we gradually forced ourselves to believe we were "colored" Frenchmen, we forgot we were simply Haitians, that is, men born of determined historic conditions, having collected in their minds, just as all other human groups, a psychological complex which gives to the Haitian society its specific physiognomy. Since then all that is authentically indigenous — language, customs, sentiments, beliefs — have become suspect, tarnished by bad taste in the eyes of elites smitten with nostalgia for the lost mother country [France]. With very strong reason the word Negro, formerly a generic term, acquired a pejorative meaning. As for the term "African," it has always been, it is the most humiliating affront[2] that can be addressed to a Haitian. Strictly speaking, the most distinguished man of this country would much prefer that one find him to bear some resemblance to an Eskimo, a Samoyed, or a Tunguse rather than remind him of his Guinean or Sudanese ancestry. It is imperative to see with what arrogance some of the most representative figures of our milieu evoke the efficacy of some bastard relationship. All the turpitudes of colonial promiscuities, the anonymous shame

[1] [Jules] de Gaultier replaces M. [Monsieur] de Gaultier for sake of clarification.

[2] The French expression *apostrophe* which is used in the original text has no equivalent in English that seems to convey the intensity of meaning. *Apostrophe* can mean interpellation, reproach, challenge, slap-in-the-face, affront bringing shame, and so on.

of chance encounters, the brief pairings of two paroxysms have become titles of esteem and glory. What can be the future, what can be the worth of a society where such aberrations of judgment, such errors of orientation are transformed into constitutional sentiments? A hard problem for those who reflect and who have the task of meditating on the social conditions of our milieu! In any case it will appear to the reader how temerarious was our venture of studying the value of Haitian folk-lore openly with the Haitian public. Our audacity will seem even clearer when we confess that we conceived of the plan for this book originally in the form of popular lectures. In fact, we offered the lure of two conferences on the part of the subject that we thought would most appeal to the public love for the new and the different. For others we judged it more advisable to retain the form of a monograph. Then, we modified the original plan and we reunited all the essays in this book. We confess without hesitation that the whole mass of folk-lore, the modalities of popular beliefs, their origins, their evolution, their actual practices, the scientific explanations which flow from this system have been the problems that have most sharply activated our research. That is why they have been given a more important place in this volume. Are the solutions to which we have subscribed definitive? We are far from claiming this. The scientific world is eternally worried that the conclusions of the study of biological phenomena based upon the most recent methods and acquisitions of science will be considered as other than tentative. At least we are striving to utilize the most learned works possible in aiding us to comprehend the essential modalities of our subject. We hope that others will plough the same furrow and spread even more seeds . . .

But, one may ask, what purpose is served in going to so much trouble over minute problems which interest only a small minority of mankind living on a very small part of the earth's surface?

Perhaps this is reasonable.

We will take the liberty, however, of doubting that either the exiguity of our territory, or the small numbers of our people, problems which concern the behavior of one group of men, are sufficient grounds to warrant the indifference of the rest of humanity. Besides, our presence on a point of the American archipelago which we have "humanized," the breach that we have made in the process of historic events in order to secure our place among men, our fashion of utilizing the laws of imitation in order to make ourselves model borrowers, the pathological deviation which we have inflicted through collective bovaryism by conceiving of ourselves as other than what we are, the tragic uncertainty that such a step stamps on our evolution at the moment when imperialism of every order disguises its lusts under the appearance of philanthropy, all of this gives a certain configuration to the life of the Haitian society and, before darkness falls, it is not futile to collect the facts of our social life, to assess the gestures, the attitudes of our people, however humble they may be, to compare them to those of other peoples, to examine their origins, and to situate them in the general life of man on the planet. They are the evidence, the deposition of which cannot be negligible in judging the value of a part of the human species.

Such is, in last analysis, the essence of our venture and whatever may be its reception, we wish that it be understood that we are aware of its inadequacy and its precariousness.

Petionville, December 15, 1927.

Jean Price-Mars

Chapter I

So Spoke the Uncle

1

What is folk-lore?

Our response to this question will be drawn in part from the numerous scholarly works which have brought such renown to Paul Sébillot and to which he has dedicated the most patient research and keen insight.

Sébillot states that, according to William Thoms, the term folk-lore is composed of two Saxon words, "folk-lore," literally folk meaning people, and lore meaning knowledge, that is: the lore of the people, the knowledge of the people.[1]

"It is difficult to explain," continues William J. Thoms, "which branches of knowledge ought to be included under this generic title. The study of folk-lore has been extended well beyond that of its original conception. In a large sense it can be said that it holds a position in the history of a people corresponding exactly to that which popular unwritten law occupies in regard to codified law, and it can be defined as unwritten history. Moreover, it is the unwritten history of primitive times. In the course of the development of civilization many of the ancient manners, customs, observances, and ceremonies of the past were rejected by the upper social strata of society and gradually became the superstitions and the traditions of the lower classes.

'It can be said that folk-lore encompasses all the 'culture' of the people concerning strange and unrefined customs, superstitious associations with animals, flowers, birds, trees, local objects, and with events of human life which have not been employed in the official religion or history of the civilization; it includes the belief in sorcery, in fairies and spirits,

[1] Paul Sébillot, *Le folk-lore: Littérature orale et ethnographique traditionnelle*, 1 volume, Paris, 1913, [pp. 1-3].

11

the ballads and proverbial sayings that apply to particular localities, the popular names of hills, of streams, of lairs, of burial mounds, of fields, of trees, and so forth . . . , and of all analogous incidents.

"In primitive life, all these things exist not as relics of past times but actually as part and parcel of society itself. Both the relics of civilization and the 'status' of the folk-lore of savage tribes, belong to the primitive history of humanity . . ."

And in circumscribing the domain of the new science, Count de Puymaigre summarized, in 1885, the reasons why it was designated folk-lore: "Folk-lore comprises in its eight letters," he says, "the popular poems, traditions, tales, legends, beliefs, superstitions, riddles, proverbs, in short everything concerning nations, their past, their life, their opinions. It was necessary to express this multitude of subjects without paraphrasing, so we made use of a new word to which we attached such a vast meaning."

So thus is set forth, according to superior references, the purpose and extent of the science which concerns us. But if this purpose as we have just seen, consists above all of collecting and of classifying masses of facts about everyday life in order to reveal its significance, to point out its origin or symbol, if most of these facts reveal a certain moment, a stage of the life of man on the planet, the first tentative and venturesome explanation of the problems that he had to confront; if, on the other hand, they no longer exist in certain societies in a state of survival that marks the depth and antiquity of primitive beliefs, if they constitute, in our opinion, the most disquieting mirror reflecting the probable common origin of all men no matter of what they boast, is it not at this time advantageous to investigate in what possible ways our society could contribute to the enrichment of this part of ethnography and, if such be the case, could we not attempt a brief judgment of the value of such a contribution?

In other words, has the Haitian society a stock of oral traditions, legends, tales, songs, riddles, customs, observances, ceremonies, and beliefs which are its own, or which it has assimilated in a way that gives them a personal imprint, and if indeed this folk-lore does exist, what is its value both in literature and in science?

This is the problem with which we are faced in writing these essays. But as we well know, the multiple aspects of the subject, the abundance of the information, its intricate character, even the newness of the enterprise would handicap our efforts and would bring about certain failure if we had not the firm purpose of limiting our field of action in advance by choosing from the confused mass of material those elements which are representative of our folk-lore.

We are well aware that we are exposing ourselves to reproaches of being arbitrary or of set purpose.

But (is it not true?), according to the word of Leibnitz, if there is no science other than the general, one cannot classify without choosing, one cannot choose without categorizing.

Moreover, two approaches are available to us. Either we can establish a long list of our legends, observances, customs, and so on, giving them detailed descriptions — which would not be without profit but would provoke the sharpest and quite reasonable impatience of the reader — or else we can choose carefully from among those that would appear to have a symbolic or typical character and inquire in what way they are peculiar to us, how they are dissimilar or analogous to those which have been acquired by other societies less civilized or more refined than ours. It is this last method of comparative ethnography that we have adopted, within the limit which we have asserted.

2

We have previously agreed that folk-lore is comprised of the legends, customs, observances, and so forth . . . , which form the oral traditions of a people. As for the Haitian people, we could sum up everything or very nearly so by saying that they are the fundamental beliefs upon which have been grafted or superimposed other more recently acquired beliefs.

All of them are engaging in a harsh and heavy struggle to gain control of the mind. But it is in this domain especially that the conflict assumes different aspects depending upon whether the field of battle arises in the mind of the masses or of the elites. Now truthfully, I do not know which of these two social entities has the advantage in this limited conception if we consider that those in the lower classes accommodate themselves more easily to the world, to the juxtaposition of beliefs, or to the subordination of the more recent to earlier ones, and succeed thus in achieving a quite enviable equilibrium and stability. The upper classes, on the contrary, pay heavily for these primitive states of consciousness which are perpetual causes of astonishment and humiliation for all those who bear their stigma, for neither success nor talent which, combined or singly, can count as traits of distinction marking social hierarchy, serve as obstacles against the possible intrusion of such and such childish and outdated beliefs, and since these demand certain external practices, it follows that the minds which are affected by it suffer from an anguish and a distress often verging on the tragic.

This state of transition and of conflict of beliefs is one of the most curious characteristics of our society. From it stems the terror and the repugnance that we experience in speaking of it in society.

Need I make excuses for this situation? Are we not obliged to submit all of the problems of social life to scientific examination?

And is it not only in this manner that we will succeed in dispelling errors, in mitigating the misunderstandings, in finally responding in a satisfactory fashion to the appeals of our curiosity, so often disconcerted by the inquietude of supposed mysteries?

But before even developing the consequences that arise from the above-mentioned premises, let us arrange the order of questions by giving primary importance to a selection of tales and legends.

Tales and legends!

Does there exist a people who have yielded a richer harvest than ours?

Are you aware of any people whose imagination has invented more drollery, good nature, malice, and sensuality in its tales and legends? And who of us can forget those unending and sidesplitting stories of "Uncle Bouqui and Ti Malice" which beguiled us in our childhood?

Are these tales true indigenous products or are they only vague recollections of other tales and legends which come from periods prior to that of servitude? Were they born on our soil as our own *Creole*, as heterogeneous products of transformation and adaptation determined by contact between master and slave?

Both of these hypotheses are easily defensible and it is possible to discover in the basic elements of our tales remote survivals of the land of Africa as well as spontaneous creations and adaptations from Gascon, Celtic, or other legends.

First, let us look at the framework and the circumstances of the tales we discuss here.

They appeal to the mystery of the night as if to soften intentionally the rhythm of the narration and to place the action in the realm of the supernatural. It is, as a matter of fact, on these clear nights at the moment when "Rabbit is on guard" (as we say in the North, to describe the limpid sky studded with stars), it is at that moment that the proud

Uncle Bouqui.

"storyteller" casts the spell on his audience.

And why is the choice of hour exclusively reserved to nighttime? Is it a taboo? Yes, undoubtedly, because transgression of the rule brings terrible punishment. In fact, it is traditional that a story told in broad daylight can cause you to lose your father or mother or another loved one. But where do we get this taboo? Is it from Africa, is it from Europe?

"The old Basuto (people of southern Africa) claim that if one tells tales by day a gourd will fall on the head of the storyteller or that his mother will be changed into a zebra." This is a point distinctively characteristic of Africa.[2]

But in Ireland also, they believe that it brings misfortune.[3]

To which place then should we look for the origin of our custom? Is it Africa? Is it Europe?

Moreover, we begin our tales with a "cric," to which the audience answers "crac." This tradition comes to us directly from the colonial period. It is very peculiar to Breton sailors and very prevalent in all of Brittany and you know that we had a great number of Bretons in Saint Domingue.

Nevertheless, we must be cautious.

According to the way of slaves, the storyteller also announces his tale with an "alo" to which the audience replies "alo."

Could there not be in our preference for the first mode of expression just a simple substitution of words without an accompanying change of customs?

We believe this without much difficulty because we usually modify the morphology of the tales which we adopt before we act upon their substance. This is why, for example, in order to impose on the storyteller a determined number of stories, another question follows the "cric-crac."

"Time, Time?"

Then, depending upon whether the narrator is more or less inclined to favor the crowd with one or more stories, he acquiesces to the demand by replying: "Bois," or "Bois sèche."

The dialogue continues.

"How many will you tell?"

"None, or perhaps one, two, or several."

It seems that this manner of testing the good disposition of the storyteller is very peculiar to us. In spite of patient research we have

---

[2] Paul Sébillot, loc. cit., [p. 17].
[3] Paul Sébillot, loc. cit., [p. 16].

not found any analogous habits amongst other peoples. This is likewise true of the moral which comes at the end of the story and invariably remains the same: Cé ça m'talé ouè moin tombé jusqu'icite.[4]

"Cric?" asks the storyteller.
"Crac," replies the audience.
"Time, Time?"
"Bois sèche,"
"How many will you tell?"
"Two!"
And the storyteller has offered to tell two tales . . .

3

And now how worthwhile is the substance itself of our tales?

In our opinion it is at the very least extremely diversified. If one makes an intensive study of it, it is not unusual to encounter quite varied literary styles mingling with each other: the epic, drama, comedy, and satire. It appears nevertheless that the last two genre dominate in being more expressive of our state of mind. Moreover, the comic and the satiric aspects of our tales flash forth most often, not in the usual simple and naive plot of the story, but rather in the realism and picturesqueness

[4] This is what I went to find out and this is what I returned to tell you. [Translation of the Creole]

of the characters.

Thus, the projection of the characters will be more or less distinctive according to the ability of the storyteller himself to enliven and intensify their roles. In other words, it is necessary that the narrator play his characters, an aptitude which is difficult to acquire, given the style of complex formation of the personnages. For everything contributes to it, all of nature is the theatre: the sky, earth, men, animals, vegetables, and so forth. These personnages express themselves in parables and in maxims. They assume almost always a symbolic character. Such, for example, is the conception of *Bouqui* and of *Ti Malice*. It has been properly said of these two inseparable heroes that one is the personification of the typical rustic, of unintelligent but sincere Force, while the other is that of the Ruse.

There is evidence of all this in *Bouqui* and *Ti Malice*, but I believe also there is something more. It appears probable to us that, historically speaking, Bouqui is typical of the "nègre bossale" newly brought from Africa to Saint Domingue whose clumsiness and stupidity were the object of frequent bullying and merciless joking by Ti Malice, personification of the "nègre créole" generally considered as more adroit and even a little sly.

Moreover, the term "Bouqui" seems to be a simple deformation of "Bouriqui," a generic name borne by a seventeenth century tribe of the Grain Coast and from which some individuals were brought, through smuggling, to Saint Domingue by the English. It is claimed that they were unmanageable and could scarcely accommodate themselves to the colonial regime.

Could they not have furnished the principal elements of the character of Bouqui by their eccentricities and the unassimilable nature of their temperament so unlike other Negroes promptly mixed into the indistinct mass of slaves?

Could they not have been, because of this, the chosen victims for mockery by the others? Be that as it may, the significance of the symbol must have evolved in proportion as recollection of the colonial regime faded in the popular tradition; and, it is only now that he appears representative to us of a certain force borne of patience, of resignation, and of intelligence, just like the expression which we are able to detect in the mass of our mountain folk.

Then again, Bouqui and Ti Malice could very well be transpositions of the names of animals.

You know what a position animals hold in the formation of the characters of fables, of tales, and of legends all over the globe. Just recall the role assigned to the sly Renard, first-class glutton, past master of deceit, and the poor Baudet, narrowminded and stupid, "hampered by his awkwardness" and yet such a good fellow, which the genius of La Fontaine has drawn from the prehistoric tales of Old Europe and immortalized in his fables.

So! What? You ask if we are about to establish some sort of comparison between such fables and our tales? I see more than just a comparison, there is perhaps a relationship between them!

To begin with, is it not strange that in naming the characters, we peasants of the North call Ti Malice indifferently "Compère Lapin or Maître Ti Malice" [Sly Rabbit or Master Rogue]?

But in addition, have not our brother-Americans also chosen the rabbit or the hare as the symbol of ruse? Over the greater part of the black continent is the hare not considered as the ingenious model of finesse while the antelope characterizes foolishness and simple-mindedness?

Moreover, is it not curious that Sir Harry Johnston, one of the most knowledgeable English Africologists, in his excellent book on Liberia,[5] relates that there is a remarkable similarity of treatment in all the tales where animals are chosen as heroes and that they are retold in all of black Africa from Senegal to the country of the Zulus, from Cape Colony to Egyptian Sudan; that they issue from the same source as the fables of Aesop of the eastern Mediterranean; that there is a striking resemblance in the structure, the choice of subject of the African tales and of the tales of the common people of European countries such as have come down to us through the delightful versions of the Low German and the Walloon . . .

Ah! You see what a glorious heritage our Bouqui and his priceless companion Ti Malice can claim!

Both are the spokesmen of our grievances and of our bitterness, both are indicative of our disposition to assimilate. Do not make too much fun of them and especially do not scorn them. Do not blush either at the foolish frankness of the one, or at the cunning of the other. They are, in their way, what life offers us everywhere on the globe of stupidity, of childish vanity, and of cunning competency. They are undoubtedly representative of a state of mind very close to nature, not at all because they are Negroes but because they have been molded in the

[5] Sir Harry Johnston, *Liberia*, 2 vol., [1906].

most authentic human clay. They should be dear to us because they amused us throughout our childhood, because they still strike the first spark of curiosity in the imaginations of our offspring, and finally because they satisfy within us the taste for the mysterious which is one of the magnificent privileges of our species.

Even though they may be neither the most picturesque creations of the popular imagination, nor even the most pungent expression of its risqué tales, it becomes easy through the assignment of coarse traits to certain of our animals to color the works of fiction of which they are an integral part.

Do you know of the adventure that happened to "Macaque" [monkey] one day?

Perched high up in a tree at the edge of the road, he watched the crowd of peasants making their way to the local market.

All of his sympathy, even a little pity, went to a good woman who was lagging behind the rest even though she was trotting along briskly under her load, because Macaque, quite shrewd, indeed roguish, could see from the beaming face of the peasant that she was counting on making tremendous profit from the enormous calabash she bore on her head.

And what filled this calabash?

That was the question which Macaque asked himself. And his imagination kept running just as the peasant under her load.

Now, just at the foot of the oak where Macaque, perched on high, sought to penetrate human thought, the poor woman stumbled over a stone and suddenly the calabash fell off, broke into pieces, letting the honey it contained run out in golden sheets.

"My God! What misery!" said the peasant in tears . . .

Macaque heard and thought about it.

Of the two expressions he understood only one.

He was well acquainted with the Good Lord, whom he had also praised for having created him, Macaque, somewhat in the image of man, a sort of second cousin so to speak. But until then he did not understand misery.

He descended quickly from his observation post and hurried posthaste to become acquainted with this thing which seemed so precious.

Prudently he sniffed the substance, then tasted it . . .

"The devil! It's succulent!" he said to himself. And at once Macaque resolved to go find the Good Lord so that the Creator could give him a little misery.

He left, walked a long, long time, crossed many a savanna until finally as evening fell,

He arrived before a closed door,
From under which passed a mysterious light,
It was the sacred place, it was the marvelous place.

From behind the door, one heard the hosanna . . .

The angels were stupefied by the daring approach of Macaque.

Since God was in a conference, the Archangel Saint Michael, then chief of celestial protocol, received the august visitor and gave him, on behalf of the Eternal Father, a big heavy sack, charging him expressly and formally not to open it until he was in the midst of one of the savannas he had just crossed.

Macaque, brisk, joyful, left enthusiastically.

As soon as he arrived at the designated spot he satisfied his curiosity.

Horrors!

The sack contained only a dog!

Macaque took off with the speed of lightning. Alas! The dog, a good runner, kept right behind him, warming the hindquarters of the over-inquisitive Macaque with his breath. A race beyond description indeed in its incredible confusion.

Finally, thanks to some skillful maneuvering, Macaque outran the disagreeable guest and reached the home of a Hougan.[6]

"What a relief! Doctor, I beg you, give me something which will permit me to rid the world of this dirty breed which is the race of dogs."

"Imagine this . . ." And he told of his misadventure.

"I am quite willing," replied the hougan. "After all, it is very simple. All you have to do is bring me . . . 'certain such and such' . . . from a dog, no matter which, the first that comes along. You understand, don't you, and before the cock crows three times, I assure you there will no longer be a dog, not a single one, left on the whole planet."

"Is that all? O.K. Let's say it will be done shortly," agreed Macaque.

And immediately, he went into the country.

Two days, then three, then five passed before Macaque reappeared at the home of the hougan, carrying a closed receptacle.

The specialist unsealed it, sniffed the contents and said to his guest:

[6] The hougan is the name of the priest in the *Voodoo* religion. He is at the same time a doctor whom rural Haitians hold in high esteem.

"Listen, my friend, 'this' has an odor I cannot detect. Aha! I am warning you. If 'this' comes from a dog, all dogs shall die, but if 'this' comes from a Macaque, all the Macaques shall die!"

"Just a minute, Doctor, just a minute! . . . Your remark worries me. In truth, I am not certain of the origin of what you have just unsealed. Give me a very small quarter of an hour . . . and I promise to bring you the real thing."

Macaque left anxiously and returned no more. And that is why the dog and Macaque, two brothers in intelligence, are still irreconcilable enemies.

4

And how would I speak, what language would I use, if it were necessary to relate the racy and lecherous adventure of Master Toad [repulsive fellow] engaged and about to be married?

Would it not be necessary that the storyteller understand Latin and perhaps also — the toad being a leg-less cripple according to the tale — that he simulate with a partner the performance of this bizarre couple so that the lascivious rhythm is not spared the audience.

Be that as it may, the tales, despite their delightful character, their awkward and zesty air, only belong after all to a very rudimentary stage of the marvelous. They are by nature neither pretentious nor self-sufficient.

Oh! Indeed our legendary heroes have a higher rank on the scale of values. They take on such an excess of detail and flawlessness in real life, they pride themselves on such a knowing air in the explanation of natural phenomena, that despite the bantering superciliousness with which they treat us, we are hard put to constrain ourselves from instantly attesting to their reality.

Would you like some examples?

Should we explain why man is so diversified around the world while we Haitians are still behind in the pursuit of progress? The legend recounts how one day God, having finished the work of Creation, summoned the White, the Mulatto, and the Negro before his throne and spoke to them somewhat like the following: "Behold, I wish to bestow upon each of you special talents. Express your wishes, I will recognize them immediately." The "Blanc" at once asked to rule the world through wisdom, wealth, the arts, and the sciences. The Mulatto wanted to be just like the White — which really placed him a little behind — but when it came to the turn of the Negro, the conversation became quite comical.

"And you, my friend," said the Good Lord, "what do you desire?"

The Negro, intimidated, stammered something unintelligible, but since the Good Lord insisted, the Negro changed his mind and ended by saying:

M'pas besoin angnin. Cé ac ces Messié là m' vini . . ."[7]

And that is why we are still behind . . .

On the other hand should we stigmatize the imperturbable audacity of Haiti-Thomas,[8] his passion for seeking positions disproportionate to his abilities, his incurable penchant for evil spells? The legend says that the Abbé M . . .,, one of our first indigenous priests, died while curé of Pétion-Ville. Since he was a saintly man, he went straight to Paradise and was warmly welcomed.

Day after day he took part in the choir of angels who were celebrating on high the glory of the Creator. But finally, after a time, the good Curé became extremely bored. He went around Paradise, yawned, idled about, and became more bored than ever. One day, unable to stand it any longer, he confessed his state of mind to the Good Lord who was grieved.

"What do you wish to do?" the Good Lord asked him.

"Oh, there is only one way of keeping me from being homesick for earth, that is to give me a "position" here and there is only one that I feel worthy of holding, it is that of Saint Peter, keeper of the keys of Heaven."

The Good Lord remonstrated with him in a fatherly manner by revealing how impossible it was to realize his desires . . .

The Abbé M. . . was very chagrined but refrained from argument.

One morning, Saint Peter, while making the rounds, noticed something unusual at the gates of Paradise. A mixture of *"feuillages,"* *"d'lo-répugnance,"*[9] of *parched corn* and other substances were strewn on the ground.

He was imprudent in pushing aside the strange offering with his foot. Immediately he was stricken with such sharp pains in his suddenly swollen lower limbs that all of Heaven became upset. But from the happy face

---

[7] *"I need nothing. I am the servant of these gentlemen."*

[8] A legenday figure that the Haitians have claimed.

[9] "Feuillages" [leafage], "d'l'eau répugnance" [odorous water] are synonomous with evil spells.

and satisfied air of the Abbé M. . ., the Good Lord knew that he was the author of this misdeed and that he was guilty of an act unbefitting a resident of Paradise. He was damned and cast into hell.

And that is why we will never have an indigenous priest . . .

5

In truth, the legend does not rest always on such a high plane, although it treats the great and humble with the same familiarity and the same good humor. Thus, it illustrated with tragic commentary the life of the precursors and the founders of our nation. Toussaint Louverture, Dessalines, Pétion, Christophe as well as Dom Pèdre, Mackandal, Romaine-the-Prophetess, have furnished immeasureable material for the legend. The popular imagination has drawn from them fanciful fables and even some of our wildest superstitions.

Be that as it may, tales and legends have found in the Creole language an entirely unexpected manner of expression, subtle and penetratingly acute.

And it is here that our capacity for assimilation and our adaptive ability are transformed into the power of creation.

Is Creole a language which can produce an original literature which will establish the genius of our race? Ought Creole to become some day the Haitian language just as there is a French language, an Italian language, or a Russian language? Can Creole be used henceforth in such pedagogical applications where in the solution of a problem we use known terms in order to arrive at the discovery of other potential terms?

These are difficult and interesting questions that we will inevitably encounter in the course of this study without ever having the leisure to discuss them in depth.

In any event we will agree without difficulty that, such as it is, our Creole is a collective creation arising from the need of former masters and slaves to communicate their thoughts to each other. In consequence it bears the imprint of the vices and qualities of the human milieu and the circumstances which developed it; it is a compromise between the already mature languages of the French, English, and Spanish conquerors and the many crude and inharmonious idioms of the multitudes of individuals belonging to tribes gathered from all parts of the African continent and imported to the furnace of Saint Domingue. But it is however neither the "petit nègre" [trading French] which the complacent and obsequious imaginations of globe-trotters so often use abusively, nor the codified language that armchair doctrinaires have impatiently been trying to make of it. For the moment, it is the only instrument that we and the masses can use for expressing our mutual thoughts; a primitive instrument in many respects but possessing a priceless sonority and delicacy of touch. Such as it is, idiom, dialect, patois, the power of its social role is a fact from which we cannot escape. It is thanks to Creole that our oral traditions exist, are perpetuated and transformed, and it is through this medium that we can hope some day to bridge the gulf which makes of us and the people two apparently distinct and frequently antagonistic entities. Do you see the importance that it assumes in the study of the problems to which we have devoted ourselves here?

Creole, for those who comprehend it, is a language of great subtlety. Virtue or fault, this characteristic derives less from the clearness of the sounds it expresses than from the unsuspected depth of the ambiguities that it insinuates by its innuendoes, by the inflection of the voice itself, and especially by the mimetic face of the speaker. Perhaps this is why the written Creole loses half the flavor of the spoken language; perhaps this is why the Haitian folk-lore has not blossomed as a written literature. On the whole, in Creole the image often bursts forth in the simple repetition of analogous sounds which, in creating onomatopoeia, accentuate the musicality of the idiom. Examples are such as the word "tcha-tcha" so expressive of the rustling produced by the leaves and the dried husks of the Swazi acacia [locust tree], the word *voun-vou* which conveys the buzzing produced by the wingsheaths of the horn-nosed beetle. Besides, if more proof were necessary to bring out the ingeniousness of Creole, it would suffice to cite baffling proverbs which, appropriately in relation to our thesis, lack moreover neither pungency nor relevancy.

Is it not true that:

"Parlé francé pas l'esprit et nègre sott ce l'événement?"[10]

Ah, well! Despite this special subtle feature of our patois, it appears, nevertheless, that people do not find this resonant instrument to their liking because the interest of its tales is stressed by interspersing them with bouts-rimés and assonances, so that in the final analysis most of these stories are long singsong chants. Most of the time these recitative chants are indescribably graceful. They sustain the action by their cadence, whether in timing the movement progressively toward a

[10] To speak French does not mean you are witty. A foolish man is quite a problem.

predetermined conclusion or whether by following the rhythm in the most fanciful patterns. A very provocative fable exists in this genre.

It concerns certain very remote countries to which women were forever forbidden access.

One day, a woman was so curious she did not flinch from the idea of donning a masculine disguise in order to violate custom and to enter the city. But the bells were on the watch and soon, in a carillon of alarm, they disclosed the artifice.[11]

Bim   Bam   ça moué la-cé famm· Biim Bam li   bel   li jo — li

What a shame that this whimsical tale does not tell us what happened next. I would wager my life that, as soon as the men saw that the stranger was a woman, and especially that she was pretty, they submitted to her wishes, which was, after all, the least homage to be rendered to her seductive power.

Besides, you know that the woman has a preponderant role in the gatherings where people tell and sing tales. If she is not always the leader of the chorus, she is at least a pre-eminent figure whom the populace call the queen of song, queen forever so to speak, given the considerable importance that the chant in all its forms holds in the life of our people. In this repect, I really think that one could justly define the Haitian: a people who sing and who suffer, who grieve and who laugh, who dance and are resigned. "From birth to death, song is associated" with his whole life. He sings when he has joy in his heart or tears in his eyes. He sings in the furor of combat, under the hail of machine-gun fire, or in the fray of bayonets. He sings of the apotheosis of victories and the horror of defeats. He sings of the musuclar effort and the rest after the task, of the ineradicable optimism and humble intuition that neither injustice nor suffering are eternal and that, moreover, nothing is hopeless since "bon Dieu bon."[12]

He sings always, he sings ceaselessly. Ah! the melancholy chants of the slave, submissive and bruised under the whip of the commander, calling out to immanent justice; passionate chants, countless wailings,

[11]   Bim, bam, what I see is a pretty woman.
[12]   "God is good."

wild chorus of half-starved rebels shouting their defiance of death in the onslaught at Vertières in the sublime stanza:

"Grenadiers à l'assaut!
Ça qui mouri zaffaire à yo!
Nan point manman nan point papa!
Grenadiers à l'assaut!
Ça qui mouri zaffaire à yo!"[3]

Marseillaise of glory which, in the flashing night of Crête à Pierrot, impressed the French army by its violence and its grandeur. O melancholy songs of the wounded who died for the freedom of the race and its reintegration into the eminent dignity of the human species; absorbing lullabies which tender lips murmur to soothe the capricious moods of little children; nursery roundelays which smooth the restlessness of little ones into universal harmony; and you, liturgical nocturnes of believers troubled by the enigma of the universe and overwhelmed in the fervent admiration of unconquerable forces, satirical couplets lashing the puppets of the moment and unmasking the hypocrisy of leading politicians; hymns of love and of faith, moving cries of the love-maddened Cleopatras and the Sapphos; all of you finally which have, in long-ago or recent times, nourished dreams, exalted hope, fomented action, assuaged sorrow, all you who were the winged thought, a fleeting moment in the consciousness of my people, can I gather you reverently, gather your brilliant frondescence into an immortal gesture whereby the race would recapture the intimate sense of its genius and the conviction of its indestructible vitality?

Wishful thinking, alas! Idle ambition! . . . Of all our popular traditions, the song is the one which persistently disappears with unaccommodating frequency because it is essentially oral tradition. I do not believe that a single one of the songs which appeased the cruelty of the hours of colonial servitude has come down to us. However they must have had a certain bitter charm if we trust the verses forming the earliest known specimens of Negro-American folk-lore.

But despite whatever existed in the colonial era, only a few satirical verses and laments of love have survived, found here and there in the

[3] In English: "Troopers, to battle!
        Those who die so be it!
        We have no mother or father!
        Troopers, to battle!
        Those who die so be it!"

old chroniclers. Here is a specimen of political song [by Jean Coquille] which dates back to the first days of Independence.

> Eh! bien ces mulâtres
> Dits lâches autrefois,
> Savent-ils se battre
> Campés dans les bois?
> Ces nègres à leur suite,
> Vous font prendre la fuite?
> Vive l'Indépendance!
>
> Brave Dessalines,
> Dieu conduit tes pas!
> Geffrard en droite ligne
> Ne te quittera pas.
> Férou, Coco Herne,
> Cangé, Jean Louis François
> Près les Cayes vous cernent
> Evacuez, Français![4]

By going back a little further in time, we can cite two beautiful love songs. Unfortunately their airs have not survived. And this is why [Ludovic] Lamothe, the delightful composer of so many melodies evocative of rosy or melancholy hours, was quite willing at our suggestion, to make a new arrangement for the tender verses about Lisette:

---

[4] In English: Aha! well, these mulattoes
  Said to be cowardly in olden days,
  Do they know how to fight
  Camped in the woods?
  These Negroes with them
  Do they make you run?
  Long live Independence!

  Brave Dessalines,
  God directs your steps!
  Geffrard right beside you
  Will not desert you.
  Férou, Coco Herne,
  Cangé, Jean Louis François
  Encircle you near Les Cayes
  Depart, Frenchmen!

Translation according
to Moreau de Saint-Méry.[5]

I

Lisette quitté la plaine,
Mon perdi bonher à moué;
Gié à moin semblé fontaine,
Dipi mon pas miré toué.
La jour quand mon coupé canne,
Mon songé zamour à moué;
La nuit quand mon dans cabane,
Dans drani mon quimbé toué.

II

Si to allé à la ville,
Ta trouvé geine Candio,
Qui gagné pour tromper fille
Bouche doux passé sirop;
To va crèr yo bien sincère
Pendant coeur to conquin trop
C'est serpent qui contrefaire
Crié rat pour tromper yo.

III

Dipi mon perdi Lisette
Mon pas sonchié Calinda
Mon quitté Bram-bram sonnette
Mon pas batte Bamboula
Quand mon contré l'aut nèguesse
Mon pas gagné gié pour li;
Mon pas sonchié travail pièce;
Tout qui' chose à moins mourri.

IV

Mon maigre tant cou gnou souche,
Jambe à moin tant comme roseau;
Mangé n'a pas doux dans bouche,

I

Lisette tu fuis la plaine,
Mon Bonheur s'est envolé;
Mes pleurs, en double fontaine,
Sur tous tes pas ont coulé
Le jour moissonnant la canne,
Je rêve à tes doux appas;
Un songe dans ma cabane
La nuit te met dans mes bras.

II

Tus trouveras, à la ville,
Plus d'une jeune freluquet,
Leur bouche avec art distille
Un miel doux mais plein d'apprêt;
Tu croiras leur coeur sincère!
Leur coeur ne veut que tromper;
Le serpent sait contrefaire
Le rat qu'il veut dévorer.

III

Mes pas loin de ma Lisette,
S'éloignent du Calinda;
Et ma ceinture à sonnette
Languit sur mon bamboula.
Mon oeil de toute belle,
N'aperçoit plus de souris;
Le travail en vain m'appelle.
Mes sens sont anéantis.

IV

Je péris comme la souche,
Ma jambe n'est qu'un roseau;
Nul mets ne plaît à ma bouche,

[5] Médéric Louis de Moreau de Saint-Méry, *Description topographique, physique, civile, politique et historique de la partie française de l'isle Saint-Dominique*, Philadelphia, 1797-1798, Vol. I, pp. 65-66.

Tafia c'est même comme d'l'eau.
Quand moin songé toué Lisette,
D' l'eau toujou dans gié moin.
Magner moin vini trop bète.
A force chagrin magné moin.

La liquer s'y change en eau.
Quand je pens à toi Lisette,
Mes yeux s'inondent de pleurs.
Ma raison lente et distraite,
Cède en tout en mes douleurs.

V

Lisette mon tandé nouvelle,
To compté bientot tourné
Vini donc toujours fidelle,
Miré bon passé tandé.
N'a pas tardé d'avantage,
To fair mon assez chagrin,
Mon tant com' zouézo dans cage,
Quand yo fair li mouri faim.

V

Mais est-il bien vrai ma belle,
Dan peu tu dois revenir:
Oh! reviens toujours fidèle
Croire est moins doux que sentir.
Ne tarde pas davantage,
C'es pour moi trop de chagrin;
Viens retirer de sa cage,
L'oiseau consume de faim.[6]

---

[6] In English:

I

Lisette, you fled the plain,
My happiness has flown away;
My tears, in a double fountain,
On all your steps have fallen.
By day as I harvest the cane,
I dream of your sweet charm;
A dream in my cabin
By night puts you in my arms.

II

You will find in the city,
More than one young coxcomb,
Their mouths artfully distill
A sweet honey full of affection;
You will believe their hearts are
    sincere!
Their hearts wish only to deceive;
The serpent knows how to imitate
The rat that he wishes to devour.

III

My steps far from my Lisette
Depart further from Calinda;
And my cincture of bells
Languishes with my bamboula, [drum].

My eye for beautiful girls
No longer notices smiles;
Work appeals to me in vain.
My senses are prostrated.

IV

I decay like the stump of a tree,
My leg is only a reed;
No foods are pleasing to my taste,
Liquor changes into water,
When I think of you, Lisette,
My eyes are flooded with tears.
My reason, slow and listless,
Yields to all in my sadness.

V

But is it really true, my loved one,
Soon you are about to return:
Oh! return ever faithful
Believing is less gentle than feeling.
Do not wait any longer,
It gives me too much sadness;
Come take from its cage,
The bird consumed with hunger.

It is also under the token of love and in a melancholy mood that an abandoned woman gives vent to her sadness in another song that Moreau de Saint-Méry has collected for our enjoyment.

I

Quand cher zami moin va rivé,
Mon fait li tout plein caresse.
Ah! plaisir là nou va goutté;
C'est plaisir qui duré sans ceese.
　　Mais toujours tard
　　　　Hélas! Hélas!
Cher zami moin pas vlé rivé.

II

Tan pi zouézo n'a pas chanté
Pendant coeur à moin dans la peine.
Mais gnou fois zami moin rivé
Chantez, chantez tant comme syrène.
Mais, mais paix bouche!
Cher zami moin pas hélé moin?

III

Si zami moin pas vlé rivé
Bientôt mon va mouri tristesse
Ah! coeur à li pas doué blié
Lisa là li hélé maîtresse.
　　Mais qui nouvelle?
　　　　Hélas! Hélas!
Cher zami moin pas cor rivé!

IV

Comment vous quitté moin comme ça!
Songé zami! n'a point tant comme moin
　　Femme qui joli!

Si comme moin gagné tout plein talents qui doux.
Si la vous va prend li; pa lé bon pour vous,
   Vous va regretté moin toujours.[13]

    Such a woman, adorned with faded and antiquated charm, is the sister of the immortal *Choucoune,* the *marabout* of Oswald Durand,[7] and she expresses in bitter echoes the plaint of the woman who waits forever for an unfaithful one. Is it not the same sentiment which inspired the quatrain of the poet of "Serres Chaudes."

   Et s'il revenait un jour
   Que faut-il lui dire?
   Dites-lui qu'on l'attendit
   Jusqu'à s'en mourir . . .[8]

---

[13]

I

When my dear friend will return
I will lavish mad caresses upon him.
Ah! The pleasure we will enjoy
Will be eternal . . .
But it is getting late
   Alas! Alas!
My dear friend does not wish to
   return . . .

II

Do not sing little birds
While my heart has so much pain.
But if my friend returns
Sing, sing like the Siren.
   Silence, Alas! Alas!
My friend has not called to me! . . .

III

If my friend wishes no more to return
   I will die,
Ah! his heart would not forget
Lisette whom he called his mistress . . .
   What news?
   Alas! Alas!
My dear friend is still far away!

IV

Why have you abandoned me
Think of it my friend! There is no
   other
Who is prettier than I. If you find one
Who may have more talents than I
   Take her . . . I do not believe it.
You will miss me always . . .

---

[7] Oswald Durand (1840-1906), considered by most Haitians as their greatest poet, is remembered especially for his immortal poem *Choucoune,* also the name of the central female character — a marabout of extraordinary charm. Written in Creole, his thoughts of amorous love and racial melancholy are mixed with characteristic Haitian sense of the droll and savory.

[8] In English:
       Greenhouses
  And if he returned one day
  What must he be told?
  Tell him that someone waited for him
  Until she died . . .

But as interesting as these oral traditions which we have briefly discussed may be, as suggestive as they may seem, they are only a very minute part of this complicated mass which is our folk-lore.

Beliefs are the most apparent and most representative expression of it. To study the beliefs not only in their actual manifestations but in their recent or distant origins, to disentangle them from the symbolism in which they are enveloped, to compare them to other states of consciousness as felt by other peoples is the task that we will pursue in the following pages.

Chapter II

Popular Beliefs

1

No study seems more worthy of testing the ambition of an observer than that which embraces the whole of the psychological phenomena designated under the generic name of popular beliefs. Undoubtedly this includes many heterogenous elements, such as relics and amalgams of old customs whose secret meaning escapes us now: the initial empiricism of juridical techniques and concepts, the idle musings of theosophists, the practices of medicasters, all tentatives from which come the rough drafts of the first scientific disciplines, but also as well the sacrifices of sorcery and charlatanical duplicity which indicate the point where ignorance clashes with the mysteries of nature. What briefly are all of these modalities of popular beliefs which as one group burst out in manifestations of trust and piety? Do they not reveal the uncertainties from which no human creature can escape in the presence of enigmas which beset us from birth to the grave? Are they not the essence of so many representations in minds which cling too close to the state of nature to accept man's most magnificent proof of nobility, this curiosity by which we are overcome in the face of the unknown and perhaps of the unknowable which floods our universe? After all, all of our popular beliefs rest upon authentic acts of faith which in the end are concretized in a religion which has its cult and its traditions.

We are going to examine these propositions in order to discuss their value and to attempt to demonstrate their exactitude and veracity. But a preliminary question delays us at the very threshold of this study.

We have just said that the practices in question are actual beliefs and are embodied in acts of faith which imply adherence to a religion.

What is this religion? Would it be *Voodoo*?[14] In admitting that it may be possible — and we believe the hypothesis demonstrable — to reduce all our popular beliefs to the modalities of the *Voodoo* faith, can we consider *Voodoo* as a religion?

Nothing seems more appropriate to us in clearing up this preliminary question than to understand from the beginning the scope and significance of the terms we use. This step will at least have the advantage of removing all ambiguity from the field of discussion.

First of all, what is religion?

The particular nature of this study prohibits us from lingering long on definitions of religion proposed by philosophers and theologians. We will limit ourselves to investigating and to retaining among the proposed meanings those which, in minimal terms, include the essence of what one is likely to experience in the universality of religious sentiment and phenomena. We intend to adopt an explanation broad enough to satisfy completely the exigencies of the most complex religions while at the same time including the simple terms of the most elementary forms of religious phenomena and sentiments.

We will immediately dismiss the definition that is usually given of religion as coming from the Latin "religio, religare," that is to say to join, thus deriving from this etymology the simple conclusion that religion is the essential bond "which links the divinity with man." (This etymology appears very questionable to us.)[15]

Ethnography and history seem to justify our reasoning. Are there not great religions in existence in which the idea of gods and spirits is absent or at least plays only a secondary and inconspicuous role?[16] This is the case in Buddhism notably. Buddhism, says [Eugène] Burnouf, places itself in opposition to Brahminism as an ethic without god and an atheism without nature. "It does not recognize any god on whom man depends," says [Auguste] Barth. Its doctrine is completely atheistic and [Hermann] Oldenberg, on his part, calls it "a religion without god." In reality, the

---

14 The spelling [French] of the word is not fixed. The reader will find variants on occasion in the course of the study. [There has been considerable effort by modern social scientists to eradicate the pejorative meaning attached to Voodoo, especially by American popular writers of the 1920's and 1930's, by using the word *Vodun* (or variations of it) when describing the religious beliefs of the Haitian peasants. In recent years however, English translations of foreign academic studies on this subject have generally employed the word *Voodoo* and American scholars are beginning to do the same. Please consult the translator's introduction for the full explanation.]

15 *Orphéus*, p. 3, [Salomon Reinach, Paris, 1900].

16 [Emile] Durkheim, *Les formes élémentaires de la vie religieuse*, p. 42, [Paris, 1912].

total essence of Buddhism is contained within four propositions which its adherents call the noble truths.

The first considers the existence of pain as bound to the perpetual flow of matter; the second shows desire as the cause of unhappiness; the third makes the suppression of desire the only means of suppressing unhappiness; the fourth enumerates the three stages through which one must pass in order to attain this suppression: they are justice, meditation, and finally wisdom bringing full possession of the doctrine. Having traversed these three stages, one arrives at the end of the road, at deliverance, at salvation through Nirvana.

Such are the fundamental elements of Buddhism, at least originally. We do not claim that this religion has not evolved into a type of religious adoration embodied in a personal god who is Buddha himself. We have wished simply to stress that if a great religion like Buddhism could arise and live during a certain time in its original purity according to an entirely secular concept, then the definition of religion given above, that is, to understand it as a bond between divinity and man, would exclude Buddhism from the realm of religion and thus bring about a paradoxical conclusion. So we will eliminate the acceptance of religion as the symbol of an attachment of man to a being or to some spiritual beings upon whom he depends, because this is more characteristic of those religions that are already highly evolved. The idea adopted by the sociological school of Durkheim contains the essential thoughts that we are seeking. It establishes, and everyone agrees, that "all the known religious beliefs, whether simple or complex, have a universal characteristic: they assume a classification of real or ideal things which men have introduced as two opposite types, designated generally by the clear-cut terms of the profane and of the sacred. The division of the world into two domains, the one including all that is sacred, the other all that is profane, is the distinctive trait of religious thought; the beliefs, the myths, the dogmas, the legends are either representations or systems of representations which express the nature of things, the virtues and the powers which are attributed to them, their history, and their affinity to one another and with secular things. But, by sacred things we do not mean just personal beings that we call gods or spirits; a crag, a tree, a spring, a pebble, a piece of wood, a house, in fact anything, can be sacred. A rite can have this quality; there does not even exist a rite which does not have it to some degree. There are words, utterances, formulas, which can be pronounced only by the mouth of consecrated persons; there are gestures, movements which cannot be performed by everyone."[9] In brief, the sacred and the profane form two distinct categories, with the difference residing in the absolutely opposite character of one from the other. If this quality is revealed by the representation of a unique spiritual being or of superior beings "to such a degree at least that man depends upon them or has fear of or hope in them, whom he can call to his aid and be assured of assistance," [17] if man worships this being with love and adoration in his heart or expresses his feelings in a public and external cult, it is not difficult to recognize in these few traits the manifestations of piety which have resulted in types of monotheistic religions such as Catholicism, one of the most imposing examples. If on the other hand man finds in the contemplation of abstinence, in the practice of charity, in humility, and in external sacrifice, the opportunity of achieving a state of holiness and blessedness which frees him from the miseries and the disabilities of the flesh without even calling upon external intervention, then Buddhism in its beginning stages has given us the proof of a religion without god.

Finally, if man, disarmed by the forces of nature because of his ignorance, venerates them through fear and submission, or if his daily relations with things cause him to place them in categories favoring alliance or tending to hostility, such an attitude will lead us toward the most elementary forms of religious phenomena and sentiments as are offered in numerous and suggestive examples from the primitives. It is this last attitude which justifies the famous line of poetry by Stacius:

"*Primus in orbe deos fecit timor, ardua coelo*
Fulmina dum caderent . . ."[18]

In any case, we have tried to demonstrate through three types of religion — going from the simple to the complex — that the formula we have adopted, however succinct the explanation may have been, is rich enough to contain in its general significance, the essence of religious sentiment. We are saying that, stripped of the symbolism that gradually enriches it as it grows in the human heart and as man grows in culture

[9] Price Mars does not indicate the closing of the quote. Presumably it ends where it is indicated by this note. See Emile Durkheim, *The Elementary Forms of the Religious Life,* translation by Joseph Ward Swain, London, 1954, p. 37.

[17] J[oseph] Bricout, *Ou en est l'histoire des religions,* p. 15, [Paris, 1912].

[18] "The gods in the world were first born of fear when the terrible thunderbolt fell from the sky." The verse is from Statius (*Thebais,* III 6660) who borrowed it from Petronius. The same thought is developed at length in Lucretius (*De Natura rerum*). Mgr. [Alexandre] Le Roy, *La religion des primitifs,* p. 20, [Paris, 1911].

and in civilization, religious sentiment is reduced more and more to a mass of rules, to a system of scrupulous exactitude, which we feel we must observe in order to achieve present or future happiness, whether this happiness is derived from ourselves or from one or more spiritual beings who are watching over us.

2

And now, in the light of this definition, will we be able to discover how Voodoo satisfies the conditions of a religion?

Voodoo is a religion because all its adherents believe in the existence of spiritual beings who live anywhere in the universe in close intimacy with humans whose activity they dominate.

These invisible beings constitute an Olympian pantheon of gods in which the greatest among them bear the title of Papa or Grand Master and have the right to special hommage.

Voodoo is a religion because the cult appertaining to its gods requires a hierarchical priestly body, a society of the faithful, temples, altars, ceremonies, and finally a whole oral tradition which has certainly not come down to us unaltered, but thanks to which the essential elements of this worship have been transmitted.

Voodoo is a religion because, amid the confusion of legends and the corruption of fables, we can discern a theology, a system of representation thanks to which our African ancestors have, primitively, accounted for natural phenomena and which lies dormantly at the base of the anarchical beliefs upon which the hybrid Catholicism of our popular masses rests.

We are aware that this statement will bring quick objection. You are, no doubt, wondering what is the moral value of such a religion and, as your religious education is dominated by the efficiency of the Christian moral philosophy, you use that as your standard of judgment. In the light of such rules you can only dutifully condemn Voodoo as a religion, not only because you reproach it for being immoral but, more logically, because you frankly declare it amoral. And since it is not known how an amoral religion can exist, you cannot accept Voodoo as a religion. Ah! Such an attitude would be worse than an intellectual injustice, it would be a negation of intelligence. For, in the end, we are aware that every religion has its moral code and that it is most often closely related to the mental evolution of the group in which this religion has been born and has taken root. No doubt, we know of such and such a religion — Christianity for example — which rose directly to a moral height that is at the least difficult to surpass. But, without entering into the development of considerations which might exceed the intent of this modest study, we know that Christianity arose in a terrain long prepared for the flowering of this magnificent culture. Even though it was preached from the beginning to the humble people of Israel, there was in the air, as one might say, such a religious fermentation induced particularly by the messianic hope spread in the Jewish milieu by the lofty reasoning of great prophets, there were so many serious ideas debated by the doctors of law in the disputes of the synagogues, the Greek philosophy had exercised such an influence on the masters of Jewish thought, that when Christ appeared this occurrence was considered from an historical angle and without mystical significance as if it were in some way the culmination, the ultimate end of a process beginning with the fervent piety of the Bedouins whom Moses was commissioned to lead toward the promised land. Interestingly enough, if we proceeded from the thought of Moses to that of Jesus it would be possible to demonstrate how the Judo-Christian moral code was refined and enriched just as gold comes from the veinstone. Is there, in fact, anything more contrary to the Jewish sentence: an eye for an eye, a tooth for a tooth, than the sublime exaltation of love that the Galilean taught in action and in love when he told his disciples that the first and last commandment of God must be to love your neighbor as yourself? Is it not this thought that Saint Paul has expressed with his "abrupt eloquence" when he wrote to the Corinthians: "Though I speak with the tongues of men and of angels, if I have not charity, I am but as sounding brass, as a tinkling cymbal." Now if in place of considering the Christian moral code in its purity and its transcendence as revealed in the evangelical doctrine, we went back to its origins or to the remote ideas from which it was derived, we would be less tempted to use it as a standard of comparison. In fact, if we were less willing to consider "our morality as *the* morality," we would see that primitive societies are restrained by a very narrow code of constraints and obligations, all of a religious origin which, by their extensive application, dominate the private and public life and express in the clearest fashion that these societies have morality.

Do such constraints, such obligations exist in Voodoo? Who would dare to deny it?

From birth to death, the adherent of Voodoo is imprisoned in the narrow web of a network of interdictions: he is forbidden to permit a fixed time to elapse before immersing the new-born in a lustral water carefully made up by the *hougan* who consecrates the infant to the divinity capable of preserving it from the malevolence of evil spirits and of helping it against "the influence of supernatural maladies"; he is forbidden to pronounce the "baptismal" name of the infant in certain circumstances in a loud voice, especially in the evening;[19] he is forbidden to act irreverently in the vicinity of the sources where "the Spirits" reside; he must show respect for the old people who are the trustees of traditions; he must not kill or steal; he must participate annually in some sacrificial act of worship; he must not practice incest; parents must not follow the funeral procession of their dead children or wear black clothing publicly as a sign of grief; he must not bury dead bodies without having previously washed them with a protective secret solution known only by the high priest; he must not bury the dead without providing them with such talismans as can be useful against a possible resurrection or even may be needful to survive under any form whatever, whether in the nature of wandering phantoms or through metempsychosis into some other human individuality, and so forth.

On the whole, all of these customs, all of these interdictions of which we have given only a small number here, are summed up in a code of taboos to which the individual submits with a reverential and quite singular fear. But, if it is true that private and public moral code is the emancipated daughter of taboo which, by definition, is a set of scruples, how can we dispute that Voodoo does not have its own ethic? It only appears to be devoid of it because, despite ourselves, we judge it in terms of a type of a higher moral law appropriate to our conception of life, because in short we judge the Voodoo ethic as a superstition injurious to our ideal of civilization. If, in place of considering it in comparison with Christian moral law, we judged it by its intrinsic value, one would see by the severity of the sanction to which the follower who transgresses the law exposes himself, how it commands a discipline of private life and a conception of social order which has both sense and relevancy.

We would thus understand how, at a given moment, Voodoo might

---

19 We find the same taboo again and again among the vast majority of primitive peoples. [Lucien] Lévy-Bruhl explains this in *La mentalité primitive*, p. 229, [Paris, 1925]. The name for primitive peoples, he says, is not just to identify individuals. It is an integral part of the person, it partakes of the person. If one disposes of the name, one is master of the person also. To betray the name of a man is to betray the man himself.

be effective enough to curb the instincts of the individual to a certain extent and guard against the dissolution of the community.

Ah! Another serious matter is the objection raised against Voodoo that it is tainted with magic and sorcery.

We willingly agree, if however it is conceded that it is singularly difficult to determine where religion ends and magic begins. For, in the final analysis, if magic is conceived as the power that is attributed to an individual over natural forces, whether he pronounces certain words or he carries out certain acts or gestures by virtue of which he believes he can attain what he desires — and that is what is known as imitative magic, the classic example being the power possessed, as we suppose, by twins or the last-born child to make rain fall merely by pronouncing the ritual formula and pouring water on trees in time of great drought — or whether after all the individual believes himself capable of exercising from a distance an influence on the life of his fellow-man simply by subjecting the clothing, nail clippings, hair, teeth or whatever else belonging to the subject to some mysterious process, and this is what is called sympathetic magic — in reality if magic is the authority that the individual confers upon himself and thanks to which he believes himself capable of controlling all things and principally the forces about him by constraining them to obey his personal desires, then we wonder by what name we should call the action of those who, strengthened by their prayers to the Christian divinity, carry the image of some saint in processions for the purpose of stopping tempests, of quieting the turbulence of volcanos, of stopping seismic shocks. Are these not also endeavors to subjugate the forces of nature to our personal designs by claiming alleged power over the physical laws that govern matter? By what name must we call the act of multitudes who, kneeling on the flagstones of the sanctuaries with wax candles in hand, wait, hoping for the fulfillment of their prayers, the punishment of an enemy, the realization of some dream of glory or of love? After all, there has been reason to say that "humanity has not remained passive in the presence of the thousands of spiritual forces by which it believes to be surrounded. In order to react against them, to subdue and enslave them to its ends, humanity has found an auxiliary in a false science which is the mother of all true sciences, Magic."[20] As, moreover, the first men had to accommodate themselves to the material conditions in which they were obliged to live without being able to dominate them — and all non-civilized

[20] Soloman Reinach, Edition 1900, p. 32.

start afresh with the same experience — they gave life to the physical milieu, deified natural forces, determined as much as possible the modalities by which they would regulate their relations with these forces. Therefrom came a system of representations, a cosmogony which is based both on religion and magic, and from thence came also this phenomenon that quite often the most complex religion is in the beginning only an ensemble, a complementary unit of magic powers from which it disengages itself very slowly by evolving towards higher and more spiritualized beliefs. And this is perhaps why it is rare to find a religion even among those richest in abstraction with beginnings that were not tainted by thaumaturgy and Magianism. Without doubt, in western civilization magic survives only as a curious relic and with an impertinence that is unpardonable, but it is especially in this respect that it appears as a caricature of true religion and that it "employs a sort of professional pleasure in profaning holy things" and that, "in its rites, performs the contrary of religious ceremonies."[21]

Nevertheless these two forms of belief — magic and religion — are distinct from and opposite to each other in many ways.

Religious beliefs are not just the exaltation of sentiment which makes us test our dependence on cosmic forces and, brought to its highest expression, influences us toward universal communion through love, confidence, and prayer; they have in the highest degree the social virtue of bringing us together in community, of strengthening the bonds that tie the people of the same country together, and beyond the frontiers, peoples, different races, and finally significant portions of humanity for the greatest flowering of the common faith which animates them.

As for magic beliefs, whether the progress of knowledge restrains the possibility of their growth, whether they belong to outdated periods of the ascensional march of humanity toward more enlightenment, they are obliged to wrap themselves in mystery in order to draw souls through fear and spread only among few followers. For that very reason these beliefs reveal a particularly individualistic character. In this sense we have observed that though there are religious communities there are no magical communities.[10]

And now, can we hope from this short discussion to be able to draw a first conclusion, namely that Voodoo is a very primitive religion formed

---

[21] Durkheim, Les formes élémentaires de la vie religieuse, [pp. 59-60].

[10] At this point we must remind the reader that Price-Mars was writing this text in the 1920's. Since mid-twentieth century, anthropologists would agree with Paul Bohannan in Social Anthropology, 1963, when he says, ". . . religion and magical institutions are raised on a foundation of social groups," p. 367, or as Melville J. Herskovits notes in Cultural Anthropology, 1955, p. 221, "that magic . . . is actually an integral part of religion."

in part by beliefs in the almighty Power of spiritual beings — gods, demons, disembodied souls — in part by beliefs in sorcery and magic? Can we anticipate that this dual nature will be revealed to us as we study its more or less pure state in the country where it originated and in our country, altered by its juxtaposition to the Catholic religion rather than to the secular, adapted to the conditions of life of the rural masses battling against the legal statute of the nation which would like to free itself of all attachment to this very ancient form of beliefs of which it no longer has any use.

And here synthetically is the position which Voodoo occupies in our society.

3

Just how did Voodoo come to us?

Unquestionably from Africa. *Africa* however implies a geographic location that is much too large for this word alone to suffice as a precise response to the concerns that absorb us. For the question is nothing less than knowing whether Voodoo spread as a concrete religion through the entire thirty million square kilometers of the old continent or whether it was confined within limited areas. This is what we are going to examine.

Let us hasten to say that nothing is more difficult to ascertain in the present state of African ethnography. However, insofar as our investigations have enabled us to further the study of mores and customs of the people of the black continent, it seems that we have found here and there, over all of African land and among the people who live there, some rites of worship which are similar though not completely identical to the rites of Voodoo. Among them appear nuances that are sometimes almost imperceptible, at other times great enough to establish dividing lines. Thus, along the entire length of the Atlantic coast, from Cape Blanc to the Cape of Good Hope, along the coast bordered by the Indian Ocean up to the land of the Somalis; in the hinterland, on all of the central plateau and the forested area, to the edge of the deserts in the Northwest and to the oriental border in the East, it is possible to collect an amazing harvest of fairly similar beliefs, while in the Mediterranean region and that bathed by the Red Sea, religious differences singularize the populations who live there and establish a fairly clear contrast between their traditions and those of the other African peoples.

Well, as arbitrary as this line of demarcation may appear to be, it does nonetheless correspond with living reality. It separates the parts of Africa which are more or less animistic from those which are more or less Christian or Muslim.

CARTE DES RELIGIONS DE L'AFRIQUE

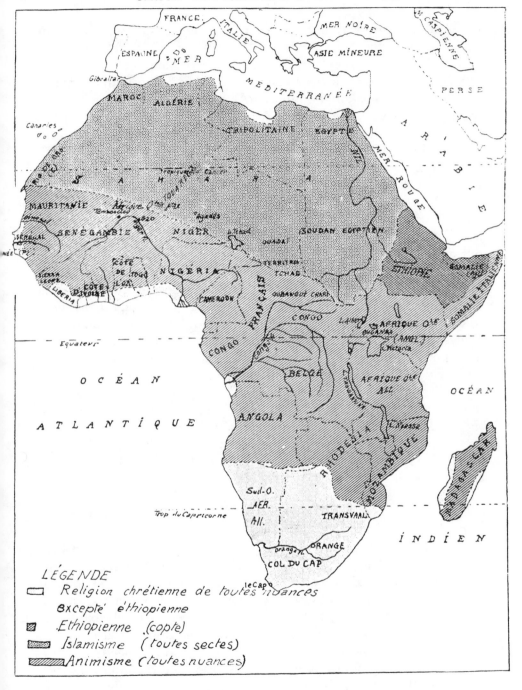

LÉGENDE

☐ Religion chrétienne de toutes nuances excepté éthiopienne

▨ Ethiopienne (copte)

▨ Islamisme (toutes sectes)

▨ Animisme (toutes nuances)

And this difference likewise imprints an ethnic stamp on all of the populations of the old continent. We know, in fact, that during innumerable centuries vast currents of invasions coming from Asia by way of Suez have led to the interbreeding of Semitic invaders with aboriginal populations of North and Southeast Africa. We know besides that the same Semites live in the north of Africa as a more or less pure-blooded dominant race, that Islamism and Christianity were implanted through them in these regions and have continued though altered by juxtaposition with the beliefs of the races that they subjugated or tried to penetrate. In view of the considerations that we have just established, it appears possible for us to construct the religious map of Africa without running into the usual danger of such an enterprise, the impossibility of marking all of the delicate shades of transition. Be that as it may, can we pick out on this map any country along the Guinean Coast in which there was a concentration of the slave trade where we can study an unadulterated Voodoo? We will refrain from dealing with it in this form because to our mind the term Voodoo carries an ambiguity that is wise to dissipate forthwith. Nowhere have we found it to signify a body of beliefs with codified formulas and dogmas. There exists in such a center as Dahomey some spiritual representations called *Vodoun* while, under varying designations, other African countries offer us quite similar beliefs derived from the same psychological base. So, if in Saint Domingue these diverse beliefs, represented by followers belonging to tribes differing in their degree of civilization and indeed in their physical structure, have received the common designation of *Voodoo*, just as we included them all ethnographically under the classification of Negro, it is due to two causes, one of a psychological nature and one of a linguistic order.

4

Since the greatest justification, the sole motive for the slave system was rooted in religious proselytism, His Christian Majesty, King of France, had enjoined his subjects by the second article of the Edict of March, 1685, known as the *Code Noir*, to obey the following injunctions:

1. "All slaves living in the Islands," said the king, "will be baptized and instructed in the Apostolic and Roman Catholic religion. We charge those inhabitants who buy newly arrived Negroes to inform the Governor and the Intendant of the said Islands within the week at the latest, under pain

of an arbitrary fine, that they will give the necessary orders to have them instructed and baptized within an appropriate time."

2. "We forbid all public practice of any other religion except the Apostolic and Roman Catholic; all offenders will be punished as rebellious and disobedient; we forbid all assemblies for this reason and declare them illicit and seditious conventicles, subject to the same penalty even those taking place under the masters who permit or suffer such out of regard for their slaves.

It follows then, according to the literal meaning of the aforementioned text, that Negroes — whatever their tastes, beliefs, or aptitudes — were forced to receive instruction in order to be baptized in the Catholic religion within the week after their debarkation at Saint Domingue. We are even able to affirm that one of the first surprises which greeted the African on the threshold of entering the New World was the demonstration of violence by which he was forced to acknowledge other gods than he had known and who seemed to be outraged and were threatening him with immediate or eventual suffering.

Could it not be the accumulation of such rancor and resentment which exploded later in the singular ceremony of the *oath of blood* on August 14, 1791? Boukman, preparing for the general insurrection, had the Negroes assembled in the Bois Caiman on the plantation of Lenormand de Mézi swear an oath of fidelity under quite impressionable circumstances. We recall the scene to mind.

In the black night, under the tangled branches of the leafy Mapou [silk-cotton tree], the conspirators in silent bands had only one mind and thought.

Streaks of lightning flashed constantly through the skies. The sound of thunder added terror to the fearful scene.

Then, in the silence of the shadows, the priestess made cabalistic signs and plunged the knife of sacrifice into the throat of the wild boar. Then she spread out the entrails on the blood-soaked earth and Boukman pronounced the sacramental words:

> Bon Dieu qui fait soleil,
> Qui clairé nous en haut,
> Qui soulevé la mer,
> Qui fait l'orage gronder,
> Bon Dieu là z'autres tendez

Caché dans son nuage.
Et là li gardé nous.
Li vouai tout ça blancs fait.
Bon Dieu mandé crime,
Et pas nous vlé bienfaits,
Mais Dieu là qui si bon
Ordonnez nous vengeance.
Li va conduit nous.
Li baille nous assistance.
Jetez portraits Dieu blanc
Qui soif d'leau dans yeux nous
Coutez la liberté qui nan coeur
à nous tous!. . .[22]

5

Moreover, according to the above texts, since the only religious demonstration permitted was that of the Catholic Church, the result was that Negroes received baptism with suspect zealousy. But to what extent was this legal regulation respected by the masters? More or less. The reason was that rudimentary religious instruction had to be given Negroes in order to baptize them. And this idea permitted monks to intrude into the movement of the workers. Although Catholic priests were also slave owners, they were accepted as having more benevolence and humaneness in their relations with these poor creatures. Certain monks — the Jesuits — were even accused of urging the desertion and revolt of

[22] Good Lord who made the sun
Which shines on us from on high,
Who raises the sea,
Who makes the tempest roar,
Hear you, people, the Good Lord
Is hidden in his cloud.
From there he looks down on us
And sees all that the white men do.
The God of the white men commands crime,
Ours solicits good deeds,
But this God who is so good (ours)
Orders us to vengeance.
He will guide our hand.
And give us assistance.
Break the image of the god of the white men
Who has thirst for our tears
Hear in our hearts the call of liberty! . . .

the workers. They inspired violent antipathy for lay authority and so on November 24, 1763, the Superior Council had them expelled from the colony.

As for the Negroes, the forced Christianization to which they were subjected, gave them a pretext for distracting their adversaries and stealing a bit of Freedom from their daily harsh labor.

Yet we should also remember that the Creole Negroes, already Catholics, took advantage of their apparent faith as a way to show superiority over new arrivals whom they jeered and who, even when they had complied with the law and came from the church provided with their baptismal paper, were welcomed by the Creoles with the derisive epithet of "baptisés debout" [baptized standing — or quickly en masse].

But the baptismal ceremony was, for most of the neophytes, an occasion of feasting and reveling with their chosen godfathers and godmothers. This is why the Negroes quickly devised the dodge of having themselves baptized more than once so that they could have several opportunities for fun. It is obvious merely through this fact that the new religious state of the slave was only a facade; that his fundamental beliefs were only slightly shaken by his official conversion and remained unchanged in the mysteries of his infrangible consciousness. His beliefs had to remain all the more mysterious in order to withstand the pressures of the law and of the human surroundings. But we are well aware of the resilient power of which any belief is capable that is supported by the whole mass of time-honored sentiment. It plunges its roots into the unfathomable depths of the subconscious all the more tenaciously as it is constrained to dissimulate itself.

Such was the psychological situation in which the Sudanese of the bush, the forest-dwelling Congolese and all the rest found themselves when, tormented by oppression, they were forced to make an ostentatious show of Christianity and to repress their secret adoration of obscure forces to which they felt bound by long ancestral traditions. It is natural that these people under such circumstances should feel united each time that a sudden emotion, a secret gesture, an act of piety revealed the persistence of beliefs within them which, if not identical, had many more similarities among them than they had with those of the masters who were so detested by all, whatever the origins, the customs, and the habitat of each before deportation to and servitude in the foreign land. Thus we have an explanation for and can understand the organization of secret societies which held nocturnal meetings in the depths of the forest for the free exercise of cults whose existence has been recorded since the first days of colonial administration.

Without doubt these assemblies eventually assumed a genuinely political character, but one can affirm that they pertained to worship in the beginning. They created in the course of time an imperative obligation sustained by severe sanctions and thus maintained the existence of a truly religious community, new in many respects, daughter of the milieu and of the needs of the moment. This is very likely, it seems to us, the probable origin of *our* Voodoo. It is pre-eminently a syncretism of beliefs, a compromise of the animism of the Dahomeans, the Congolese, the Sudanese, and others. By being able to assimilate the modalities of all these varieties of beliefs to the point of giving them an apparent unity of rites and customs under a common denomination, it essentially did recapitulate within itself the essence, the substratum of all the other cults and was furthermore the form most comparable to the religious traditions of the tribes disseminated from northern Guinea to Cape Lopez, including the Grain Coast, the Ivory Coast, and the Gold Coast, the kingdom of the Ashanti, of Dahomey, and so forth . . . , and extending from the coastal regions into the hinterland, to the Sudanese plateau, as far as 20⁰ north latitude.

It was the closest expression of the beliefs of a large category of peoples whose totem was the serpent and who, even when they did not carry on the worship of it, knew that the serpent was the eponymic animal of their ancestors.

Moreover, Voodoo was readily diffused among the members of all the tribes wherever the beliefs were related as well as where the dialect was more or less similar. Now, the greatest number of Negroes imported to Saint Domingue belonged to the linguistic family of the Bantus or that of the Mandingos.

Which language of these two groups, Mandingo and Bantu,[23] prevailed among the plantation Negroes?

We would surmise that it was the Bantu, not only because it constitutes the linguistic group which occupies the greatest part of inhabited Africa extending from one ocean to the other and from the upper basin of the Nile and of Lake Chad down to the Orange, but also because the slave traffic was most fruitful among these people that spoke only one

[23] From the personal prefix "Ba," and from the root "ntu," meaning "the men," according to Dr. [Wilhelm Heinrich Immanuel] Bleek, *Comparative Grammar of South African Languages*, cited by Mgr. Le Roy, *La religion des primitifs*.

tongue, the Bantu. We have corroboration of this in a large number of historical documents. Moreau de St. Méry[24] tells us that most Negroes in the colony were from the coast of the Congo and Angola, that is, that they were taken from an area between Cape Lopez and Cape Nègre, which was close to three hundred leagues in a straight line. They belonged beyond all question to the linguistic group of the Bantu. And among the qualities that St. Méry recognized about them and which marked them particularly for domestic service was their great ability to speak Creole with ease. Therein lies one of the most characteristic causes of the power of the Africans to adapt to their new milieu.

For this precious faculty of asimilation enables us to understand the reason why Creole rapidly absorbed the diverse African dialects, including the Mandingo,[25] since the most important group numerically had made it, like the masters themselves, the surest means of communication. And this explains equally why so few words of African origin, deformed or pure, have survived in our present Creole. Would the word *Voodoo* be an African survival or is it a Creole term?

6

English-speaking Africologists lean toward the second hypothesis.[26] They think that the expression derives from the word "Vaudois" and they draw, from the analogy of Voodoo rites and of the unrestrained actions to which the Vaudois sect surrendered, the conclusion that the colonists of Saint Domingue simply applied the name of the heretical cult created by Pierre de Vaux or Valdo to the African religion.

We recall that this rich merchant of Lyons, at the moment when the religious ferment of the twelfth century produced the reform movement in favor of a return to primitive Christianity, gave up all his worldly goods to the poor, had the gospels translated into the vernacular, and preached a doctrine very akin to the apostolicism which had been condemned as heretical by Boniface VIII. The extemists nonetheless con-

---

[24] Moreau de Saint-Méry, *Description topographique, physique, civile, politique et historique de Saint-Domingue.* Original edition, Philadelphia, 1797, Vol. II. [Should be Vol. I, p. 32].

[25] "Although the Mandingo was the language of a tribe of upper Senegal it was understood to be an inter-tribal dialect by the majority of the Sudanese people." [Maurice] Delafosse, *Haut-Sénégal-Niger*, 3 Vol., Vol. I, page 368.

[26] Cf. *The Negro Church: a social study*, (The Atlanta publications, [Georgia, 1903], p. 5); W.E.B. Du Bois, *The Negro*, [New York, 1915], p. 189.

tinued their propaganda and among them were inspired ones who claimed to be possessed by the Spirit. It is in these troubled times that there suddenly arose one called Eon de l'Etoile, a Breton gentleman who claimed to be the Son of God coming to earth to judge mankind.[27]

Up to what point do these remote analogies of the Vaudois cult with the African religion of the *Obi* or *Obia* which has spread almost everywhere in Africa under different names and is really only one of the many forms of animism, up to what point have these more or less vague resemblances given birth to the confusion of terms and of thought from whence has emerged the word "Voodoo"? This would be difficult to explain, just as it is most difficult to account for linguistic transformations or alterations. In any event, what would give a certain consistency to the hypothesis of English-speaking Africologists is that the cult of African animism under one form or another was known and described by the oldest chroniclers of Saint Domingue, such as the Jesuits Le Pers and Charlevoix for example, and starting from the moment that the slave trade discharged great numbers of Negroes into the colony the term *Voodoo* was scarcely encountered in the eighteenth century until Moreau de Saint-Méry first employed it around 1789.

However one serious objection prevents us from adopting the Anglo-Saxon hypothesis. There exists on the coast of Guinea a little country called Dahomey, of little importance if we compare its diminutive territorial extent to the area occupied by the Bantu, but exceedingly enterprising through the power of its military organization until conquered by the French. In Dahomey there is a religion with a structure made of the same elements as our *Voodoo*. In Dahomey certain deities, the *Spirits*, are generally called *Vôdoun*, and according to the translation of A. Le Hérissé, it is curious how one finds in certain formal rituals, almost word for word, the most common expressions in the "language" of our Voodoo adherents. Here are, for example, two versions which show a striking resemblance.

Vodoun e gni Mahounou	*Mahou ouè do Vodoun*
The spirit is a thing of God	God possesses the Spirit[28]

But by what process were a handful of men, tied to the same ignominy, bent under the same yoke of infamy, able to exercise a sort of domination over the rest of the group to the point of leading it to em-

---

[27] Cf. [Maxime] Petit, *Histoire universelle des peuples,* [Paris, 1913], Vol. II, p. 30 and following.

[28] A. Le Hérissé, *L'ancien royaume du Dahomey,* Paris, 1911, [p. 96].

brace some of the rites and forms of the Dahomean religion? This is what we will attempt to demonstrate.

Let us remember henceforth that it is highly probable that the forms of incantation, of chants, of prophesy in which the same words often were repeated, engraved themselves on the minds of the sect followers as much as on those of the occasional spectators; that these forms have lost their peculiar meaning little by little in past ages to the point that those who repeat them at the present time are totally ignorant of their original sense; that in the end it was at this moment of colonial life that the term was adopted which defined the syncretism of beliefs and at the same time gave concordance to the religious rites and dances of the slaves of Saint Domingue; that if for more than a century we found no reference authenticating the term "Voodoo" neither in the official acts of the Superior Council, in the official reports of the various Governors, the Lieutenants of the Kings or in the police reports of the marechausée, nor in the Remonstrances of the Colonists or the exhortations of the Jesuits, we should recall that the colonial world, in Saint Domingue as well as in the other French islands, did not begin to take umbrage at the religious demonstrations of the slaves until they seemed to become the symbol of revolt around 1740-1750. We know that this was the time when a great many slaves escaped into the hills and the mysterious drum summoned numerous nocturnal meetings.

Do we not have figures which progressively show the growth of this movement of revolt? A thousand runaway slaves around 1700 and more than three thousand in 1751.[29] They acquired leaders: Michael in 1719 in the mountains of Bahoruco; Polydor in the plain of Trou; Noël, Canga, and many others in the neighborhood of Fort Liberty about 1775.[30] We all know the story of Mackandal, executed in 1758. He was the most famous of the leaders who exercised a genuine fascination over his associates. Revolt was the objective of every one of them. They did not recoil from any means to realize their purpose, and if by chance they were taken and delivered to the executioner, they accepted their torture with the proud faith of the martyr. The masters multiplied the punishments in vain: castration, quartering, the stake, the wheel, but nothing could check the mystical fervor of the mutinous rebels. "They

[29] Report on the Negro runaway slaves in Saint Domingue documents at the National Library cited by Vayssières [Pierre de Vaissière], *Saint-Domingue*, Paris, 1909, [p. 235].

[30] Decree of the Council of Le Cap, October 2, 1777.

suffer without uttering a word," writes M. [Monsieur] de Machault, a colonial administrator, and M. de Sezellan adds: "They endure the cruelest torments with a steadfastness that has been unequalled, appearing on the scaffolds and the funeral pyres with fierce tranquillity and courage."[31] But how could there be such insouciance, such stoicism in the face of suffering if it were not for the absolute certainty, the unshakable confidence with which the victim submitted to a force that increased his will tenfold and placed him above his actual misery, assured moreover that, whatever the fate that would befall him, the ultimate triumph of his actions was certain and undoubtedly so was the realization of his hopes. It was the power of faith which led Negroes to martyrdom. It was at the same time the supreme guide which compelled them to accept the discipline ordered by the ringleaders. You see, these commanders did not exercise just religious authority.

Because of the audacity and energy of their action, they wielded political and religious power simultaneously. Thus they were in the position of provoking and of accomplishing the ruin of the regime through the double mystical influence that they exercised over their followers. From this proposition follows a logical outcome. Only those among the conspirators who had been known in their tribes as leaders of people and doctors of the faith offered the greatest guarantee in the eyes of their co-religionists. The Dahomeans answered both criteria. It is therefore highly probable that they served as leaders in these political and religious movements and that it was through their influence that the term *Voodoo* (the Spirit) has been attributed to the whole religious manifestation of the slaves because the word conveyed the essence of their beliefs and embodied all the nuances of African animism. Therein it seems to us lies the double genesis and the evolution of African beliefs that we designate as Voodoo.

In order to understand the mechanism well, we believe it necessary to study its birthplace, that is Africa, its races and civilization.

---

[31] Letter of M. de Sézellan of Le Cap, June 7, 1763 (*Documents of Saint Domingue*, Carton XV).

Chapter III
Africa, Its Races And Its Civilization

1

One of the most salient characteristics of African ethnography is the close relationship which exists between the habitat of races and the stage of their civilization. If we survey the black continent from the North to the South, from the East to the West, we will find that where the peoples have believed or do believe in material and moral prosperity, where they have created states of some importance and are developed in social culture, there also the physical and economic conditions of habitability have been, not the sole, but the principal factors in the development of civilization.

These are the temperate regions of North Africa, such as Morocco, Algeria, Tunisia with their colonial settlements peopled with indigenous races who have achieved a remarkable state of culture, or such as the Egypt of the Pharaohs, the august mother of Mediterranean civilizations, or such as the interesting beginnings of civilization in the coastal regions bordering on the Atlantic Ocean and on the high Sudanese plateau where long ago so many Negro kingdoms and empires blossomed with a high degree of economic prosperity and moral progress.

Let us now examine the other side of the picture.

In the west, along the great expanse bathed by the Gulf of Guinea from the Ivory Coast to Angola, beyond either side of the equator, vast forests unroll and stretch toward large lakes. What is its precise area? It does not appear that such a calculation has been made. All that can be said is that the equatorial forest affirms its power and extends its area of darkness over millions of square kilometers and imprints a character *sui generis* [unique] on all this section of Africa. It is the habitat of a rich variety of races very different from each other but on the whole contrasting with the other races of the Sudanese plateau as much by morphology as by the resultant psychical elements called character.

It is these contrasts, among other motives, which have led geographers and ethnologists to divide Africa *grosso modo* [roughly] into three natural regions: a moderate region to the North and South of the Equator, followed by steppes and deserts; a tropical and subtropical region, extending from the fourth to the seventeenth parallel; and finally the equatorial region covered with tangled forest of such an abnormal and inextricable density that it alone helps explain why Africa was surnamed the mysterious. And how did the division of the continent into such distinctly contrasting zones arise? We will have a clearer understanding if we consider the orographical structure of the country.

We are aware that, save in its eastern margin, Africa is destitute of lofty mountainous ranges with peaks covered permanently with snow as in Asia and in Europe. It is composed, on the contrary, of a succession of plateaus which are higher toward the south. "Each plateau, hollowed into a shallow basin, has a slight rim around it. The passage from one plateau to the one immediately behind it is accomplished rather abruptly up a sharply inclined slope. It is, as we advance from the ocean toward the interior, like a giant stairway, each step being two to three hundred meters higher than the preceding one and varying in width from hundreds to thousands of kilometers. The first ascent is under the ocean and runs parallel to the coast. The second forms a sharp rise which is called, according to the respective district, the Crystal Mountains, the Mountains of Mayombé, Palabala, and so forth . . ."[32]

The result of this orographical arrangement, given the absence of glaciers and of a central mountain system of high altitude which would influence its meteorology, is that the climatic physiognomy is expressed only through its latitude. But the superimposition and the vastness of the plateaus, the abrupt slope which sometimes forms the passageway from one plateau to another, the shallow depression which hollows them; on the other hand, the proximity of the equator influencing the rate of seasonal rains — whether rain falls in torrential abundance during most of the year, whether it orders the rhythmical march of seasons by alternating periods of drought and humidity, finally whether the rainfall becomes infrequent and almost entirely disappears near the desert — all of these meteorological conditions impose a unique character on African hydrography. In any case, on the high plateaus the waters accumulate

[32] Dr. Ad[olphe Louis] Cureau, *Les sociétés primitives de l'Afrique équatoriale*, Paris, 1912, [p. 4].

in the depressions forming immense lakes which are much like inland seas. Are they seeking a path to the oceans? The waters hurl forward in great swirling sheets forming enroute enormous and innumerable cataracts or else roll massively and silently over long distances, always ready to let loose, at floodtime, avalanches of ruin through the savage grandeur of their power. And this is how, by two or three features, the general physical structure of the African continent is made clear.

Should we illustrate these general remarks with a concrete example?

Let us consider for a moment the immense extent of the equatorial region conventionally known as the basin of the Congo. We know that it is distinguished by the constancy of astronomical influences rather than delimited by a territorial conformation. As it is, it covers more than 4,500,000 square kilometers, which is an area somewhat smaller than half of Europe but seven times larger than France and more than sixty times larger than the island of Haiti. How does nature supply the water for such an expanse? There is such a prodigious amount. Is it not in this region that the most powerful river of all Africa, the Congo, rises? According to Elisée Réclus, probably as much water rolls along in the Congo as in all the other rivers of the country combined. It is calculated that at its mouth in normal times, that is between floods, the Congo discharges more than two million cubic feet per second (de Preville). Do you realize that it rises both from Lake Bangweulu and somewhat further on from the overflowing Lake Tanganyika by way of the Lukuga [river]?

We find ourselves on the high plateaus, around 800 meters in altitude and about 10° South latitude and 20° East longitude. The river is searching for a way to the sea. The last slopes of the plateaus of the South, the last foothills of the mountains of the East and the plateaus of Chad force the river to describe an immense curve above the Equator toward the North. It bends to the low regions of the West. In its upper third it receives from the slopes of the southern zone, the flow of innumerable tributaries, the smallest of which is larger than our Artibonite. Rich contributions come equally from the little rivers of the West. These are no more than little brooks and lagoons intersecting each other in many moving paths. Then the river, swollen by so many tributaries, concentrates its strength and hurls itself against obstacles which it destroys in its charging course toward the lowlands. From mountainous heights it spreads toward the plain, sometimes in tumultous cataracts, sometimes in shining sheets of water. It is probably the Congo that Dr. Cureau is describing in these moving words . . . "For hundreds of kilometers along the flank of the plateau there is chaos, a confusion of rocks, trees, and furious waters, the tumult of a wild river filled with roaring, with swirling eddies, with enormous spouts of flashing water, with the awesome gliding of an entire river, with alternative swelling and contraction of its mass similar to the quivering or the panting of an exasperated fighter against an obstacle.

"Higher, on the plateau, the river stretches out imposingly and majestically . . . The rivers of Africa, which no civilization has touched, have the severity, the massiveness, and the savagery of the picturesque formed by capricious and ungovernable chance.

"The greatest overwhelm the imagination with the volume of their flow, the violence of their current, and the awesome kinetic energy of their mass. These giants know no middle road at all; they are calm and apathetic; then, abruptly, they shoot forward on a mad course to the abyss in a milieu of desolation and ruin which they have themselves precipitated along the way.

"By day, under the oppressive noonday sun, their surface resembles a heavy bath of mercury, without a quiver, without a ripple, reflecting as if a mirror the pitiless heat of a glittering sky,"[33]

If we relate this magnificent description to the Congo we will easily imagine the frightening mass of running and stagnant water that fills the region, the amount of humidity that is released from such a milieu. But to all that we must add the constancy with which water vapor builds up in the atmosphere and resolves into almost daily torrential rains. Then, it is equally easy to understand how such meteorological conditions will produce the expansion of a flora surprisingly unusual in its species.

In the muddy swamps of the seaboard grow the many varieties of mangroves, with long roots emerging above the mire and entangled as the threads of a broken loom. Further inland is the realm of the immense forest. And here appear the baobab, the giant palms, the bombax with enormous trunks rearing up and spreading into space with exasperating exuberance. Their dark foliage forms a dome of thick greenery which the rays of the sun pierce with difficulty. At their feet are entwined a maze of tropical creepers, as supple as spider webs yet as resistant as metal shanks.

At times the undergrowth becomes more compliant. A clearing renders the gloom of the forest less mournful, while under the sun, the

[33] Dr. Cureau, *op. loc. cit.,* [pp. 8-10].

accumulation of dead leaves in never-ending fermentation, accumulate, shrink, and weave a padded, velvety carpet.[34]

There is no need to investigate the details of the picture any further in order to draw a clearer fresco of the physical milieu.

We can imagine, is it not true, that such physical conditions are only appropriate for the development of a singular and wild animal life.

Let us leave to their empire of water and slime the monstrous amphibians, melancholy witnesses of a prehistoric era; leave to their errant course the wild beasts big and small, the various troops of monkeys, the silent band of vampires, the countless multitude of snakes. The history of this fauna is well-known to us. What is less familiar perhaps is the pullulation of truly miniscule creatures whose existence appears to be justified only by their continual assault on other organized beings. These are the innumerable hordes of ants, termites, weevils, ferocious devourers of seeds and fruits, ruthless ravagers of the smallest harvests, untiring demolishers of miserable human habitations. These are the shock troops of mosquitoes and the tse-tse flies, vengeful agents of deadly illnesses for man and livestock, propagators of swamp fevers and of trypanosomiasis, all so much the cause of ruin and destruction as to render this region inaccessible to human life. And yet mankind has clung and developed there through the incredible phenomenon of adaptation. Ah! if all the secrets of biology are not forbidden our curiosity, is it not true that all adaptation of an organized being to a given environment is summed up, speaking in familiar terms, as *give and take;* that life is impossible without an internal reaction to external influences, that the maximum adaptation of an organism to its surroundings is the greatest capacity of its malleability and resistance to the forces of annihilation; that in the end, an equilibrium, a harmony, a sort of biological mimesis is established between creature and environment?

If these propositions are true, we can corroborate them in the history of man on the planet. Of all organized beings, man is the only one in truth who, by the power of his intelligence, possesses "the original élan, the internal drive," not only to adapt himself to the environment, but to use it in such a way as to keep the little flame of his superiority burning and to preserve in himself the divine essence of eventual evolution.

This is the moving history that the races who live everywhere on the African continent and more particularly those that inhabit the

[34] Cf. [Sir Henry] Stanley, *Dans les ténèbres de l'Afrique,* 2 vol.; *A travers le continent noir,* 2 vol., [1879].

equatorial zone, even the area of the forests, reveal to anyone who knows how to question them.

2

For the mass of ignorant persons and even for the greater share of refined people whose distinction is to put up with nonsense that is so much the more assertive since it rests upon information gathered at random from reading, there is no doubt that Africa is the original cradle of the black race. It is anything but that.

It is not necessary to discuss here what is illusory and erroneous regarding the concept of race itself as applied to human nature, to linger on the question of whether the human specie derives from a single origin or divergent ones, if it is the resultant of evolution or better yet the product of an "explosive" transformation, because we are aware that authoritative scholars and ethnographers since the studies of de Quatrefages to the more recent work of Delafosse,[35] of Desplagnes, of Sir Harry Johnston, and so forth . . . , acknowledge that southern Asia has been the probable point of departure of races which people the African continent.[36] It would be interesting to follow the itinerary if we could mark out their routes with positive landmarks. From all that we have been able to compile of this far-off time, it is probable that "the vibratory center" of ethnic migration was somewhere around the plateau of Iran and that the wave surged forward in two directions, one to the East and the other to the West. This would explain the presence of consequential Negro populations, with a current count going beyond 30 million, which one finds south of the Godavari, along the coast of Coromandel, of Nizam, of Jaipur, on the plateau of Mysore, on the coast of Malabar, and so forth. From the Hindu peninsula the infiltration of the Negro continued always toward the east, and would have reached the southeastern islands and through Burma the straits of Malacca and the Malay

[35] Maurice Delafosse, Les noirs de l'Afrique, 1 vol., [Paris, 1922]. Delafosse is of the opinion that the settlement of Africa has perhaps come from migrations originating within the boundaries of the Indian and Pacific Oceans; Lieutenant [Louis] Desplagnes, Le plateau central nigérien, Paris, [1907]; Sir Harry Johnston, The Negro in the New World, 1 vol., London, [1900]; The Opening up of Africa, New York and London.

[36] Noted paleontologists such as Matthew, (W.D.), "Climate and Evolution," (Annals of the New York, tc. of sc.) XXIV, 1915, ["Climate and Evolution," Annals of the New York Academy of Science, XXIV (February 18, 1915), pp. 171-318]; Marcelin Boule, Les hommes fossiles, Paris, [1923], p. 467 and following, also acknowledges that southern Asia is the point of departure of ethnic migration.

Archipelago.

The other stream would have flowed toward Anterior Asia, through the Iranian plateau to Arabia, and from there across the isthmus of Suez to Egypt and all parts of Africa. Is it not due to this infiltration of Negroes that a Nigritic element is found in Europe during the Mid Quaternary period as indicated by the discoveries of the caves of Grimaldi by Professor Verneau?[37]

Such would be, in any case, the hypothetical itinerary of the migration of races which have populated Africa in a very early age. It is easy to realize that, given the present state of science, it is impossible to support these reflections with any proof. We can only suggest that they are highly probable.

We ask ourselves, uneasily, by what phenomenon we can explain the influence of Negro blood, traces of which are very visible in a great many populations of Anterior Asia and even a little of Asia Minor, if not as the sequel of a black migration beginning either in Africa or in Asia. On the other hand, so meagre are the given paleontological facts that we are inclined to think, according to the words of Boule, that "India appears more and more as a very old center of prehistoric culture."

However it may be, and no matter what our wish may be, we will be excused for not lingering on this discussion since, wherever we stop, there will still remain another aspect of the problem to resolve. To which human types did or do the races who populated Africa belong?

A momentous question, in truth, and one which almost seems like squaring the circle.

We have not, alas! any solid criterion for settling the eternal debate about the problems of our origin. All we know positively is that the present groupings of the genus *homo* on which we confer, inappropriately moreover and with a simplemindedness, attributes of species and subspecies, of races or of varieties, all being the only tangible realities by which our investigations can be exercised, nevertheless fail to comply with strict, zoological classification, and we know further that for thousands of years these ethnic groups have intermingled with each other despite their specific differences to such an extent that none exists in a pure state, even if theoretically such a phenomenon ever did exist at a

---

[37] "It should be admitted that a more or less Nigritic element lived in south-western Europe around the Mid Quaternary period, between the race of Spy and that of Cro-Magnon." Report of [Dr. René] Verneau cited by Marcellin Boule, *op. cit.*, [pp. 284-285].

moment of time at some place on the planet.[38]

So if migrations of peoples coming from the Orient in prehistoric ages chose Africa as their dwelling place, it is perhaps possible that by interrogating the ethnography of the old continent as it is at present and in spite of the inadequacy of data, we would find in the surviving types the primitive origin of races which migrated in olden times to Africa.

3

Aside from all theoretical considerations, there is agreement of interpretation on some essential facts.

Three types emerge from the amalgam of African races. One type is very clearly dwarfish, with the figure varying from 1m. 25 to 1m. 45 [4'1" to 4'9"]. These are the Negrilloes, the Pygmies of the forest. They also look the least Negro according to the color of their skin, if by *Negro* we mean *black* as the etymology of the word signifies. They are clear chocolate and even a little reddish-colored.[39] By contrast, they have wooly hair, twisted in peppercorn fashion, upper limbs that are more developed than the lower, the prognathism very accentuated, "that is, the protrusion of the jaw-bone," so that the chin seems receded. They are closely related to the Bochimen or, more exactly, the Bushmen, who have a lit-

[38]   The "negroid type would seem (judging from the skeletons of Grimaldi) to have penetrated the north-west as far as Great Britain and from there into Ireland. In the east there are traces in Switzerland and Italy, and from the neolithic to the historical period it penetrated the northern races. From modern times to our day, the influence of an old negroid element is readily discerned in the populations of North Africa, of Spain, of France, of Ireland, of western Britain, of Italy, of Sardinia, of Sicily, and in the populations bordering the eastern Mediterranean." Sir Harry Johnston, *The Negro in the New World*, p. 26. And further on the eminent Africologist speaking of the mixture of Caucasian with Negro blood expresses himself in these terms, "It is from the mixture of all these elements in different degrees" that have come the people of Africa such as we recognize them today. "Very few of them" are free of some drops of Caucasian blood originating from the persistent invasion of Africa by peoples of the white race since 12,000 years before Christ to our time. *Loc. cit.*, p. 30. In a marginal note on "fossil men" Boule points out that, since the discovery of the Negroid skeletons of Grimaldi, others have been found from the Neolithic period in Illyria and the Balkans. "The prehistoric statuettes, dating from the Copper Age, of Sultan Selo (Bulgaria) seem to represent Negroid figures," according to [?] Zupanic, "Les premiers habitants des pays Yougoslaves," *La Revue Anthropologique*, 1919, p. 32.

[39]   The skin color of the Bochimen is a tawny yellow while that of the Negrilloes is the brown of a chocolate tablet or slightly roasted coffee. [Joseph] Deniker, *Les races et les peuples de la terre*, Paris, 1926.

tle taller figure (1m. 50), [4'11"], a lighter skin, and a woolly shock of tousled hair. The habitat of both extends throughout all equatorial Africa and into southern Africa. They live in a miserable state, in roving bands, occupying temporary encampments in the immense forest areas or in the desert-like steppes of the eastern region. They possess nothing, do not practice any kind of industry, and live only by gathering, hunting, and fishing. They may well be "the pygmies" of which "the father of history, Herodotus of Halicarnassus" speaks.

In any event, when one chances to find them now in a pure state, they represent certainly the last survivors of the most primitive type of man whose history has been preserved for all times by the earliest written accounts and by the most persevering oral traditions of the African tribes.[40]

"On this sub-stratum was deposited, at a distant and indefinite period, the so-called Hamitic element of Asiatic or European origin (supposed continuators of the Cro-Magnon race). This element has been preserved in a rather pure state among the Berbers, and perhaps has been transformed by the interminglings with the Negroes, into a new race, analogous to the Ethiopian with which we must connect the ancient Egyptians." (Deniker, page 521) The southern Semites, who came since the Egyptian neolithic period from another continent, mixed with the new race and further modified the types of the North-East. But it happened that another characteristic — the influence of language — apparently seemed to unify all the agglomerations of more or less black men living in most of southern Africa and bordering on the Congolese center. Nevertheless, such startling diversity of types left no doubt of the amalgam of ethnic strata from which they were derived. In short, all the people who speak Bantu, whether they are Kaffirs of Zulus, from Matabele or Nyasaland, whether they live in the Upper Congo or on the shores of Tanganyika are known as the Bantu race because their languages offer a certain linguistic unity in that the principal characteristic is the formation of words derived ordinarily from a prefix.

Finally, to complete our analysis, we envisage the case of the third ethnic group also formed of composite types and which, for the sake of convenience, Deniker calls "the Nigritian race" from which is drawn the popular or classical type of Negro. Their area of habitation is limited on the North by an undulating line from the mouth of the Senegal to the great curve of the Niger, then from the fourteenth parallel North

[40] Lieutenant Desplagnes, *loc. cit;* Stanley, *loc. cit.;* Deniker, *loc. cit.*

to Bahr-el-Ghazal and the Nile; in the South, from the coast of the Gulf of Guinea to the Cameroons, then from the mountain range of Adamawa, seventh degree of latitude North, to the countries occupied by the peoples of the Foulay-Sandeh group, and further to the East to the basin of the Upper Nile. This great river constitutes the limit of the Nigritians while to the West the boundary is clearly indicated by the Atlantic Ocean. (Deniker)

"One can divide the Nigritian group into four large sections: 1st, the Nigritians of eastern Sudan or Nilotic Negroes; 2nd, those of French Central Sudan (that is, the Hausa-Wadai group); 3rd, the Nigritians of the French Western Sudan and of Senegal; 4th, the coastal Nigritians or Negroes of Guinea." (Deniker)

It is probably from this group that Africa draws its traditional ethnic physiognomy because it outnumbers all the others, and it is perhaps this peculiarity which has caused the continent to be called land of the blacks since Antiquity. In any case it is they who have largely supplied the slave market of the Americas and the West Indies. In part, we Negroes of Haiti are their more or less authentic descendents.

But what are the fundamental characteristics of the Nigritians and how may they be distinguished from other Negroes?

First of all, they are truly black in skin color. Here also, the physical human figure developed fully. Although the Nigritian group may be formed of very diversified ethnic classes, although it may be subdivided into many important human varieties, with each doubtlessly using different idioms, yet in the general language structure, contrary to the Bantu language, the derivation of words comes through the use of suffixes. The best ethnographers agree that the diverse specimens of this group resemble each other only through analogy. In fact, who would not differentiate between the Nilotic Nigritian and the other types? The Nilotic is one of the greatest specimens of known man. Clearly crossed with Hamitic blood or mixed with that of the equatorial forest-dwellers, he embodies sometimes a beautiful specimen with fine and distinguished features, sometimes a symbol of latent strength with a stocky appearance and broad-nosed face . . .

The central and western Sudanese share with the Negroes of Guinea the common characteristic of being dolichocephalic and tall (about 1m. 70 [5'7"], with either dull or shining black skin. However they are composites to an extreme, not only because they have interacted with one another for thousands of years but because they have mixed with the

Caucasian blood of invaders coming from the Mediterranean coasts or Asia, thanks to the isthmus of Suez or the straits of Bab-el-Mandeb. Is there not quite a difference between a Guinean of the coastal forests, whose oval-shaped head of hair, large flattened nose, thick lips, torso with bulging chest and rippling muscles, whose whole thick and massive appearance evokes the image of a true athletic specimen, reputed for his bravery and his fierceness — and the delicately jointed, looselimbed Mandingan or Lybian Negro, with curly hair, gentle features, broad forehead, agile and solid at the same time? These diverse types are all considered as being of the same Nigritian race, though they differ greatly in their general morphology. In the final analysis, all of them, Pygmies, Bushmen, Bantus, Nigritians from the coasts or the plateaus — all generically called Negroes — reveal such an amalgam of types, that to consider them as one offers such a diffuse and complex picture that it is, to say the least, erroneous to speak of *one black race* in Africa, since it is impossible to sustain or to justify this thesis from either an historical or an anthropological point of view.

The dissimilarity of African races is even more striking if, in order to demonstrate the cogency of our original proposition that the possibilities of social culture are primarily daughters of the physical milieu, we direct attention to the centers of original civilization revealed to us by African history.

We will see how the psychological conditions of human development endure the determinism of material conditions.

4

But how do we talk about African civilization?

In what labyrinth of sophisms will we be led astray?

Do not the two terms conflict with each other as two incompatible substances repel each other in the crucible of the experimenter?

Is not black Africa considered as the classical land of savagery? How can one speak of Africa without paradox? This is, at any rate, the somewhat simplistic conception that we ourselves have of our ancestral country from the singularly brief information contained in overly succinct handbooks.

Now, for some thirty or forty years, scientific missions from Europe have explored the old continent with great hopes of becoming enlightened about the past life of its races, research enterprises of colonial governments have collected facts and traditions of the greatest interest, and from these studies as a whole there has appeared an African history, extraordinary in its revelations and quite suggestive as to the conclusions to which it leads us.

It brings us to a basic observation. If by the civilization of a country, of a people, of a race, is meant the social and political organization, the intellectual culture which this country, this people, or this race has attained, if it includes the whole of its institutions, beliefs, customs, and mores, if all these things reveal that these people have a sense of collective and private life, the guiding principle from which law and morals proceed, then there have been at a given point in time on the African continent centers of Negro civilization whose remains have not only been found, but also whose renown has radiated beyond the limits of the steppes and the desert.

These cultural centers took on most often the form of a State — empire or kingdom — owing to the ingenuity, perspicacity, and audacity of an energetic leader. Most commonly this State had as a nucleus a city whose prosperity extended to the neighboring village in such a way that the empire was, in the end, a series of federated towns obedient to a governing leader. The most brilliant of these empires was the one that the Songhaï established on the banks of the Niger, whose moving history is recalled for us by Félix Dubois in his monograph on *Tombouctou la mystérieuse* according to the testimony of *Tarikh-es-Soudan*[41] written by the Arabian historian Abderraham-es-Sadi. "The empire of the Songhaï extended to the North from the salt mines of Thégazza, in the middle of the Sahara, to Bandouk or the country of the Bammakou in the South; from Lake Chad in the East to the shores of the Atlantic Ocean in the West. To cross this extensive kingdom would take six months of walking."

One of the emperors of the Askia dynasty to whom history accorded the glorious title of Askia the Great, brought to the empire an extraordinary degree of prosperity and moral grandeur. This Muslim is remembered for a famous pilgrimage to Mecca in 1495, in the company of scholars and pious commentators of the Koran. He was escorted by 500 horsemen and 100 footsoldiers. He had brought 300,000 pieces of gold. During his sojourn of two years outside his states he distributed

---

41 Félix Dubois, *Tombouctou-la-Mystérieuse*, Paris, 1898; [al-Sadi, 'Abd al-Rahman iban 'Abd Allah], *Tarik-es-Soudan: La chronique du Soudan*, (Translation of [Octave Victor] Houdas, [Paris, 1898-1900]).

100,000 goldpieces in the holy cities of Medina and Mecca. He dispensed a similar sum to provide for his maintenance and that of his numerous following, then he used the rest of his money for luxurious purchases which he brough back to Câo [Gâo], the capital of his Sudanese empire in 1497. He had organized his country with the rare clairvoyance of a prudent and circumspect administrator. Thus the security of the State resting from the first on superior armed forces was in essence truly an army of well-trained professionals, always prepared to pounce upon predatory tribes and to spread the rule of the master wherever circumstances demanded. The empire was divided into vice-royalties, each having as its leader a faithful lieutenant of the emperor, chosen from members of his family or his immediate entourage. During the thirty-six years of his rule he maintained peace and justice throughout his empire, which was as big as half of Europe. He was particularly diligent in the promotion of agriculture; thus he utilized the waters of the Niger in a system of canals which permitted the cultivation of arable land as far as the edges of the desert. Since the Empire was the center through which passed the routes of caravans which exchanged cotton-cloth, silks, small glassware for gold, ivory, and other precious materials, the sovereign organized a system of weights and measures in order to regulate commerce against abuse. But where the splendor of the empire attained its greatest brilliance was in the domain of arts and sciences. The ruins of Timbuktu attest to a peak of development of an architectural artistry somewhat resembling Egyptian art. The arts and sciences, cultivated by knowledgeable men, were taught at the University of Sankore, a grand mosque whose imposing ruins still existed some thirty years ago. Foreign scholars flocked to the Sudan, says Dubois in quoting the Arabian historian, knowing that the best welcome awaited them. They came from Morocco, Touat, Algeria, Ghadames, Cairo. The arts and sciences developed rapidly and soon a series of the most interesting Sudanese writers arose. The author of *Tombouctou la mystérieuse* concludes: "A work of that period brought the highest honor to the genius of the Negro race and therefore merits all of our attention. During the sixteenth century, this land of the Songhaï, which bore the seeds of ancient Egypt, was throbbing. A marvelous thrust of civilization arose there, in the heart of the black continent." [p. 134]

This civilization was not the result of chance, as one might be tempted to believe, not a state of prosperity because of the happy initiative of a series of able princes. The fact is that western Sudan, because of its geographical position, has been at all times the crossroads where the elements upon which civilizations are founded have coincided with one another: facilities for economic cultivation, markets for products of the soil and of the subsoil, industrious and enterprising peoples, finally, fermentation of beliefs and religious proselytism. In this moment of gestation the rise of leaders who embodied the genius of the race and who were drawn to the needs of the country was sufficient to set in motion the movements of intellectual expansion and progress of every kind, as is strikingly exemplified in the most ancient civilizations.

The written history and the oral traditions of the Sudanese offer us a complete illustration of this point of view.

If the empire of the Songhaï was the magnificent center of a culture, whose flowering we have just verified, and was able to make strides in moral and material progress at a time when civilization everywhere was still groping in the dark, it would be a grave mistake to pretend that this movement was no more than the flash of a meteor. On the contrary, it seems to have been the materialization of more or less fruitful endeavors that go back to the foundation of Ghana around 300 A.D. by white princes whose dynasty reigned for seven centuries.

Following this dynasty came a line of black Soninke princes who not only brought under their dominion the country of Blad-es-Sudan but also pushed strongly forward into the desert to subdue the Berbers of the white race. The Arabian historians and geographers, Bekri and Edrissi, give very pertinent details on the organization of the empire of Ghana. Such was the result that around the year 1000 it had attained a rather high development of political power as well as material prosperity. It owed this good fortune to its position as an intermediary marketplace between the countries of the North and of the South. It was the storehouse of salt extracted from the mines of Tatental, situated in the Sahara. We know how highly the populations of central Africa valued salt because of its scarcity in these regions. It was used sometimes as a medium of exchange as if it were gold or money.

Ghana was also the great market of gunpowder and nuggets of gold from the gold-bearing regions to the south of Senegal. This is why, at a time when surprise attacks, or razzias, were the symbols of power, this rich and prosperous black empire was a temptation for all conquerors desperately anxious for glory or in need of prisoners. A white leader, Aboubekr-ben-Omar, ruler of the Almoravides, who had succeeded in establishing his domination over southern Morocco and had conquered all of the Sahara, invaded the Negro empire of Ghana and destroyed it around 1076.

Now let us glance quickly at the history of the countries at the bend of the Niger. We will find there a development almost parallel to that of the countries we have just studied, and perhaps our interest in them will be even keener if, though we may be faulted for treating our subject too loosely, we do not forget that the principal object of this very succinct study of African civilization is to find the origins of certain customs and beliefs which the Haitians have retained after four centuries of transplantation.

Ah well, among the distinctive features of empires at the bend — empires of the Mossi — we ought first to point out their resistance to external causes of destruction because of their superior density of population and their greater ethnic homogeneity, fundamentally Negro, and finally the saving influence of a religion that was more thoroughly national.

A remark appropriate to make concerning this last characteristic is that like the Sudanese the rulers were fervent followers of Islamism and the principal tendency of their government was the constant preoccupation of adapting the customs of their subjects to the regulations of the Koran, thus requiring them to surround themselves with Muslim scholars of letters and sciences who served as both political counselors and spiritual guides.

But to what extent did the people assimilate the prescriptions of the Koran and how many were superficially Muslims? This is certainly a question which should be asked each time that leaders attribute their motives of action to religious inspiration and especially when this religion is of foreign importation. Here in the empires of the river bend, principally in those of the Ouagadougou and the Yatenga, religion has the force of a national sentiment concretized in a doctrine "which regulates minutely all acts of public and private life based largely upon the ancestral worship by which the emperor as descendent of the great universal forefather retains complete control, participating himself in some way in the quasi-divinity attributed to his deceased predecessors and which he is to enjoy after his death.

"In this respect a somewhat remote but real analogy may be drawn between the institutions of China and of the Mossi in that what made up the strength and long life of the first also powerfully aided the second in maintaining their integrity throughout the revolutions within neighboring countries."[42]

In fact, these empires which rose in the eleventh century, lasted eight hundred years before they were destroyed by French conquest at the end of the nineteenth century. Though they have never had the brilliance nor the renown of the states of the left bank which we have already discussed, they were none the less distingished by their intelligent as well as practical organization. Thus the division of the empire into five provincial governments and three vassal kingdoms, the strict dependence of the governors on and their submission to the central power, the regulation of the relationships between the sovereign and his subordinates, all testify to a truly remarkable sense of political organization. And it is thanks to this administrative aptitude, to this competent direction that the emperors of the Mossi safeguarded the integrity of their country against threats of absorption or of annihilation from without . . .

Finally, to conclude our historical incursion into the Sudanese area, there remains a last word to be said about the empire of the Mali (of the Mande or Mandingo), a vast country lying to the south of the Mossi. It had its hours of glory from the eleventh to the seventeenth century.

The Mandingo form a Negro population predominant for both their language and their physical type which distinguished them amongst the diverse peoples who inhabited most of the western Sudanese plateau. In remote times they had intermixed with their neighbors the Peuhls, who are themselves the descendants of Judo-Syrians and also of the invading Arabian Berbers whose ethnic influence is so strong in the basin of the Niger. Like the Peuhls, Moors, or the Tukulors they have often been called "red men" because of their hybridization. According to ethnographers, they are intelligent, industrious, proud, and courteous.[43] They are all Muslims and, according to Leo the African, their conversion goes back to 1050.

It seems that the first ruler to adopt Islamism might have been converted by an Almoravide prince, the uncle of the Sultan Youssef-ben-Tachfine, founder of Marrakech. The Mandingo succeeded in establishing a stable empire which lasted for almost six centuries. Several of their sovereigns, like all good Muslims, made the pilgrimage to Mecca and

[42] Delafosse, op. loc. cit., Vol. II, p. 124 [See Haut-Sénégal Niger]. Cf. Lieutenant [Lucien François] Marc, Le pays Mossi; Louis Tauxier, Le noir du Sudan; pays Mossi et Gourounsi, Paris, 1912.

[43] Sir Harry Johnston, Liberia, 2 vol., London, Vol. II, p. 928; Delafosse: op. cit., Vol. II, p. 171.

several marked their reign with enterprises and works of great interest. Kankan-Mussa (1297-1332), one of the most famous, drew attention to his generosity and intelligence during a trip to the holy place. He had the good fortune of meeting worthy men, such as the Arabic Spanish poet Es-Saheli and the historian El-Maner, whom he attached to his retinue and brought back with him to the Sudan.

He used their services in the administration of the empire and it was under their direction that the two mosques were erected in Timbuktu and Gâo, which had been annexed to Mali at that time.

Ibn-Batuta, the Arabian geographer, has left us a minute description of customs and of the ceremonies in honor of the court of the Mali rulers. He has portrayed the luxury and the grand pomp in which the emperors took pride, the order and regularity of the administrative divine services, the observance of the principles of the Koran. From all of this we get the impression that the empire of Mali had achieved in a black country a type of organized state comparable to many realms all over the world.

In summary, when we include the whole period of history of black peoples disseminated in the Sudanese area watered by the Niger and its tributaries — whether it is a question of the federation of cities of which Ghana was the center or the empire of the Songhaï that the Askia made famous, whether it concerned centralized monarchies typified most strikingly by the Mossi, or the states which had their moments of brilliance on the Mandingo plateau — we find in an examination of historical facts that a certain social culture, a conception of public life, essentially a form of black civilization had been developed at one time in the heart of Africa. If we were to compare this civilization to that of other peoples on the three continents and notably to that of eastern European peoples at the same time period, we would not find that the Negroes were the ones with the greatest inclination toward barbarism or the least aspiration to a higher ideal of social life.

But then another problem presents itself and impels us to discover why the Sudan seems to have been the only center of a cultural movement. Were there any others? And if others did exist, why did they not last as long as those of the Sudan whose history we have just sketched?

Such questions seem to be applicable enough to the study to warrant them a brief moment of thought.

Chapter IV

African Societies and the External World

In order to understand the evolution of African societies of which we have sketched two or three very brief historical portraits, in order to explain the deadly obstacles which all the others have encountered and the long silence surrounding the mystery of their existence, in order finally to comprehend the sense of heavy prejudice which weighs upon the Negro, we must study the African question further, not only by recalling the structure of the age-old continent as we have just done, but also by completing our data on the history of African communities with a history of their relations with the external world. So we will try to reconstruct — fragmentarily it is true — the framework of the most moving drama that has been staged in a part of the world.

We recognized earlier in the text that Africa is topographically divided into natural regions. We showed that these regions varied climatically from the temperate to the tropical and then to the equatorial zone. We have broadly delineated the very special characteristics of this last region. From this diverse research we are now able to extract a first precept, namely that it is certainly not by happy coincidence that the superior or potential forms of civilization were found only in temperate or tropical Africa. It seems possible that we can explain the general pattern of these social movements by the contingencies of the physical milieu. This is too succinct a judgment for us to make without supporting its validity with some preciseness.

We know that noble efforts have been made to discover what some have called *laws of civilization*;[44] however it does not seem, to our knowledge at least, that these attempts have achieved results concrete

[44] Cf. T[héophile] Funck-Brentano, *La civilisation et ses lois*, [Paris], 1876; [Walter] Bagehot, *Lois scientifiques du développement des nations*, [Paris, 1885].

enough to permit the establishment of iron-clad laws according to which the life of a people are bound to develop and which indicate, depending on whether this group succeeds or fails in realizing them, its aptitude or incapacity to adopt superior or crude forms of civilization. Nevertheless, it is understood that among the many ideas accepted about the evolution of peoples, one of the most evident is embodied in the close correlations existing between man and the physical milieu in which he lives, particularly when we consider man in the primitive stage of his existence. Often his ability is heightened or diminished as his adaptation to the milieu is conditioned by the extent of the intelligence he exercises, or maybe as the physical forces mold him in a way that establishes a perfect equilibrium of action and reaction between the human being and nature. This is what Miss Semple expresses successfully in the following form:[45]

"The geographical foundation upon which a state rests encompasses a complex set of physical conditions which can influence its historical development. The most important among them comprise the size of the state and the zone in which it is situated, its continental or insular position, mediterranean or maritime, open to the vast ocean or confined to some interior sea; its frontiers, whether they are contained by the sea, the mountain, the desert or the sinuous lines of some river; its mountainous forests, its rich plains and its arable lowlands, its climate and its drainage systems, the richness of its minerals or the poorness of its indigenous or imported flora and fauna. When a state has benefited from all of these natural conditions, the land becomes a constitutive part of this state modifying the people who inhabit it or being modified by them until their affinity through reciprocal interaction is at the point where the people cannot be understood if they are detached from their milieu. Any attempt, theoretically, to separate one from the other reduces the social or political body to the situation of a cadaver still useful in the study of anatomical structure according to the systemic thought of Herbert Spencer but projecting little light on the vital process."[46] No human group could illustrate more forcibly the validity of these remarks quoted above than the peoples of Africa. Whatever we conjecture about their origin or however we may envisage their present or past way of life, there is an easily perceptible difference that distinguishes the man of the forests

[45] Ellen Churchill [Semple], *Influences of Geographic Environment on the basis of Ratzel's System of Anthropo-geography*, New York and London, [1911], p. 59.
[46] Cf. Camille Vallaux, *Géographie sociale: Le sol et l'état*, Paris, 1911.

from the man of the plains.[47] This difference has been affirmed throughout the ages, here by a certain sense of social and political organization, by the creative effort of a certain intellectual culture, there by the disorderly dispersion of wandering tribes and the effort of adaptation to the depressing conditions of an uncontrollable natural world. Is it not true that the inventive genius of man is completely foreign to the geographical position of the Sudan which in the past was made as much the limit for commercial incursions over the continent as it was the region most accessible to ethnic migrations coming from Asia and Europe? Is it not true that the wild barrier of the impenetrable forest at the threshold of the equatorial zone has resisted the curiosity of the outside world with a mysterious sphinx-like smile?

If such are the acceptable ideas of geography, let us see how history has utilized them.

And to begin with, it goes without saying that the real world has not always been what it is today. Transformations of the earth from the prehistoric age to the present time have profoundly and gradually changed the appearance of the globe.

Thanks to the hypotheses of geology and the allied sciences[48] we are able through bold induction to reconstruct the changes on our planet. Thus paleo-geography calculates that approximately fifty thousand years ago, North Africa and southern Europe may have been connected by a kind of isthmus that joined Morocco to the southern end of Spain, and Tunisia to Sicily and the peninsula of Malta.[49] Likewise toward the southeast, Asia and Africa formed only one land mass since the straits of Bab-el-Mandeb were of later creation. However in contrast to this picture, perhaps the Mediterranean and the Red Sea were connected to each other by means of a canal which, becoming obstructed, later became the isthmus of Suez. On the continent of Africa numerous water-courses, shallow lakes, sort of like inland seas of a size far larger than those existing now, occupied the same central region just as today and abundantly fed the basins of the Upper Congo, of the Chari [River], of the Zambesi [River], of Lake Chad and of Hausaland. Moreover, the Sahara itself was probably sprinkled with marshes and shallow lakes fed by mountain streams. It is easy to understand that such an abundance of water could have made the face of Africa, from North to South and East

---

47   Cf. Dr. A. Cureau, *op. cit.,* [pp. 23-33].
48   Notably tectonics, stratigraphy, and paleontology.
49   Sir Harry Johnston, *The Opening up of Africa,* p. 22.

to West, totally different from what it is today. A luxuriant vegetation covered the regions which are now but an empire of sand.

This must have been what the Sahara, the Libyan, and the Nubian deserts once were. If this pleasant picture has not survived to our times it is because geological transformations in this part of the planet have gradually brought about a process of change, a drying out of the land through the diminution and retreat of ice in Europe and a corresponding lack of cataracts. Add to this, in the same setting, another phenomenon which must have accentuated the drying process. This was the question of the drainage of flowing streams into the ocean. In short, all of these actions combined have contributed much to the growing scarcity of water and even to the final exhaustion of this element. It is readily apparent from these diverse changes on our planet that during an approximate period of fifty thousand years, a larger habitable area was available to man in Africa than is so today. All of this justifies the law credited to Jean Brunhes[50] that the rate of human settlement of any area on earth is closely related to the capacity of its water supply to contribute to economic wealth and the natural vigor of plant life. There must not be too much or too little of it. As soon as the equilibrium is broken in one way or another there is a repercussion on the ecumene [the permanently inhabited portion of the earth] and human settlement follows the same curve of decrease. Thus it is likely that the habitability of Africa, during an indeterminate period after the paleolithic age, offered conditions assuring the equilibrium that human geography required. But, with the slow transformations of the earth, the conditions also slowly changed. Now, in this vast expanse between the Red Sea and the Atlantic, "nature pursued an extreme course in erecting a barrier between the Sahara, Libyan, and Arabian deserts and the fertile countries of Mauretania, of lower Egypt, and of prosperous Arabia, abundantly watered by heavy rains. The shallow marshes dried up leaving deposits of salt and soda in their beds, the rivers disappeared, the forests thinned to nothingness, and the denuded soil was exposed to the occasional ravages of thunderstorms which washed it, and the absence of trees and vegetation brought about extreme changes in climate from torrid heat by day to intense cold at night. This alternation of heat and cold made the soil dry and crumbly and broke up the bare rocks. The same causes created winds of extraordinary violence which reduced the broken rocks to sandy dust. So were formed the deserts in Arabia and northern Africa

[50] Jean Brunhes, *Géographie humaine,* [Paris, 1912], p. 67 and following.

which became barriers between tropical Africa and the Mediterranean countries and little by little isolated the people and animals of this land from those of temperate Europe and Asia. In this way *tropical Africa distinguished itself from others.* The great mass of subspecie Negro was trapped in the region to the south of the deserts and was unable to interbreed at all with the Caucasian races of Europe, of North Africa, and western Asia."[51] This was the tragic adversity which, for thousands of years, kept a part of the black race crushed under the horror of the worst abominations. That they did not regress to downright simple animality is to believe — holding to the most probable hypotheses on the evolution of species — that the link by which man is attached by some common ancestor to real Simians is forever buried in the mists of time, it is to believe that the cosmic conditions which probably produced man from some lowly quadrumane at a moment in time will never recur. And if some varieties of species handicapped by relentless influences of the milieu have been or are still burdened by such heavy fetters that they appear to the observer to be leading an absolutely primitive life, we would be tempted to attribute the possibility and the persistence of such a state of things to some irony of nature desirous of reminding us of the lowliness of our origins in spite of the gifts it has bestowed upon us elsewhere. However that may be, we are the only living creatures who, according to the rhythm of our existence, can fluctuate between the most staggering progress and the most degrading submission. Nevertheless, as low as we may descend, we preserve within ourselves the magnificent aptitude [ability to acquire knowledge] which perpetuates our lineage above the balance of creation. This perhaps is the great misfortune of human nature but it is also certainly its inalienable mark of nobility. And this is what the Negro of Africa has retained as the co-heir of the eminent dignity of human nature despite whatever the best of authorities have said to the contrary.

In any case, of all that we know of the struggles of man on this planet, of all we know of his reversals and his triumphs, of his painful biological and social evolution, no circumstance, no fact, can properly illustrate with more acuity and realism the harsh battle that he had to lead against natural obstacles than the way of life of the Negro relegated, confined, trapped in the area of the equatorial forests for thousands of

[51] Sir Harry Johnston, *The Opening up of Africa,* p. 24. We have italicized this phrase of the quotation for a purpose. It is a question of understanding clearly that the black mass was blocked up in the forested area in the extreme southern part of the desert region and not strictly speaking in tropical Africa.

years. This was the dark tragedy which kept him outside history until the dawn of modern times, and when the era of discoveries and of heavy maritime trading brought this fraction of humanity into contact with the rest of the world, it was to create the most odious form of exploitation of man by man: slavery.

Those who reproach Negroes for their inferiority or their so-called inaptitude for civilization disregard too easily the terrible conditions of Negro life in the equatorial zone. For the conclusion of these superficial critiques clashes with contradictory facts found in other black communities favored with better climatic conditions. Is it not an established fact that wherever the modes of habitat have offered some possibilities of social culture to the indigenous population, there arose on the age-old continent some societies which organized according to their genius in coping with the resources at their disposal and which were always quick to secure the best benefit from their relations with the external world. This explains the success of the Sudan which, because of its position, became the intermediary center of two worlds. It is, in reality, accessible from one side to the people of the Mediterranean through the Barbary States[52] and Egypt, and on the other to the people of the Orient through Suez and the straits of Bab-el-Mandeb.

Moreover, its topographical situation has always made it the marketplace where bold caravaneers ventured in search of gold, ivory, and slaves coming from the impenetrable regions of the West. It was pre-eminently a crossroad of ethnic migrations. Thus it is not surprising that we found there not only more or less civilized communities but an amalgam of peoples, of customs, of mores, and of beliefs fashioned according to the individual genius of the black races implanted there.

Have we proof to support this point of view?

"In referring to the *Ora maritima* of Avenius," says Desplagnes,[53] we see Hanno of Carthage scattering 30,000 colonists along the oceanic coasts of Mauritania, around 414 B.C. Thus we can already sense that the North African populations of Libya were formed from a mixture of indigenous black tribes and immigrant Asiatic tribes. Moreover, Utica was founded as early as 1100 B.C. and numerous Phoenician colonies already dotted the Libyan coasts. Herodotus described this confederation of diverse tribes to us by the name of *Nasamons* or Nasamous which preceded the federation of the *Marinids;* now, this name of Nasamons

[52] The Barbary Coast: Tripolitania, Tunisia, Algeria, Morocco.
[53] Lieutenant Louis Desplagnes, *Le haut plateau central nigérien,* p. 113.

is Egyptian and expressly denotes the crossbreeding of blacks *Nashi* and Asiatics *Amon*. Indeed this definition can easily be traced from a hymn to *Amon-Ra* dating back to the time of the *Rameses* where we read: "Men come out of his two eyes and spread over the surface of the earth, the flock of *Ra* divides into four races: the Egyptians *Rotou*, the Negroes *Nashi*, who are under the patronage of *Hor*, the Asiatics *Amon*, and the peoples with white skin *Sokhit*, the goddess with the head of a lion extends her protection."

Besides, in all Sudan there is a tradition that men with light complexion and long hair were the first to become accustomed to the use of a kind of jewelry or precious stones called *aggry beads*, "pierres d'aigris," for personal ornamentation. At one time these glass beads were the object of very brisk trade in African countries. They still may be found now on living people as well as in the tombs or Tumuli, so Delafosse informs us.[54]

Where did they come from? From Europe or from Asia? They have been found both in Assyrian and in Phoenician tombs, in certain regions of eastern Asia and of southern Europe. The Egyptians decorated their mummies with them. This great diffusion into diverse and faraway places marks the extent and the influence of this ancient custom and lends credibility to the hypothesis that the trade of "pierres d'aigris" existed in the basin of the Mediterranean in early antiquity and that perhaps they had been introduced into Africa by the Phoenicians whose African colonies were very prosperous. In addition, we know that their successors, the Carthaginians, advanced far to the south in searching for ostrich plumes, gold, ivory, and slaves. The commercial relations that these Mediterranean people established with the Negroes of the Sudan did not stop with the exchange of merchandise. It is highly probable that they also remained to establish stations in the Sudanese villages and that they left there something of their race, customs, arts, and industries. Besides, the same phenomenon occurred in eastern Africa.

Abyssinia was a center of civilization in direct contact with Egypt. Its influence like that of Egypt, extended far to the West over the peoples of eastern Sudan. The dispersion of Semitic people coming largely from the Arabian peninsula and mixing quickly with the indigenous element along the coast of eastern Africa contributed to the civilization of this part of the Sudan which is merely an extension of the temperate zone of the Northeast.

[54] Maurice Delafosse, *Les noirs de l'Afrique*, 1 vol., p. 28.

It seems to us that two observations arise from this short analysis. If Africa is an immense peninsula largely inaccessible along its coasts because there are few bays and capes, which are protected moreover from all outside attack by sandbars; if the narrow isthmus that once linked it to Asia played only a secondary role in its relationship with the world, then black Africa, forced to rely upon herself, could only develop according to her own genius and even these cultural possibilities would be dependent upon the climatic zones. We mean that where nature offered man an existence in which the physical elements were less deadly, there he received an undeniable advantage in the expansion of his energies to the fullest. But it is also true that in the North and East at a time when civilization was a gift of the Mediterranean, its less precipitous coasts and milder climate sheltered people whose sailing ships, crossing the bountiful and hospitable sea between Europe and Africa, brought back not only European goods for consumption and ornament, but especially that intangible something that brings about a mental exchange between man, most often without their knowledge, through which mankind asserts and distinguishes itself above the rest of nature.

Is this all?

We have only considered so far the life of African societies born under the sky of the Sudan and set in the grassy savannahs as the testimonials of a supreme effort of indigenous creation. When we view attempts at civilization in this perspective we are seeing only one side of the phenomenon. It is different in reality, it even appears that we can assert that the greatest, if not the only obstacle to creation of society in ancient Africa, lies in the tragic grandeur of physical nature. In that case the Sahara, because of its immense area of shifting sand dunes and extreme aridity, would symbolize regions that were uninhabitable by the very dryness of the soil, while in the equatorial forest the unusual strength of natural forces through a superabundance of water and humidity offers little chance of lasting success for the gradual development of human societies. Here and there, in rare places where nature is less severe, there may be a temporary settlement. The oasis and the glade are the only places suited to the exceptional conditions of the milieu — conditions of a temporary nature because they are constantly subject to abrupt transformations. One comprehends that no human society, tied down by such restrictions, can grow progressively — since the fundamental base of all progress is stability and duration. The wandering life required by such a fortuitous existence is a consequence of these peculiar habitats in which man is doomed to a perpetual displacement while the erection of temporary shelters in isolated villages, in perpetual battle with the harsh encroaching forest, is the other constraint of physical determinism.[55] But the picture would be incomplete if we were to limit the forms of indigenous civilization, real or potential, to the Sudanese plateau.

In the vast region along the Atlantic coast some social groups with interesting organizations have arisen.

Should we not point out the theocratic state of the Fulani of Futa-Jallon in French Guinea? These people, crossbred of Peuls, of Mandingo, and of all colors [Tukulors], have constantly shown an inclination for the humanities to the present day.[56]

Is it not appropriate to call attention to the tribe of Vai scattered along the coast of Liberia? From this tribe came the ingenious Doalu Bukere who invented an alphabet still used by his people. He told the Reverend Sigismund Koelle, the celebrated missionary philologist, how the revelation of the writing came to him from a divine messenger through a dream.[57] Upon awakening he gathered together some of his kin and marked out the signs of his alphabet; then after a long period of study spent in adjusting and perfecting it, he gathered his disciples about him and won the approval of the king who imposed the new tool of communication upon the people. A school was founded at Jondu for the propagation of this system of writing which survived all the vicissitudes of intertribal warfare and still constitutes today an unquestionable witness of the intellectual aptitude of the Vai.

From an artistic point of view we should not disregard the countries of Benin and Yoruba whose inhabitants have long been recognized for their works in bronze and clay. The ancient pottery of Benin reveals a perfectly remarkable sense of the beautiful.[58]

But the most interesting country of the coastal zone is Dahomey [Benin] because of its influence and organization. Its political and social constitution which is so rigidly hierarchical with four classes — the nobility, the high officials, the people, and the slaves — all *Danhomenou*, people or things of Dahomey, properties of the king; its civil administration; its army so firmly organized by a division of services and absolute spirit of discipline, have placed the Dahomeans above all other peoples

[55] Cf. [Georges] Hardy, *Vue générale de l'histoire d'Afrique*, [Paris, 1926].
[56] Delafosse, *Les noirs de l'Afrique*, p. 89, Paris, 1922.
[57] Sir Harry Johnston, *Liberia*, *loc. cit.*, p. 1108.
[58] Cf. [Leo] Frobenius, *Voice of Africa*, [London, 1913 translation, esp., pp. 292-349]; W.E. Burghardt Du Bois, *The Negro*, [pp. 48, 62-68, 153].

of Africa.

In the European world Dahomey has unfortunately become famous through the gruesome stories of the yearly mass murder of hundreds of slaves, captives of war, which was celebrated in a ritual known as the "great custom."

However one regards these abominations, it is significant to point out that Dahomey, thanks to the cohesion of its social organism (political regime, family institutions, religious system), has remained independent under one dynasty, feared greatly by her neighbors from the sixteenth century to the French conquest of 1894 when the last king of the country was dethroned.

Through these synthetical terms it has seemed possible to recall the life of the black peoples of Africa. This is how we thought we could schematize their efforts to create societies, the organization of their political communities, their utilization of raw materials appropriate to the industrial or artistic needs of their milieu, and especially their power of assimilation to all that the external world could offer them and which was consistent with the fundamental qualities of their genius. What is all of this, if it is not an ideal of collective life realized in a corner of the habitable area of the globe, the testimony of a unique conception of civilization. And this conception of social life has not only manifested itself in material works. It attained its highest value in the support of spiritual forces. The study of African beliefs enables us to grasp the most visible expression of that imponderable, the Negro mind, and to follow, moreover, the patterns of its eventual transformations, the unconscious survivals in this colossal ethnic transplantation which became Negro slavery in the Americas.

Chapter V

African Animism

1

A very old tradition based on misconceptions and on an interpretation that is as superficial as it is arbitrary, grips most of black Africa in the mesh of fetishism. But what is fetishism?[11]

[11] In this chapter, Price-Mars is quite clearly presenting arguments against the then popular conceptions of fetishism, animism, and religion, as well as notions about the mental capacity of "primitive peoples." Although the African continent had become the center of imperialism, the general populace of the Western World actually knew little about the peoples who lived there. There was, in addition, much controversy among social scientists at the end of the nineteenth century concerning the meaning of animism in relation to religion as offered by the eminent British anthropologist Sir Edward Burnett Tylor. Most accepted his simple definition of religion as "the belief in Spiritual Beings," but raised objections to his position on animism. He said,

"It is habitually found that the theory of Animism divides into two great dogmas, forming part of one consistent doctrine: first, concerning souls of individual creatures, capable of continued existence after death or destruction of the body; second, concerning other spirits, upward to the rank of powerful deities . . . Thus Animism, in its full development, includes the belief in souls and in a future state, in controlling deities and subordinate spirits, these doctrines practically resulting in some kind of active worship." (*Primitive Culture*, 1874, pp. 424-7; cited in Melville J. Herskovits, *Cultural Anthropology*, 1955, p. 210.) Simply put, Tylor assumed that animism was the basis of all religion.

Price-Mars does not mention Tylor in his text but it is interesting to study his analysis of African animism. He does follow the concept of "collective representations," originally introduced by Emile Durkheim and also used by Lucien Levy-Bruhl, but with considerable acuity he refuses to accept Levy-Bruhl's use of the term "prelogical" in reference to "primitive mentality."

Since the middle of this century, anthropologists have accepted the idea that animistic thought may be part of any culture, old or new, but do not talk in terms of whether animism, animatism, fetishism, or social experience is the original or universal source of religion. Rather they stress understanding ritual thoroughly in reference to the creed of a society and this relationship in turn to the culture of that society. This same procedure is used to compare one culture with another. And as E.E. Evans-Pritchard has reminded us, the "savage" acts as he has been taught to

In a paper[59] that the president [Charles] de Brosses presented to the Académie des Inscriptions in 1787, he employed this term for the first time to characterize the worship in which Negroes seemed to materialize natural objects. He considered it the origin of religious sentiment among all peoples by defining it as follows: "I call in general by this name (fetishism) any religion that has animals or inanimate earthly beings as the object of worship." Now, this word comes from the Portuguese *feitico*, a derivative of the Latin *factitius*, meaning artificial. It was applied as we know by seafaring Portuguese who, in their voyages of discovery along the western coast of Africa, thought they saw the natives rendering homage to shells, to stones, or other natural objects. They called these symbols of worship "fetishes."

The observation as it was established is not only incomplete, it is false because it is the result of misleading appearances. Unfortunately the doctrine to which it gave birth has sanctioned an error which is now ineradicable.

No, it is not the shell, or the stone, or the image of sculptured wood, or even the animals that the indigenous of Africa worship. The most backward of these men can be convinced that an imponderable element, an occult force is sometimes embodied in this object or that animal, just as the Forest, the Thunder, the River, the Sea, the Earth appear to him to be endowed with a will, desires, passions, and likewise are empowered to act as Forces. Moreover, is it not an established fact that death, a daily and inevitable event, harbors a mystery which is, to say the least, synonymous with fear and terror? Do the dead not return? Can they not exercise a good or bad influence on the living? Are they not themselves also forces of which one should be beware?

As many questions probably arose in the mind of primitive man. Left defenseless against the hostility of these forces, powerless to suppress often unfriendly manifestations, is he not prudent in devoting to them a cult of veneration and respect so as to curry their friendship? Such is the approach of his uncertain reason and, as emotiveness is the governing inclination, the dominant quality of his personality, he is

act. His ideas are the sum and substance of the collective experiences of his society. (See also Paul Bohannan, *Social Anthropology*, 1963, pp. 313-326.)

[59] *Du culte des dieux fétiches ou parallèle de l'ancienne religion de l'Egypte avec la religion actuelle de Nigritie*. This paper was judged too incautious and never received approval for official publication by the Academy. It appeared three years later without the name of the author. Cf. H [enry] Pinard de la Boullaye, S.J., *L'Etude comparée des religions, Essais critiques*, Paris, 1922, [1929 edition, Vol., I, p. 234].

always on the point of reacting with fear and anxiety in the presence of the least phenomenon that he cannot explain. Is not the most immediate explanation to recognize an intelligence in things and to believe them possessed by some Spirit? Though the bent of such reasoning is faulty, it none the less indicates a certain chain of ideas — insufficient, inferior, prelogical perhaps — but capable all the same of leading the individual or the group to imagine a kind of cosmogony [model of creation or evolution of the world]. This is, in my opinion, the way to explain the fundamental concept of the primitive concerning the world in which he lives, what is, definitively, his response to the enigmas which torment all of us. We judge this response to be puerile, because we have gone beyond this stage of mental development thousands of years ago, because moreover, the maturity of our thought permits us to link effects with their causes and thus to reassemble one by one the materials from which we have formed the structure of sciences. And besides, what are we boasting about?

Do we not find ourselves — many of us at least — helpless and apprehensive each time that certain phenomena go beyond the limit of our actual knowledge? What is the purpose of life, its origin and its end? Have we not meditated painfully on these eternal questions for as long as there have been men who thought? And on whom shall we rely to find an explanation of these problems that is worthy of our intellectual pride?

Those who take refuge in a prudent wisdom find that most of these questions border on the extreme limit of our investigations and of our ability to understand — at the unknowable of things, while others, the great majority of men, believe in the omnipresence of a superior being, master of all things in this world and director of its harmony. In fact, almost the same problems of human destiny, of the relations of man with the world in which he lives, have led the primitive and the civilized to consider a theogonic system in which both, for the most part, invoke one or more formidable, mysterious powers whose anger and hostility they fear. Both choose the modalities [general patterns or customs] most appropriate for realizing their objective. The first, the primitive African at least, believes that the tutelary divinity has too high a position to be engrossed in the petty affairs of his creatures. Having accomplished his work, this divinity has established between men and himself a class of invisible intermediaries (spirits, manes) who alone are accessible and consequently must always be addressed in order to obtain favors and blessings from on high. Civilized man, on the contrary, acknowledges implicitly that a modification of the divine plan, however minimal it may be, is virtually possible only by a direct intervention of God. In any case, it seems to us that this conception of the relations of man with the world in which he lives constitutes the starting point, it is one of the fundamental elements of religious sentiment. Consequently it is comprehensible that the worship of Providence externalizes itself, on the one hand, by multiple manifestations consistent with a sensorial intelligence as yet unable to form abstractions, and that, on the other hand, the worship of Providence matures into representations freed from the material matrix and affirmed by totally spiritual constructions. However it may be, one will agree that, in both cases, the measures of reason denote less difference in nature than in degree. In the final analysis, they mark the slow evolution of human thought from the level of rough representation to superior forms of abstract ideation. The animism of Negroes is therefore nothing other than a religion of primitive men. I do not know if all primitive peoples in all ages have worshipped the Unknowable in the same ways. It is probable — with nuances that show the wealth or poverty of imagination or again, and to a certain extent, according to the habitat of peoples favored by the beauty and hospitable clemency of the physical milieu or oppressed by its fierce hostility. Is it not true that Greek mythology is the daughter of the mild atmosphere of Attica "where the nine sacred Muses of Pieria cherish Harmonia of the golden curls" according to the magnificent symbolism of Euripides?[60]

Moreover, I do not know if, at a moment of time, God revealed himself to all humans in various forms "and many ways" *multifariam, multisque modis,* according to the text of Saint Paul.[61]

I do not know if some have preserved the purity of the original import of this revelation while others have altered it to the point of having retained only the fundamental propositions soon masked moreover by a thick layer of errors. These are but the fine distinctions of theologians.

[60] "In order to have the sentiment of the divine, one must be able to distinguish, through the precise form of the legendary god, the great, permanent, and general forces from which it was born. One remains an unfeeling and narrow-minded idolater if he does not perceive vaguely that beyond the personal figure there lies the physical or moral power symbolized in the figure. The comparison of mythologies has shown recently that the Sanskrit myths originally expressed only the play of natural forces, and that language, little by little, made gods from the diversity, fertility, and beauty of physical elements and phenomena." [Hippolyte] Taine, *Philosophie de l'art,* [Paris, 1865].

[61] Letter to the Hebrews, chap. 1, in [Alfred] Loisy, *Les livres du nouveau testament,* [Paris, 1922]. Cf. Mgr. Le Roy, *La religion des primitifs,* Paris, [p. 475].

What seems certain to us is the fundamental unity of Negro animism, despite its apparent morphological diversity. Whether one studies it on the Sudanese plateau where it is sometimes influenced by the probable contribution of foreign elements, whether one considers it as a religion of the State in certain social organisms, such as the Mossi, or better yet in its harsh form on the western coast in Dahomey, African animism may be summed up in a few very simple propositions: 1st, each man is composed of a double personality, one physical, tangible, material — the body; the other, intangible, immaterial, embodied in the first as its animator — the soul; 2nd, death is the operation by which these two elements are broken apart — the soul is separated from the body. What does this soul or spirit become after death? According to the Bantus of Loango, the *M-Zimu* or *Mu-Zimu* (soul or spirit) searches for another habitat immediately after the cessation of life in the corporal body,[62] which is after all only a reincarnation, while for other peoples this element wanders about randomly or remains near human habitations.

Moreover, the Gabons accept a dual spiritual principle, the *Mu-Zimu* and *l'ombwiri* (from which perhaps came the Haitian word *zombi,* although the words do not have the same meaning at all). This ombwiri is a tutelary spirit which is attached to each individual although it may be independent of him. It vanishes from the person at his death and remains invisible although it devotes itself to guarding the tribe. It is a superior spirit among good spirits. The Mandingo, on their part, establish a difference between the *dia,* vital breath, and the *niama,* spirit. Death is the cessation of the vital breath while the *niama* survives the destruction of the body . . .[63]

On the whole, it seems indisputable that the African Negro made a very clear distinction between the body and the soul of humans.

It is, at least, the most plausible interpretation that can be drawn from the mass of facts collected by innumerable writers who troubled themselves with such questions, notably missionaries, colonial administrators, explorers, and so forth.

2

Nevertheless, the Durkheim sociological school has risen against this

---

[62] Mgr. Le Roy, *op. cit.,* p. 153 and following.
[63] Cf. Mgr. Le Roy, *op. cit.;* Delafosse, *op. cit.,* [pp. 148-149]; Cureau, *op. cit.,* [pp. 355-403].

interpretation with considerable force and authority. In his celebrated book on "how natives think,"[64] [Lucien] Lévy-Bruhl points out how observers end in dangerous confusion when they try to penetrate the psychology of primitives by the same method used to analyze the mentality "of an adult white."

It is a matter of two distinct categories. The principal difference between them lies in their incomparableness, indeed in the divergent nature of their perception.

For "an adult white" — and this very likely pertains to any normal individual whatever his color may be who, having attained mental maturity, is capable of discernment, adaptation, of judgment in short, and is apt thereby to react and behave in most circumstances in a sensible and reasonable manner — for this individual, to perceive is to devote himself to the complex process of becoming conscious of the external world and realizing the representation of it in his mind. Now, this process, which seems to have only a specifically individual significance, most often hides a collective character. We mean that, even though no representation is known to exist without the mechanism of the nervous system peculiar to each individual, every representation nevertheless has to externalize itself from the common experience which is an attribute of the social milieu. Such, for example, is the act of expressing an impression. In using language — a collective medium — one uses necessarily a vehicle which is the property of a determined group. Therefore it is understandable that the value of the collective representation be in close correlation with the society for which it reflects the degree of intellectual culture, beliefs, sentiments, and so on . . .

Is this not how we should understand the definition that Lévy-Bruhl has given us?

"The representations which are termed collective, defined as a whole without entering into detail," he says, "may be recognized by the following signs: they are common to the members of a given social group; they are transmitted from generation to generation; they impress themselves upon the individuals and awaken within them, according to the circumstances, sentiments of respect, fear, adoration, and so on, for their objects. Their existence does not depend upon the individual. It is not that they imply a collective subject distinct from the individuals composing the social group, but rather that they present themselves in forms

---

[64] [Lucien] Lévy-Bruhl, *Les fonctions mentales dans les sociétés inférieures*, Second edition, *loc. cit.*, Paris, 1912; Lévy-Bruhl, *La mentalité primitive*, [Paris, 1925].

that cannot be accounted for by considering individuals merely as such. Thus it is that a language, although it only exists properly speaking in the minds of the individuals who speak it, is none the less an incontestable social reality, founded upon an ensemble of collective representations. For it imposes itself on each one of these individuals; it exists before him and it will survive him."[65]

But we should refrain from believing that the mode of representations takes place in the same manner with civilized as with primitive peoples. The first usually use a preliminary intellectual process. It is an "intellectual or cognitive phenomenon." The second, because of a sort of weakness in their capacity for abstraction, are only able to draw emotional elements from it.

In their little differentiated mental activity, elements such as ideas and emotions, which are distinct elsewhere, become confused — whence comes their inability to objectify their representations. For each time that thought evokes the image of the object perceived, this is enveloped, colored by an atmosphere heavy with passions or sentiments. The intellectual phenomenon is completely effaced, obscured by the emotional element. In addition, the exceptional circumstances by which primitive peoples acquired most of their collective representations — dances, initiation ceremonies, rites of puberty, and so on — the oppressive force of traditions and taboos, makes them in essence sacred acts or obligations which, by their reverent character, confer the supremacy of the society upon the individual. In these conditions, the individual, plunged into a troubled atmosphere in which float the modes of thought and belief that are the collective attributes of his group, comes to envisage reality under a special form. His perception makes no distinction between image and object. The pursuit of causality which is the distinctive mark of the reasoning "of the civilized" leaves him indifferent or, at least, he does not even surmise its existence. He ascribes all to an occult power which is always present and manifest in everything. His mentality is molded, fashioned by an affective complicated system that places it in a world both unreal and convincing, in any case outside common reason and logic. His mentality is *mystical*. And this mystique is at one and the same time cause and effect. For the primitive, it is from this mystique that the unique conception of the external world develops. Nothing that exists can have an objective character. Whether it is a question of physical things and facts — a mountain, a river, a plant for example

[65] Lévy-Bruhl, *Les fonctions mentales*, p. 1, *Introduction*.

— or maybe a question of interpreting events of a biological nature, as sickness, sleep, death, the mystique intervenes to create confusing liaisons in the understanding of the phenomenon. It is the complete sequence of thought of the mystical mentality that Levy-Bruhl very precisely calls *prelogical thought.* One law, the law of participation, seems to preside in this intellectual operation, by virtue of which "objects, creatures, phenomena can be, though in a way incomprehensible to us, both themselves and something other than themselves. In a fashion no less incomprehensible, they give forth and they receive mystical powers, virtues, qualities, and influences which make themselves felt outside them, without ceasing to remain where they are." Thus one conceives that this conceptual form embraces the physical and moral world as one complete unit, that all the operations of the mind may be profoundly impregnated by it and that they take the place of our concern to attach everything to a cause, whether the law has already been revealed to us or whether we suspect its potentiality.

This then is the grand doctrine of the sociological school, reduced to its principal elements, but too narrowly compressed within the bounds of a simple summary. We do not wish to dispute either the fine logical order or the sound structure. But should we not ask ourselves if the doctrine is incompatible with that of animism since the latter does not delight in a systematic and obliging interpretation of facts.

First, even if no one did contest the domination of collective representations in the formation of thought, it is certainly extreme to confine the individual within the pressure of society as if to forbid him any other form of thought than that emanating solely from the group. It has been called to our attention[66] that "the community life, the social assembly, the collective state exalt individual powers, that society, as the guardian of traditions, transmits to successive generations the acquisitions [culture] existing prior to the individual but, in the final analysis, society does not create intelligence." Consequently, the individual is susceptible to rising above his group by a power of personal thought which magnifies his personality. Such especially is the origin of genius. Is it forbidden to believe that the elites, even among the primitives, can truly think in the logical form common to groups differentiated *sub specie oeternitatis*? [from the aspect of eternity; consideration of things in their relation to the perfection of God (Spinoza)] Is it forbidden to believe that, between

[66]   H[enri] Delacroix, "Les operations intellectuelles," in *Traité de psychologie* by Georges Dumas, Vol. II, [Paris, 1923], pp. 145-146.

them and us, the difference of reasoning resides less in the nature than in the degree of development?

We have acknowledged since the beginning of this study that the thought process of primitive man is poor in abstraction and, moreover, that it is still entirely sensorial, controlled by the imagination, and that consequently "it goes beyond the real."[67]

It is the principal characteristic that we have recognized in him. But the reasoning of the primitive, quickly satisfied by approximative explanations acquired when incited by the curiosity of the unknown, demonstrates that its structure is not specifically different from ours.[12] It is in an embryonic phase of its development and nothing will make us admit that it is incapable of breaking out of the shell of collective representations in which its particular mode of perception imprisons it. In addition, what appears more evident to us than the ingenious arrangement of the above mentioned theories is that the term animism, generally used to refer to the propensity of primitives to endow all of nature with a spiritual energy, expresses their frame of mind very incompletely. In our opinion, it manifests a dynamism which seems to characterize the thought of primitives more concretely or, at least, the thought of the Negroes of western Africa with whom we are particularly concerned in these essays. This is the opinion of Dr. [Eduard] Pechuël-Loesche[68] who has dealt with the question in his study of the Bafioti on the western coast of Africa. He concluded that we had to reject the doctrine which attributed to Negroes the belief of spirits embodied in objects or in living things and that, in order to express their sentiments, it would be better to substitute the more widely used term dynamism. Thus we return to the Artistotelian formula that the divine envelopes all of nature. But this dynamism is expressed, is explicit in particular forms of worship. It has

[67] J. Bricout, *Où en est l'histoire des religions,* [p. 68].

[12] Price-Mars is particularly astute in his analysis of "prelogical principle" as introduced by Levy-Bruhl. In all fairness, however, it must be added that Levy-Bruhl later rejected the idea of "prelogical." He went so far as to regard the term "primitive mentality" as invalid. It may be that, as Paul Bohannan suggests, he meant to imply "prescientific" rather than "illogical" (as many interpreted it) as the meaning of "prelogical," to which argument Price-Mars would probably have agreed. Melville Herskovits says, ". . . all peoples think in terms of certain premises that are taken for granted. Granted the premises, the logic in inescapable." In other words all human beings think "prelogically" at times. We do not in everyday living adhere rigidly to the wellknown "pattern of scientific thought" in our own culture. (Herskovits, *Cutlural Anthropology,* 1955, pp. 360-363.)

[68] *Die Loango-Expedition,* III, p. 356-357, cited by Lévy-Bruhl, *Les fonctions mentales,* p. 107.

found in Delafosse its most astute and discerning analyst. Already, in the authoritative work that the eminent Africologue published about fifteen years ago and from which we have drawn the best of our documentation, he has stated and affirmed the essential part of the doctrine[69] and in his recent monograph on "the Negroes of Africa"[70] he has brought to this matter definitive evidence of his thorough knowledge of African mores and customs. "Animism or the worship of spirits," he writes, "is the true indigenous religion of western Africa. It is divided into the cult of the dead and into dynamism.

"The Negro considers that, in every natural phenomenon and in every being containing harmful or latent life, there exists a spiritual power or a dynamic or efficient spirit (niâmi in Mandingo) which can act by itself, and from this comes the veneration of spirits personifying natural forces and those of the souls of the dead, spirits which have been liberated by the death of their momentary human receptacle. The Negro attributes both reason and passion to each of these genies or spirits: if he finds a way to convince his reason or satisfy his passion, he is thereby associating the genie or spirit with his own desires."

In addition, he believes "that every animated being contains two immaterial sources in addition to his body. One, a sort of breath or vital fluid, has no other role than to animate matter and to communicate life and movement to it; it is a source without its own individuality or personality, which is eternal in the sense that it existed prior to the body that it animates at the time and will survive it and go to animate another one, and so on until the end of time. Like matter, it is infinitely divisible and can dissociate itself into diverse elements each of which suffices, alone or combined with an element coming from elsewhere, to animate a given body. When a man dies, it is really the vital breath abandoning its carnal envelope [body] in order to proceed immediately to create a new life either in a human or an animal in gestation, or in a germinating vegetal shoot. Of course this kind of fluid, without personality, intelligence, or will, that may be compared to an electric current, is not the object of any cult. It is a spirit, if you wish, but only in the etymological sense of the word (spiritus [meaning] breath).[13]

"The second principle is quite different: born with and at the same

---

[69] Delafosse, Loc. cit., [Haut-Sénégal-Niger], Vol. III, p. 165.
[70] Les noirs de l'Afrique, Payot et Cie, p. 149-150, 1922.
[13] Though not shown in the printed text, the quote continues through the next two paragraphs. Ibid., p. 150.

time as the body that harbors it, it constitutes the veritable personality of the being to whom it communicates the thought, will, and force to act; the vital breath permits the members of a man or an animal to move, it permits the sap of a tree to circulate in its veins, but this movement and this circulation cannot be accomplished if they are not ordered by the spirit.

"If it happens that one day the control of the vital breath escapes from the spirit and that, as a consequence, this breath leaves its envelope and death follows, it is because another, stronger spirit has neutralized the first: that is why all death is attributed by Negroes not to material causes, which for them are only secondary and chance causes, but to the psychic influence of an evil-minded spirit, alone the first and real cause of death."

Such is, in its breadth and clarity, the conception of African animism explained in terms of the latent or formal beliefs of black peoples from one end of Africa to the other.

Of course this animism is concretized here and there in formal rituals, in more or less organized worship and in oral traditions. It impregnates the mores and the customs, presides over the family organization and the systems of social and public life. Finally, it colors the rhythm of all existence from birth to the grave. A few examples of organized worship will help us to illustrate our thought.

3

The populations of the high Sudanese plateau, which Lieutenant Louis Desplagnes has described for us in a detailed monograph,[71] believe in the existence of a supreme divinity *Ammo* or *Amma*, residing in the incorruptible region of the heavens, creator of the universe. From this divinity emanate the active male and female forces which govern the world. The moon, a male divinity, and the sun, a female divinity, personify them. To these two stars must be added the earth in order to form a triad similar to the Theban triad. It is this that the Habbés of the central Nigerian plateau worship. It is to this triad that they erect altars with three points formed by arranged stones at which the priests come to celebrate the rites pertaining to worship. These stones are most often conical or "rough-hewn" monoliths placed in the courtyard of each familial home.

[71] Lieutenant Desplagnes, *Le plateau central nigérien*, Emile Larose, 1907.

Not all the Sudanese tribes revere the astral forces under the form of the Triad. It is said that all those with the name terminated by the suffix *ngo*, as *Karo-ngo* or *So-ngo*, adopt the female divinity. Thus "the *Hougho-Ouango* of the Mossi sacrifice to the Sun in order to attach it to the earth at dawn and dusk, at its rising and setting, during the first week of the winter season, then afterwards, only on the sixth day in the morning at sunrise.

"They go to the altars formed of three conical stones to offer sacrifices and libations always surrounded by all the people, the heads of the families, the tom-tom players, and the familial masks."[72]

On the other hand, the tribes who form the confederation of those who sacrifice to the male Force, can be designated by associating the letter R with their name; thus one would have the name *Sara-Kolle*, *Sor-Kos, Mar-Kas*. Be that as it may, they consider the moon as the symbol of their divinity.

It is within the jurisdiction of the priests "to announce solemnly the phases of lunar evolution and to determine the succession of happy or ill-omened days in the week by the position of the star in the firmament; finally this planet aids them in dividing time and designating the seasons."[73]

Aside from the celestial triad, the Sudanese tribes believe in the existence of other spiritual forces which find themselves in daily communication with humans and make themselves known in every circumstance and in the least incidents of life. Finally, in order to assure the perpetuity of the cult, the Sudanese have achieved a half-political, half-religious organization. The treasures of tradition and the defense of the community rest on the authority of a Council formed of all the heads of families whose advanced age constitutes a guarantee of venerability. Under certain determined conditions, this council of elders elects a chief called *Bougho* or *Hogon*,[74] "a name which signifies fire or the heat of the fire," to preside over their deliberations and to take charge of the higher interests of the tribe. This individual acquires, from this act, a considerable power. His political and religious powers are absolute. In rising to supreme honor, he becomes *Har-Boughô* or *Hougon-Dale*, high priest of Fire, presiding over the Council of Elders. As possessor of these titles and privileges, the right to interpret the designs of the divinity reverts

[72] Desplagnes, *loc. cit.*, p. 270, [275-276].
[73] Desplagnes, *loc. cit.*, p. 271.
[74] One recognizes readily that these two terms have been altered to form *Bôcor* and *Hougan*, priests of Haitian Voodoo.

to him. His person is thenceforth sacred. He lives alone in a corner of the village, usually on the top of some hill. His house, ornamented with moldings, is a true temple where the tribal symbols of alliance are deposited. He draws the attention of the crowd by the priestly insignia that he wears. These consist of a dark blue flowing garment which covers him completely, on the breast a huge opal attached at the neck, a twisted "large iron bracelet on the right leg, copper earring on the right ear, and silver ring on the middle finger of the left hand." He wears a red miter adorned in green on his head which must always be close-shaven.

"While performing his official duties, he carries a walking stick of hammered iron with three bulges or a staff ending in three branches, emblems of the servant of the divine Triad." [p. 322]

"Throughout the year, in a small highly decorated niche hollowed in a wall of their house, these priests tend the sacred fire with which, at the end of rainy season, they are obliged to light the great purifying fire made of brushwood."[75]

Next to these high dignitaries, there is another who is inferior in rank because of the different quality of his tasks. This is the *Laggam* or *Leggué* who is the interpreter for abandoned and malevolent earthly divinities. Feared very much because of the mystery which surrounds the exercise of his functions, the Laggam also carries certain symbols: a huge agate suspended from the neck, a bracelet on the left ankle, an iron ring on the little finger of the right hand, and finally, a silver ring in the left ear.[76]

All these personnages are assisted in the performance of their official duties by subordinate officials whom they install in office. But, they themselves can attain the dignity of office only through a true religious ceremony. When the Hogon-Dale dies, this event must be kept secret for three years. The privileges of his office are fulfilled during this lapse of time by his eldest son. But, with the end of the delay, the Council of Elders meets on a night with a full moon. Then officials climb to the roof of the temple and announce loudly to the people: "The Hogon-Dale is dead," and utter lamentations. The Council of Elders, having offered goats and chickens to the spirits of the ancestors, implore the gods to reveal the one who appears to them to be most worthy of filling the vacant office. For three days they devote themselves to ceremonies consisting of sacred dances before the altar of the divinity and of mysterious

[75] Desplagnes, p. 276.
[76] Desplagnes, p. 333.

consultations. Finally, on the fourth day, the Council proclaims the chosen one who then receives the sacred insignia and is conducted in grand procession to the dwelling reserved for him. The final phase of the ceremony symbolizes the death of the recipient who henceforth ceases in effect to exist for his family, being consecrated to the service of the gods and to the safekeeping of the people.

Desplagnes, who with [Charles] Monteil has given us the description of these curious customs, is inclined to think that they are due to the infiltration of Asian customs and ideas. However that may be, they are neither systematically adopted nor systematically similar among all the composite peoples of the vast Sudanese plateau. Here and there they undergo some transformation and deformation although their essential nature remains practically unchanged. Moreover, three great religious festivals are part of the ritualism of these tribes: first, the festival of ancestors; second, the festival of sowing; and third, the harvest festival.

The festival of ancestors takes place at the option of the Hogon, on a favorable day in May when the moon is full. As the head of the Council of old men, the high priest goes to the cave which tradition claims as the dwelling place of the first ancestors. There he sacrifices some chickens and a black or black-spotted male goat on whose head the plate of sacrifices has been placed. Then he burns up the remains of the propitiatory victims and tosses the ash to the wind. He keeps only a piece of chicken liver which he eats while invoking the ancestral spirits. During this ceremony the people, standing apart, observe the most devout silence.

The sowing festival is held during the period of the heavy summer rains, in July. It consists of ritual dances, of offerings of seeds to be sown, and of animal sacrifices.

As for the harvest festival, the most sumptuous of all, its actions are largely those of thanksgiving to the divinity for having favored the community with the blessings of happy days and abundant harvest.

Thus, toward the end of the year, the Hogon conducts the offering of the first fruits in the presence of the crowd assembled before the temple. Then, in the midst of the faithful, he presides over a great meal of fellowship where "they all eat, as the main course, enormous cous-cous" made of the first fruits of the harvest. This feast is thus known as the "feast of the bellies."

We can observe without difficulty that the organization of worship on the Sudanese plateau, such as we have just summarily described, assumes a rather demonstrative dynamic character. These are the forces which are spiritualized: the sunlight, abundant and energetic; the earth, maternal and protective; the moon, regulator of the seasons, symbol and rhythm of time. If there are other elements near this triad to which the Sudanese imagination lends mysterious and formidable power, it is those responding to the character of Laggam, servant of malevolent divinities. It is probably the dualism of these two dissimilar cults, the one more spiritualistic, the other more animistic, which reminds people of some strange influence in the religious conception of the Sudanese.

In any case, such as it is, this organization clearly displays an intelligence and a concern for religious things which has to be noted and compared with other conceptions. It induces us to search among other people living further to the southwest for another model of cultural organization from which we will draw similar beneficial information and experience. Let us choose the Dahomean religion to which we have already referred many times. It lent its design and form to Haitian animism in the historical conditions which we made clear earlier in the text. A detailed study will enable us to analyze its structure.

4

The Dahomeans possess a system of theogony in which we notice, first of all, their belief in a Supreme Being, *Mahou* or *Sê, Intelligence.* Mahou is the creator of the heavens and of the earth.

If they invoke him at times as if to give witness of his supremacy over every visible thing, the Dahomeans, as most of the other black peoples, do not translate their veneration of the supreme god into a tangible worship. Mahou is too highly placed to attend to human beings; in return, humans are not troubled if they do not reach him. Besides there is no way to do so. They believe that Mahou cannot be approached through their prayers, their sacrifices, and their offerings and they feel that he is indifferent to things immediate to this world. But, below him, on another level, there is another category of divine beings, derived from him and upon which he has bestowed omniscience and complete power. These are the Spirits, the *Vodoun.* Nothing on the earth or in the heavens happens without their participation. Their wrath arouses fear and their benevolence spreads over all who merit it. It appears that Mahou expresses his will through the Vodoun: *Vodoun e gui Mahounou, the Spirit is a thing (a creature)* of God. The Vodoun are embodied in human beings whom they use to make known their wishes as well as in natural phenomena which represent manifestations of their anger, vengeance, and power.

There are Vodoun of the sea, rivers, mountains, sky, earth, thunder, wind, smallpox, and so on . . . It is the divinization of natural forces and phenomena as a whole dynamic process. Outside these diverse incarnations, Vodoun are sometimes devoted to the protection of a city, a tribe, or a family. As such they may dwell in a famous or sacred place, may assume the material or symbolic form of a rock or an eponymic animal; they may personify the ancestral totem of a family. Thus the *Tô-Vodoun* are the protective spirits of certain collectivities and reside particularly in trees, bushes, or rocks and are venerated in the places where they have revealed their presence and their power. The *Ako-Vodoun* or *Hennou-Vodoun* personify the ancestral founders of such tribes and receive pious hommage.

A cult which came from Savi and took root in Quidah, capital of ancient Dahomey, has contributed more than any other to make the religion of the Vodoun well-known. This refers to the worship of Dangbé (the good serpent). He is honored under the form of a harmless python of medium size.

In the nomenclature which we have just given, we have only included (except for Mahou) divinities of a dynamic character, the protective deities of collectivities as families, cities, and tribes. To these categories we must add *Legba* and *Fa* who play a particular role in the Dahomean theogony. They are personal gods. "Legba is the companion hidden in each individual. Like an elf, he is always ready for some sly prank or even the worst maliciousness; but, he is easily softened to compassion by prayers and sacrifices."[77]

His dwelling place is the navel, hence the name *(Homêsingan)*, chief of anger. Is he also a kind of priapus?

Some people believe so.[78] In any case, at the entrance-ways of the villages one always encounters the symbol of Legba represented by a small statue burdened with an enormous *phallus.* As for Fa, he is

[77] A. Le Hérissé, *L'ancien royaume du Dahomey: moeurs, religion, histoire,* Emile Larose, editor, 1911, p. 137.

[78] Dr. [Justin Chrysostome] Dorsainvil, *Une explication philologique du Vodû,* [Port-au-Prince, 1924]. [*Priapus* was the Greco-Roman god of procreation, guardian of gardens and vineyards, personification of the erect phallus. Le Hérissé says, "The phallus that one notices in the statues of "Legba" leads to the assumption that this vôdoun (god, spirit) was analagous to the ancient Priapus. We do not completely agree with this view . . . His powers are not restricted to this." *Ibid.,* pp. 138-139.]

something like a guardian angel vested with the protection of the masculine sex. As "messenger of *Mahou,* he forsees destiny." He is honored and consulted habitually as the oracle of destiny. To all these divinities, to their symbols, to their multiple and varied incarnations, the Dahomeans dedicate a public worship which is completely organized. In order to conserve tradition and to resolve theological difficulties, there exists a hierarchical priestly body composed of four categories: the *Vodoûn-non,* the *Houn-so,* the *Vodoun-si,* and the *Vodoun-legbanon.*

The *Vodoun-non* (*non* meaning embodied in him, he possesses *Vodoun,* the spirit) is the high priest and the principal sacrificer. He is the supreme depositary of the wishes of the divinity. He lives in the sacred enclosure where the temple is built. He is the one who instructs disciples in the sacred and esoteric language (formed from the early Dahomean). Through tradition, he knows the virtue of plants, prayers, and incantations. He alone sacrifices at the altars. For any ceremony outside the temple, he invests his minister the *Houn-so* with special authority by which he confers upon him the privileges attached to the exercise of his high office, *Houn-so e so Houn, il porte l'esprit* (meaning, he is the transitory agent of the spirit). For in the ceremonies of worship, his role as Houn-so consists of dancing some ritual steps while carrying the sacrificial victim on his shoulders. Then the spirit descends upon him to sanctify his gestures and his action.

The Vodoun-si are the apprentices, the scholars destined for service to the divinity. They are instructed under special conditions by the high priest and live in the sacred enclosure until the end of their studies.

Finally, the Legba-non (*non,* signifying embodied in him, he possesses) is the individual who is possessed with the spirit of Legba. In the religious dances he performs the role of an obscene buffoon.

That is, in a few words, what makes up the priestly organization. One will easily understand the exceptional importance which these personnages enjoy if he remembers that their theological science is not to be found in any sacred book, but is transmitted from age to age by oral tradition, that it assumes ipso facto an esoteric character, and that initiation is obtained only through procedures which submit their nervous systems to ordeals of extreme severity.

But what are these so-called ceremonies of worship? We could do no better than to transcribe the impressive description of one to which Le Hérissé has devoted a page in his fine monograph. It concerns a commemoration to the dead.

On the fixed day, the veil of the *Asen*[79] having been lifted, the *Hôdeto* and the *Tansinon*[80] began the ceremony (p. 176).

"In the first place, the celebrant calls the dead; at each name the assistants clap their hands softly, then touch the ground with the right hand and immediately thereafter carry it to the lips or forehead. In the second place, the celebrant names the head of the family of the important personnages present, that is, all those who have shared in the expenses of the commemorative festival. Finally, he demands the protection of the ancestors for the well-being of the country and of the family."

After these rites which recall to mind a recitation of litanies because each word of the celebrant is repeated by the assistants, the offerings begin. The female celebrant takes a calabash filled with water and decorated with allegorical figures in metal. She presents it to the male celebrant who, while standing, pours a little of its content on the *Asen.* In this same fashion, drops of different liqueurs, pinches of flour and foods prepared with any product of the earth not forbidden to the family are offered to the ancestral spirits; after that the assistants divide the remains of this feast of the dead, according to the familial hierarchy.

Then comes the moment chosen for the sacrifice of the animals. Butchers lead a tightly bound ox before the sacrificial place, cut its throat, and collect a calabash of its blood which their leader carries to the celebrant to sprinkle over the *Asen.* With a turn of the hand, voluntary sacrificers twist the neck and break the wings of the chickens, they pull out the tongue and feathers which they toss in the air while others place the entrails of all the victims on the altar and cut up the flesh to offer to the important assistants. It is finished. The dead are satisfied. The living have fulfilled their duties toward them which obliges them in return to assist the living, an inalienable privilege belonging to them even in the country from whence no one returns.

The two models of organized worship in opposite regions of the continent whose detailed activities we have just used as illustrations, justify the propositions that we made at the beginning of this chapter, namely that the Negroes, in their religious thought, respond to any other directive than that of adoration of natural objects. If their religion at times assumes a material form in acts of fetishism, one can say that it slips

[79] Asën: object of worship made of metal, vaguely resembling an umbrella. It is consecrated to the spirits.

[80] "Dèho-prier," to speak to the dead, to the "spirits." "Hodéto," he who speaks to the spirits. The "Tansinon" is generally a woman devoted to the celebration of an identical worship.

under the influence of such and such determinative causes, just as do all the others, into ruts where superstition empowered by good luck enjoys being the caricature of religion. Such incidents occur in the lifetime of all religions; they verge on the true doctrine and infiltrate it like a foreign substance, destroying the purity of its essence. But if on the other hand, doctrinal interpretations, thanks to collective representations, have brought about better comprehension of the psychological substratum, the source of the Negro mystique, we have pointed out that these interpretations have in no way been inconsistent with a better understanding of animism. At this point of our inquiry we must, in giving a quick glance at what we have examined, extract the knowledge which is pertinent to the clarification of the ultimate purpose of our research, namely, the explication of the beliefs of the Haitian masses.

5

From the ethnographic journey that we have taken across Africa, we have aspired to reconstruct not only the prehistoric past of the age old continent but also the moving past of the races who peopled it from both a biological and social evolutionary point of view. And this effort to probe obscure origins has aided us in rendering an account of the actual conditions of the black races of Africa. Finally, by relying on the best references in this attempt at synthesis, we have tried to penetrate the Negro mind by coordinating the diverse composite mass which forms the mainstay of his beliefs. Thus — so we flatter ourselves — by objective observation the African mentality has appeared to us less ephemeral, less impervious to intelligence.

If this is what we have accomplished by our efforts at reconstruction then we can more readily begin the explication of Haitian beliefs whose most disturbing aspect has always seemed to us to be their link to the African mystique.

Chapter VI

The Religious Sentiment
of the Haitian Masses

1

All Haitians are Christian, Catholic, Apostolic, and Roman. In the large cities and more rarely in the country, there are also some followers of reformed religions — Baptists, Adventists, Methodists, Wesleyans — who form an active and zealous minority.

One is correct, however, in assuming that the authenticity of the above proposition is of little relevance. And if we needed to be convinced of this fact, it would be sufficient to recall to mind the mode of social and ethnic formation of the Haitian nation which has had a logical repercussion on the development of religion.

We know, do we not, what elements have produced the Haitian society. We know how gangs of slaves imported from the immense expanse of the western coast of Africa to Saint Domingue presented as a whole a microcosm of all the black races of the continent.[81] We know how the promiscuity of the white and of his black concubine, how the unauthorized conditions of a society governed by the caste system, gave birth to an intermediate group between masters and the captive mass. We know, furthermore, how the conflict of interests and passions, how the confrontation of egoisms and principles created by the revolutionary mystique, precipitated the revolt which led the former slaves to found a nation. This is, very briefly, the origin of our people. It can be said that, since the distant time around 1506 when the first Negroes were introduced into Haiti in order to substitute their legendary endurance for

---

[81] Cf. [Jean] Price-Mars, *La vocation de l'élite*, 1 volume, [Port-au-Prince, 1919]; "Le sentiment et le phénomène religieux; chez les nègres de Saint-Domingue," in *Bulletin de la Société d'Histoire*, Volume II, [May 1925, pp. 25-55].

Indian weakness, those among them who endured the precarious life of gold seekers in the gorges of Cibao or under the protection of Spanish conquistadors, afterwards those who, taking part in the smuggling trade of the Dutch, Normans, Bretons, and other sea pirates, participated in the foundation of the first French settlements in Saint Domingue, all those who, in small numbers of course, joined in the life of the buccaneers or filibusters until the uninterrupted flood of the slave trade poured out during more than two centuries the mass of two million individuals hideously consumed by its horrible regimen, all of these people [Negroes] constituted the sedimentary bed out of which came the primitive elements of the Haitian people. They are the millions of settlers who changed the ancient virgin forest, where the savage grandeur of the tropics dispensed an intemperate superabundance of life, into the hospitable and attractive land of Saint Domingue. The enormous annual hecatomb [human sacrifice] by which they paid for the prosperity of the colonial regime, was the principal condition for the enrichment of the land. In any case, not a bud, a breath, a cell can actually escape from the biologic solidarity which binds the living matter of today with the raw energy expended by African Negroes with their tears, sweat, and blood in the soil of ancient Quisqueya in order to transform it into our country of Haiti. And if it is true that humanity is formed more of the dead than of the living,[82] if the dead impose on us not only their physical constitution but also the pattern of our thought, even the aggregates of our ego, by what absurd wager would one try to disengage our Haitian society from its racial origins of four or five centuries ago. Besides, is it not an established fact that this society as a whole has kept its time-honored character? Does it not reproduce in most respects and with a surprising fidelity an enlarged and more beautiful image of the society of Saint Domingue?

Obviously, the old orders have been solemnly abolished. In the glow of the conflagration that enflamed the former colony, the basic system was broken up, dismembered. But, by nature, social phenomena are rather irrepressible. The will of man condensed in legal texts, translated into administrative measures is for the most part powerless to alter their free development. Violence itself which disrupts the arrangement, only masks its irreducibility all the more. Thus, despite the severity of bloody battles which revolutionary factions undertook on our soil and which generated a transformation of the colonial social status, despite the suc-

---

[82] Gustave Le Bon, *Lois psychologiques du développement des peuples*, Paris, 1900; *Les opinions et les croyances*, Paris, 1906.

cessive upheaval which led to the ruin of the old regime and the advent of the new nation, one is astonished to find that the change has been more apparent than real, that it was realized much more on the surface than in depth, that the mutations were brought about in a displacement of political power which slipped from the hands of the white aristocracy to those of the sangs-mêlées [mulattoes, of mixed Negro and Caucasian ancestry] and the black populace. But again, there was only a substitution of masters. As radical as this change of regime appeared to be, it was only accomplished through a monopoly of public authority by an audacious and energetic minority. In fact, the social system remained unchanged. The possession of large seigneurial estates which was the principal mark of power and fortune, preserved its age old traditional meaning. The great planters of the past were simply dispossessed by the new political leaders who gave themselves these privileges and prerogatives with a certain prudence consistent with unpredictable conditions in the public life.

As for the common people in whose name the creation of the principle of equality had been proclaimed, it was considered expedient to testify to their participation in the new order of things by assigning to each the right to vote and the possession of a few acres of land. But, confined by economic necessity to the task of producing without a supply of tools and technical knowledge, reduced to the cultivation of small and isolated farms, their situation, in a century of liberty and political independence, is that of servitude minus the presence of the Code Noir and the whip of the commander. Yet the moral philosophy remained quite unscathed since the magic formula — liberty, equality, and fraternity — was inscribed on the facade of the reconstructed edifice. But, for the one who is not reluctant to raise the veil of appearances, the Haitian society of the present time closely resembles the one from which it issued. We know that the arrogant vanity of our elite forces them into an obstinate and fierce denial of this. The elite closes his eyes to the evidence. He has only to note, however, the demographic development of our people in order to realize how vain is his stupid claim that he alone typifies the whole Haitian society. For the bourgeoisie, as they exist now, are no more than a symbol. Having fallen from their historic role as leaders of the nation because of inertia, cowardice, or failure to adapt, although they still illustrate through their thinkers, artists, and industrial chiefs the height of intellectual development to which a part of the society has risen, yet by shirking their duty to mix with the rest of the nation they exercise only a sort of mandarinate which weakens and atrophies more each day. But even if they have lost their grand vocation of leadership, they should jealously guard their role as representatives of our intellectual potentialities. Further, in being aware of what they represent ought they to inflate their dignity to the degree that they misrepresent the meaning of their role? But now in our case, a simple geographical observation takes on the significance of a fact of human geography, namely the population is divided according to the topography of the island. We realize that the western part, which interests us, is merely a network of mountains from north to south and east to west. The plains and valleys of this section are distributed parsimoniously in comparison to the part which fell to our neighbors in the Dominican Republic.

At the feet of these mountain ranges the ocean has developed a fringe of bays and promontories where our principal cities have risen. They are always along the coast or very close to it. Urban agglomerations are rare indeed in the hinterland. It is in one or the other of these that the bourgeois classes, refined expressions of the community, live.

About how many people do we estimate live here?

From an official publication[83] we have extracted the following information. Eight of the largest cities might possess a total of 207,000 inhabitants. All of the cities together would not reach a figure beyond 250,000. And with the entire population of the Republic estimated at 1,500,000 inhabitants, the proportion of townspeople would be approximately 15 to 17 per cent. Assuming that the official evaluation is underestimated — and this is our opinion since the above-mentioned figure has not been established by reliable statistics — it is nonetheless established that the country is really rural in nature with the number of peasants very likely reaching 2,200,000 in a total population of 2,500,000 inhabitants.

Ah! but it is the religious sentiment of the rural masses that holds our attention. It is toward them that our inquiry has been directed since the first pages of this book. It is toward them that we have addressed our curiosity and sympathy, certain of finding in them a candor and spontaneity which is beyond the crushing odious legends created by the adventurous imagination of short-sighted journalists and by the

[83] *Géologie de la République d'Haiti*, edited by Wendel P. Woodring, John S. Brown, and Wilbur S. Wurbank for the census of the Department of Public Works (Service géologique), p. 73, 1925. [I have added the complete names of the authors. The book was published in English by The Lord Baltimore Press, Baltimore, 1924, and there is evidently a French version published in Port-au-Prince, 1925.]

unintelligent defense of timid bourgeoisie.

Obviously, it will not be impossible for us to question the presumptious mind of the elite. We will see if it remains intangible on the rock of its Catholicism or if instead through a reverse shock the popular beliefs have obsessed it with uneasiness because they are enveloped with an indescribable something of the mysterious and the esoteric.

2

From all the analysis which we have conducted so far, we can readily guess that the religious sentiment of the popular masses derives from the same psychological substratum which formed the faith of the humble and ignorant in every country of the world.

It seems that one can assert as a rule that faith, a phenomenon that is more affective than cognitive, draws the materials that compose it from the tendency of man to search for an external support against the weaknesses and infirmities inherent in his own nature.

For however little he knows about the more or less plausible explanations of causes which govern natural phenomena and, it might be said, in proportion to his ignorance, he adopts a concept about the things of this world that is very appropriate to his mentality. It is consequently comprehensible that, between the peasant and the educated man there may be a certain disparity from the standpoint of religious beliefs and that even when their faith seems based on the same information, indeed on defined dogma — each adapts according to the degree of his own culture. As for the Haitian peasants, or the modern descendants of the Negroes of Saint Domingue, we believe we have shown at what stage of colonial servitude that compulsory Christianization was conferred on them en masse as supreme justification of the regime. We dwelt upon the ineffectiveness of the initiation rites performed under such conditions, given that they were not acts of spontaneous acceptance by the neophytes. Besides, they were no more than an occasion for feasting and revelry since they would justify certain hours of respite from the constraint of labor. We indicated, at length, how these unpolished souls remained attached to their primitive faith despite everything and we followed them to the moment where, because of the revolutionary crisis, their ancestral beliefs became the leaven of the revolt against odious oppression. It is truly during the beginning of these troubled times, at the nocturnal meetings in the woods that the Haitian cult called *vaudou* [Voodoo] was organized. But of what did this cult consist?

It will be difficult to provide a response to this question that will not be attacked. We have, at this moment, no decisive document which would permit us to analyze the diverse cultic elements of colonial Voodoo. Moreover it would be unintelligent to expect a serious and thorough study of the matter from the era in question. The history and science of religions did not exist. Nor would it be advisable to lose oneself in comparisons which would be considered as brazen sacrileges against the truths of the Church.

Moreover, serious exploration of Africa was not undertaken until two centuries later. Scientific observations and ethnographic research on the aged continent were rare in the eighteenth century. And, even now, agreement is far from being reached on the origins, the significance, and the interdependence of certain beliefs. Hypotheses concerning these matters are still uncertain. Heavy prejudice prevented seeing anything other than superstition in all religious sentiment among Negroes which was not an act of Christian devotion. And this is why all the chroniclers who have left travel accounts, notes, works on Saint Domingue have pointed out nothing worth being retained.

Two texts, however, have reached us from which we can glean some interesting information. The first is taken from the *Essai sur l'Esclavage and Observations sur l'état présent des colonies.*[84]

It concerns the anxiety of the white caste provoked by the many nocturnal meetings of the slaves wherein conspiracies against the colonial regime were fomented. In this regard, the author makes the following remark: "Their plans were impenetrable so long as they were not discovered by women who were mistresses of white men to whom they were very strongly attached.

"The dance called in Surinam *Water Mama* and in our colonies *Mère de l'eau,* is severely forbidden to them. They make it very mysterious and all that anyone knows about it is that it fires their imagination. They become excessively excited while contemplating an evil scheme. The author of the plan becomes entranced to the point of losing consciousness; when he revives he claims that his god has spoken to him and has commanded him to undertake the enterprise, *but since they do not all wor-*

[84] Arch. col. F. 129, cited by L[ucien] Peytraud, *L'esclavage aux Antilles françaises avant 1789,* [Paris, 1897, pp. 187, 447]. The "Essai" is an anonymous work. It is attributed to Lafond de Ladebat, to Barbe de Marbois, or to Billaud Varennes. [See also] Moreau de Saint-Méry, *loc. cit.,* p. 46 and following.

ship the same god, they distrust and spy on each other and these projects are almost always denounced."

From this very curious document we can extract significant information. At the time to which we are referring, probably around 1760, the religion of the slaves had not yet received any particular name and, without realizing it, the author of the Essai is explaining the reason when he informs us that the Negroes do not worship the same god.

It is obvious that until this time, despite the great number of maroons [runaway slaves] — the stimulus of necessity and the pressure of external events have not yet brought about the appropriate concessions that would produce unity of political action. "They distrust and spy upon each other," relates the text, — so it is even less possible to conceive of the uniformity of religious ceremony. The unconscious force of syncretism, however, operates silently and less than thirty years later we will find under the name of "Vodou" a religious manifestation which Moreau de St-Méry was the first to analyze in detail. This analysis grew famous and became the theme, amplified and plagiarized, for most of the accounts which have been made of the cultic ceremonies of "Vodou" by writers who have not even had the opportunity to observe them.

The author of the *Description de la partie française de Saint Domingue* [Moreau de Saint-Méry] first points out the external conditions of the worship — the decor. The ceremony requires the complicity of darkness and unfolds only in an exclusive spot safe from any indiscretion. "There, each initiate puts on a pair of sandals and places around his body various numbers of red or predominantly red handkerchiefs. The Roi Vaudoux has more and finer handkerchiefs with a completely red one encircling his forehead as a diadem. A twisted cord, generally blue, completes the mark of his eminent office." For there is a King and a Queen of Vaudoux who exercise the most effective influence over the faithful of the cult. They preside over the ceremonies and order the ritual. They are themselves the interpreters of the divinity and this divinity is no other than the grass snake. "Understanding of the past, knowledge of the present, prescience of the future, all are the privilege of this grass snake who consents nevertheless to communicate his power and to prescribe his wishes only through the voice of a high priest chosen by the followers and even more through that of the Negress whom the love of the high priest has raised to the rank of high priestess."

But through what medium is this communication obtained? Might it be that the grass snake has recovered the privilege of using the human language as of old in the Garden of Eden, "being the most artful of all the animals of the field that the Eternal God has made," as expressed in Genesis?

No, the times have changed. It concerns an infinitely more subtle operation, it is a question of nothing less than a spiritual incarnation, as we shall see.

"The King and the Queen take their place at one end of the room near a sort of altar on which is a box where the serpent is kept and where each follower may see it through some wooden bars.

"When it has been confirmed that no prying persons have penetrated the place, the ceremony begins with the worship of the grass snake, with assurances of being faithful to him and of submitting to all that he will prescribe. Each renews the oath of secrecy, the fundamental principle of the association, before the King and Queen, and this act is accompanied by the most frightful frenzy imaginable in order to make it more impressive." All this is only the outward aspect of the ceremony — we mean that part which demonstrates the profound influence of the faith — the trust which unites the faithful with his god.

A counterpart remains, the rite which shows the god becoming incarnate in his representative and being identified with him. Here accordingly the followers of the cult have rendered homage to the divinity, each has placed at the foot of the altar his offerings and his prayers, each has murmured the wish of realizing that for which he longs by invoking the almighty power of the god. It is the propitious moment for supernatural intervention.

"During all of these invocations, the Roi Vaudoux meditates, the Spirit moves in him. Suddenly, he takes the box which contains the snake, places it on the ground, and has the Reine Vaudaux stand on it. As soon as the sacred sanctuary is under her feet, instantly pythoness, she is imbued with her god, she becomes disturbed, her whole body shakes uncontrollably, and the oracle speaks through her lips.

"At times she is soothing and promises happiness, at times she thunders and bursts into reproaches, and at the whim of her desires, self-interest, or caprices, she dictates as final laws anything it pleases her to prescribe, in the name of the grass snake, to the simple flock which will never have the least thought of objecting to the preposterous nonsense and will only obey what is despotically prescribed for them.

"After all the questions have led to some sort of response from the Oracle, who is also somewhat ambiguous, a circle is formed, and the snake is replaced on the altar."

This is the first act of the drama.

The second, which intensifies it and augments its value, follows immediately. This is the dance.

"If there is a new member, the dance is opened with his admittance. The Roi Vaudoux traces a large circle with a dark substance and places within it the person who wishes to be initiated and puts in his hand a small packet of herbs, coarse hair, kernels of corn, and other such revolting objects.

"While tapping him on the head with a small flat piece of wood, he intones an African song:

Eh! Eh! Bomba, Hen! hen!
Canga Cafio té
Canga moune délé
Canga doki la
Canga li[85]

[85] Compare this with the song for which Drouin de Bercy presents the music, the words and their translation: A ia bombaia, bombé,
    Lamma ramana quana,
    E van vanta,
    Vana docki

Translation: "We swear to destroy the whites and all that they possess, let us die rather than give up." I consider this translation to be somewhat suspect. First, we are not told to which African dialect it belongs. Also several words such as "Aia bombé" seem to originate in the language of the Aborigines of the island. In any case, a local translation attributes these lines to them as a war cry meaning:

"Better to die, than to be enslaved." This is how the scholars of the court of King Henry Christophe put it to rhythm and had it adopted by the entourage of the proud monarch.

which those who surround the circle repeat in chorus, and then the new member begins to shake and dance what is called *monter vaudoux*. If he becomes carried away by his frenzy and steps by chance outside the circle, the chant ceases immediately, and the King and Queen *Vaudoux* turn their backs to dispel the omen. The dancer regains control of himself, reenters the circle, becomes agitated again, drinks, and finally reaches a convulsive state which the Roi Vaudoux regulates by tapping him on the head with his wooden paddle or spoon, or even by a blow of a bull lash if he deems it appropriate. He is led to the altar to take an oath and from this moment on he belongs to the sect.

"The ceremony is finished. The King puts his hand or foot on the box containing the snake and soon he is moved. He communicates this sensation to the Queen and, through her, the agitation spreads circularly and everyone experiences movements in which the upper part of the body, the head and shoulders seem to become disjointed. The Queen especially is a prey to the most violent agitations; from time to time she goes near the grass snake to renew the spell; she shakes his box and the little bells that adorn it, creating the effect of the cap and bells of the fool; the delirium grows. It is augmented further by the use of spiritous liquors which the initiates do not use sparingly in the ecstacy of their imagination and which helps, in turn, to sustain it. Exhaustion and fainting fits overcome some and a sort of fury overcomes others but within all there is a nervous agitation that they cannot seem to control. They whirl themselves about unceasingly. And while there are some who, in this kind of bacchanalia, tear their clothing to pieces and even bite themselves, others who have only lost their senses and fallen on the spot are carried, while the dancing goes on, into a neighboring room . . .

Finally, weariness ends these scenes which are distressing for the reasonable mind."

3

This page of Moreau de St. Méry, in our eyes, is of primary importance not only because it is the only authentic document which contains substantial data on the religious manifestations of the Negroes of Saint Domingue but also because in the abundance of details, the precision of references, and the general expression one immediately recognizes the stamp of authenticity. Although the author tells us that the sect was a secret one — and it still is in our time [1928] — his report to us leaves the impression that he was an eye witness. Moreover, in our opinion and according to that which we will establish later, even if the ritual of worship has been perceptibly modified since the colonial era, those peculiarities pointed out in the famous description still remain intangible. They appear to us to constitute the funadamental elements of Voodoo.

The most characteristic of these traits is the state of *trance* into which the individual possessed by the god is plunged. We will have an occasion to discuss this more fully later.

The second trait which imparts tonality to the ceremony is the dance, a dance made rhythmic by the sound of a trio of tall drums to the cadence of the *assons* [sacred rattles], performed according to the syncopated tunes improvised by a leader whose voice is echoed by an enraptured audience.

As for the rest, which seemed to be the essential part of the belief — we speak of the worship of the grass snake — this part of the rite has been eliminated from Voodoo or relegated entirely to the background of the ceremony. We believe it has been almost abolished. On this point, we would like to cite our personal evidence. In the course of our investigations, we had the opportunity to be present at numerous Voodoo ceremonies — a hundred at the least — some of which were performed in distant regions, and we have never seen homage being given to a snake, not even once. And, by notable coincidence, Haitian or foreign writers who have seriously applied themselves to the question have unaminously made this observation, either by expressly stating it or by never even mentioning such a ceremony. We will cite with pleasure the thoughts which D. Trouillot has assigned to this subject in his interesting pamphlet: *Le Vaudoun.* "It has been a long time," he writes, "since the reptile has fled from his *canari*, the little clay vase which forms the *sobagui* (that is, the altar).[86]

Other writers, such as Hannibal Price,[87] Dr. J.C. Dorsainvil,[88] Antoine Innocent,[89] Eugène Aubin,[90] and the Drs. Léon Audain[91] and Elie Lhérisson who have described the ceremonies of Voodoo or analyzed the data which condition its belief have not, at any time, given

---

[86] D[uverneau] Trouillot, *Esquisse ethnographiques: Le Vaudoun,* Port-au-Prince, 1885.

[87] Hannibal Price, *La réhabilitation de la race noire,* posthumous work, Port-au-Prince, 1900.

[88] Dr. Dorsainvil, diverse studies, notably those published in *Haiti Médicale,* under the suggestive title, *Vaudoun et névroses,* 1912, 1913.

[89] Antoine Innocent, *Mimola,* Port-au-Prince, [1935].

[90] Eugène Aubin, *En Haïti,* 1 volume, Paris, 1900, Armand Collin.

[91] Dr. Léon Audain, *Le mal d'Haiti,* 1 volume, Port-au-Prince, [1908].

an account of the grass snake in their works. Does this mean that the ophidian cult has entirely disappeared from the religious traditions of our masses? One would have a poor understanding of the evolution of beliefs to hazard such an opinion. As we have already demonstrated above, in Dahomey, within the cult of materialized spirits ophiolatry [snake worship] was, in a certain era and probably is still, a venerated custom. We have also noted as well how it spread across the black continent in a latent or an explicit form. Further, it is useful to remember that we recognize it almost always in the formation of the ancient Asiatic theogonies and that we accept its infiltration into the beliefs of many an occidental people. Can we forget that "the serpent of Epidaurus which the Romans worshipped as much as fire, was considered as a divine representation of Aesculapius, the child of the Sun."[92]

Did not Moses transform his magic rod into a brazen serpent called Nehushton which was worshipped in the temple of Jerusalen until the coming of Ezekias, 700 B.C.?[93] It is well understood that in a certain period of its evolution, humanity found a concrete form of deification in ophiolatry. It is not astonishing to find, as Sir James Frazer says,[94] that the cult of the serpent is still honored by a good many peoples, notably in India with the Mirasans of the Punjab. It would be even less conceivable that the Dahomean tradition had disappeared without leaving vestiges in Haitian beliefs. It survives in a rather indistinct form.

We understand that the fear observed in our peasants of killing snakes (variety of water snake, *water boa ungalia*)[95] is the most pronounced expression of this survival.

And in that case, if we were to set aside the serpent worship on which the whole scheme of colonial Voodoo was established probably because of its very close Dahomean relationships, what would remain of the original beliefs? Nothing except the dance and the ecstasy, both corroborated by the sacrifice.

May we be permitted to point out that these three elements: the *dance*, the *ecstasy*, and the *sacrifice* did form or do form the most persevering parts of religious rites and that we experience them, either

[92] Dr. Elie Lhérisson, Studies published in *La Lantern Médicale*, [March 20, 1899, pp. 19-23].

[93] Ovid, *Metam [orphoses]*, Book XV, 736, cited by [Alexander] Hislop, *Les deux Babylones*, Paul Monnerat, ed., Paris, [1886].

[94] Sir James Frazer, *Le rameau d'or [The Golden Bough]*, new abridged edition, translation by Lady Frazer, Libr. orientaliste Paul Guthner, Paris, 1923.

[95] Sir Harry Johnston, *The Negro in the New World*, p. 194.

joined together or separately, in the most exalted religions. Need we be reminded that in Greco-Roman antiquity, that the dance very often had a sacred character? Did not the Nabis, the Nazirs of Israel, resort to music to provoke possession of the Spirit so that the Eternal God could speak through their lips? Since the Hebrews used the one word "chag"[96] to express both festival and dance, does not the Bible teach us that David danced and leaped before the ark of the Eternal God, at Obed-Edom and that the ceremony was consummated with a burnt offering and sacrifices of riches.[97]

In regard to the black man, it seems to me there is reason to determine the role that music and dance perform in his spiritual life. However much these two arts are intimately associated among all the primitives, their influence over the organism assumes a clearly biological character for the Negro. We mean that even under the form of the very simple melodic line and the rhythmic step which are their most common expression, Music and Dance become an organic need for the black man, they become substantial, although imponderable contributions to nourish his nervous sytem bent under the weight of the most extreme emotivity. They color all the modalities of Negro life, whether in a mourner or a grave-digger chanting in rhythm the lamentations in funeral processions in order to avert a spell, or be it in the crowds where joyful exaltation brings forth gay songs and the explosion of superabundant emotions in spinning rhythmic steps. After all, dance and music are the two tutelary muses who hold priority in the development of Negro life in its primitive mode. One can easily imagine what particular form, what specific nuance is assumed by a religious conception that develops in such a psychological mold. Moreover, if one adds to the already mentioned conditions, the same quality of perception which, far from being the preliminary act of understanding as observed in the civilized adult, is here most often only a state of emotivity, it is not difficult to comprehend how the Negro religion makes use of the double cadre of Music and the Dance to express a moment of racial feeling.

But Music and Dance equally condition another manifestation of religious sentiment, the study of which offers a scientific interest of the first order.

This concerns the ecstacy, the trance, or possession.

What, then, are all of these?

[96] Alfred Loisy, *La religion d'Israël*, Paris, 1908, [English version, 1910, p. 88].
[97] II Samuel, Chap. VI, 12-16; II Kings, Chap. III, 15-16.

4

Through these different words we are identifying a universal phenomenon in the diversity of religions and one in which the individual, under the influence of ill-determined causes, is plunged into a crisis sometimes manifested by confused movements of clonic agitation [spasmodic convulsions], accompanied by cries or a flood of unintelligible words.

Other times, the individual is the object of sudden transformation: his body trembles, his face changes for the worse, his eyes protrude, and his foaming lips utter hoarse, inarticulate sounds, or even predictions and prophecies. Finally, oftentimes the subject, without any apparent sign of physical trouble, reveals an abnormal state through the bizarreness of his words, the mysterious air he adopts, the way he views his personality as estranged from his self. In every case, the state of trance, ecstasy, or possession appears as a delirium in which the delirious idea is characterized by a form of hallucination.

In the cult of Voodoo, this delirium has received various names.

In the West and in the South of the Republic, an individual tormented by this crisis is said to be possesed by his *loi* or his *mystère*, in the North, that he is *monté par les Anges ou les Saints*. It is well understood that the terminology is not absolute or exclusive, that it is interchangeable in any part of the country. For in the end, to have *his loi or his mystère, to be mounted by the Angels or Saints* signifies merely the possession by a spirit[98] which dominates you and dictates his will to you. We will note, by the way, that these expressions have borrowed from the French as well as some Catholic terminology. Does not obeying the *laws* of the Church, humbling oneself before the *Mystères* of Religion, performing one's devotion *to the angels and saints* of Paradise, form part of the teaching of the Church? The fact that the Voodoo cult uses its own terms to convey one of the essential modalities of the faith is not as banal as one might believe. It denotes one of the forms of influence exercised by Catholicism on the evolution of Voodoo and which will also furnish us later with the opportunity to acquire an ample harvest of observations. For the moment it is expedient for us to consider the position in religious phenomenology of the attitude of the follower who displays the aptitudes we have just described.

The Haitian people are preoccupied with the "loi" or the "mystère"

98 The term "possessed by the spirit" is likewise employed.

of Voodoo to an indescribable degree.

The believers see it as a proof of the supernatural character of the cult and they are unperturbed by this.

The others — and these form the greatest number — grant freely that while these phenomena do not reveal rational explanations, they are not to be included whatsoever in the ensemble of demoniac acts condemned and prohibited by the Church.

In a word, for both, denial like acceptance rests on the same process of reasoning which transfers what is only one of multiple psychiatric problems into the realm of the mysterious.

It is from this exclusively scientific point of view that a few rare researchers have examined the question and shed some light on it.

5

In an authoritative study published in *Haiti Médicale* in 1912 and 1913, Dr. J.C. Dorsainvil attacked the subject with the sagacity of a clinician and the clairvoyance of a sociologist, an approach which we find very laudable. As a clinician, he defined the crisis of the initiated known under the name of *loi* or of *mystère* as a psychoneurosis which he described as follows. "Voodoo is a religious, racial psychoneurosis characterized by a division of the self into two parts with functional alterations of sensibility, of motility, and the predominance of pithiatic phenomena."[14]

Does this definition grasp all the complexity of the problem? Is it indicative of the solution to which a revision of his data will lead us?

Despite the high regard we have for the scientific knowledge of Dorsainvil and with all due respect, we can only accept his definition with certain reservations.

It is true that he attempted for a long time to justify it for he was the very first to perceive that it was somewhat ambiguous. And in addition, if we refer to the last monograph that he devoted to the subject entitled *Une explication philologique du Vodû*[99] in which he has recalled perhaps too meticulously the solution which he stressed in 1913, it

[14] This quotation may be found in *Vôdou et névrose*, Port-au-Prince, 1931, p. 111. The phrase "pithiatic phenomena' refers to phenomena caused by suggestion and curable by persuasion.

[99] Dr. J.C. Dorsainvil, *Une explication philologique du Vodû*, Port-au-Prince, 1924, (published by the author). [This monograph is also contained in *Vôdou et névrose*. The quotation in paragraph three above is on page 172.]

seems to us that the total development of his recent thought is in con-
tradiction with his conception of fifteen years ago. In his latest publication, Dorsainvil has demonstrated, as we did, that the word "vodoun"
is a Dahomean term meaning *esprit* [spirit]. All religion of the Fon
[African tribe], he writes, issues from the worship of the Vodoun (that
is, of the spirits) out of which has come our popular cult.

With a wealth of details, the sociologist in the manner of Delafosse
revealed to us that this worship is as exalted as the most spiritual ones.

"Would it be saying too much," he exclaims at the end of his
monograph, "to affirm that this religious conception represents some
metaphysical ideas which give credit to Negro intelligence? Unquestionably it is not a trivial phenomenon for a primitive tribe to arrive
at such a clear and precise monotheistic conception, is it?"

But then how can we accept, on the other hand, that the same worship is only a racial, religious psychoneurosis, and so on? The contradic-
tion lies not only in the conflict of terms, it seems to be in the conception itself that the author has of Voodoo.

However, if we stress the general sense of the two statements, we
will observe that there is something justifiable in either aspect of the thinking of Dorsainvil. In our opinion, he has considered from the first only
one aspect of the problem by refraining from establishing the principal
difference which exists in the worship of Voodoo between the general
mass of believers and the very small group of initiates who participate
in the Mystères of the divinities and are overwhelmed by "lois." The latter refer to themselves by the generic term of "servants" or of "serviteurs"
of the gods. It is to this little group and to it alone that one would apply
if need be, the term of psychoneurotics which is unacceptable for the
body of believers and adherents constituting the cult of Voodoo. However
many of the latter observe commandments of the cult with as much
religious fervor as the "servants" but grace has not touched them and
there is nothing in their bearing which would indicate psychoneurosis.[100]

Having stated this postulate, it remains to us to classify the
psychoneurosis which is the phenomenon of possession in the category
of psychopathies[101] to which it belongs. Here again, we regret that we
cannot accept the theory of Dorsainvil without serious revision. It is ob-

---

[100] Psychoneurosis: Generic term which is used to designate a certain number of nervous affections whose beginning is especially psychical: neurasthenia, psychastenia,
hysteria, hypochondria, and mild melancholy. (Dubois de Berne)
[101] Psychopathy: Mental malady.

viously evident that the one who experiences the crisis of Voodoo presents for consideration the spectacle of dissociation, of profound alterations of sensibility and motility, that his trance resembles in many respects the syndrome of epilepsy and also differentiates itself from it by a symptomatology which indicates the neurological character of epilepsy but is linked, unlike epilepsy, to some non-lesional psychosis. But then in analyzing the signs by which the crisis of the "servants" of Voodoo is distinguished, one succeeds, quite easily through differential diagnosis, in making it into a simple manifestation of hysteria. Although Dr. Dorsainvil has not used this word, his theory as it is explained in the definition given above comes to this conclusion. Yes! But this solution to the problem is far from being satisfactory.

In the first place, the old conception of hysteria according to the doctrine of [Jean Martin] Charcot has been almost disproved by that of [Joseph François Felix] Babinski.

Undoubtedly you may recall that the Director of La Salpêtrière [Charcot] described hysteria as a mental malady which reveals itself in two ways: *stigma* discernible even apart from the attacks to which the affected are subject and which consist especially of sensito-sensorial hemianesthesia[102] more frequently on the left side than on the right, pharyngeal anesthesia, ovarian hyperesthesia,[103] the hysterogenic zones, and so forth; and *accidents* composed of minor or major attacks of an epileptiform character with its diverse tonic, clonic, and resolvent phases, then finally the *passionate attitudes*, the *contractions*, the *paralyses*, even *deliria*, and so on.

It is against this conception of hysteria that Babinski protested with the growing authority of a therapeutic method supported by successful experimentation. Babinski discovered that hysteria according to the doctrine of Charcot had indiscriminately invaded most of the nosological categories of mental maladies. It had resulted in such confusion that according to the wit of Lasègue, hysteria had become "the wastebasket into which were thrown all the maladies that one could not explain."

And so the great neurologist began to eliminate from the symptomatology of hysteria every sign that had been unduly attached to it and succeeded gradually in considering it from the angle of a morbid entity provoked by suggestion — auto or heterosuggestion — and suscep-

---

[102] Anesthesia of half the body with partial loss of general sensibility and of special sensibility, as gustatory, olfactory, visual, and so on.

[103] Ovarian hyperesthesia: Exaggeration of the sensibility of the ovaries.

tible to cure by persuasion, hence the name pithiatism (from the Greek *peithô*, I persuade; *athos*, curable; pitiatos, curable by persuasion) by which he proposed to replace the term *Hysteria* which he considered inadequate to describe the true character of the illness.[104]

The fact is that since this new conception was recognized, not only has it won the approbation of the great majority of neurologists and psychiatrists by its clarity and simplicity but it has proved its practical effectiveness through therapeutic application.

Moreover, the world-wide war [World War I] which enabled us to record an incalculable number of observations has largely confirmed its appropriateness.

However at the other pole of neurology, Pierre Janet, whose works and teaching at the Collège de France have caused a great stir, opposes the doctrine of Babinski with a theory which demonstrates its inadequacy to explain the whole complex problem of hysteria. According to the eminent professor, this malady is encountered only in subjects with an obvious psychological deficiency. He gives proof of their incapacity to realize mental synthesis which is the definitive phrase for the ensemble of all the imponderable elements constituting consciousness or the unity of self, so that among these subjects there results the latent possibility of a partial or total disaggregation of the personality, the stricture of their field of consciousness, the weakness of their power to react, the loss of their power of volition, and finally therefore their tendencies to act only on the level of automatism.[105] The depression so often verified in such subjects denotes above all their *psychological hypotension*. So, granted that they may be abnormally susceptible to suggestion, it would not necessarily testify to the specific quality of this suggestibility that Pierre Janet calls *suggestivité*. By this term, he designates the special aptitude of the patient to reproduce the ideas which exist independently of his will, beyond the control of his consciousness, foreign in some way to his own personality. Such a course is only possible through distractibility which is itself only another manifestation of the stricture of the field of consciousness. In his own way, the hysteric is suggestible [abnormally susceptible to suggestion], totally, absolutely. Such a weakminded spirit, a

---

[104] *Etat mental des hystériques*, by B.J. Logre in *Psychiatrie*, vol. 1, in the *Traité de pathologie médicale* [*et de therapeutic appliquée*, ed.,] Sergent, Ribadeau-Dumas, Babonneix, Paris, Maloine, 1921.

[105] Cf. Pierre Janet, *L'automatisme psychologique*, ninth edition, [Paris], 1925; G. Dumas, "La pathologie mentale," *Traité de psychologie*, second volume, [pp. 811-1006, esp. 923-932, "Théorie de Janet"].

phobiac,[106] a nosomaniac[107] can be affected by a lecture, a conversation and reproduce in behavior, in attitudes, the ideas which have been suggested to him by this authority, but here suggestion assumes a character of achievement and perfection that is met only in the mental state of these individuals. Hysteria therefore has been correctly called not only a pathological suggestibility but the suggestibility of the pathological. Thus may be explained the sensorimotor disorders with their corollaries of contractions, paralyses, anesthesias, and so forth, in reproduction of similar disorders provoked by the special receptivity of the subjects. In summary, and to the extent that a doctrine developed in so many famous books with great dialectical precision supported by numerous medical observations can be schematized, Pierre Janet defines hysteria as a malady "characterized by the narrowing of the field of personal consciousness and by the tendency to dissociation and the emancipation of systems of ideas and functions which, through their synthesis, constitute the personality."

These are the two doctrines which hold the attention of psychiatrists and neurologists concerning the problem of hysteria and on which we are little qualified to pass judgment.

However that may be, if the phenomenon of possession — the trance or the ecstasy — in those who experience the crisis of Voodoo is a psychoneurosis, can it be classified in the category of hysteria according to either of the doctrines stated above?

We do not believe so. Those possessed by the loi [or mystère] do not have the type of crisis in which the attack is provoked by suggestion and cured by persuasion. In this the definition of Doctor Dorsainvil appears incorrect to us when, in reconciling the two doctrines of hysteria, he places voodooistic possession in the order "of a separation of self . . . with a predominance of pithiatic symptoms."

On the other hand, because the dissociation of the constitutional elements of personality with concomitant disturbances of sensibility and motility form the symptomatic trilogy of the crisis of "serviteurs" of voodoo, does it follow that it is a manifestation of hysteria according to the theory of Janet?

We do not believe this either. Without doubt, here also, here especially, the realization of crisis operates only on the level of the subconscious, therefore beyond any participation of the will of the believer. Here also,

[106] One who has irrational fear.
[107] One who has obsessive preoccupation with his health.

such a course of action is only possible in a mentality where psychological hypotension plays the principal role. The pathogenic mechanism is thus the same in the one or the other. But once a certain point is reached, the parallelism ceases. Though hysterical disturbances of a highly theatrical character have just about disappeared from nosological classifications because they were the result of a process of suggestion determined by the physicians themselves, it is nevertheless established knowledge that the malady is revealed by almost identical signs everywhere. First of all, there is the attack. Most often it happens unexpectedly because of some annoyance. The subject puts his hand on his breast, collapses in a heap, rests motionless and stiff on the ground, with teeth clenched, eyes shut, or else he jerks about erratically. At other times, the body arches stiffly with only the heels and the head resting on the ground. According to the spectators, the crisis may end as abruptly as it was begun. In a few minutes, in a few hours with or without the intervention of the doctor or those in attendance, normalcy returns unless, however, there is a series of subsequent crises or the malady is associated with some other clearly organic morbid phenomenon. Here one may encounter a series of sensorimotor difficulties: contractions, hemianesthesia, dyschromatopsia,[108] all of which are susceptible to cure by persuasion.

Such is the usual course of an hysterical crisis free of all simulation — which is, moreover, extremely difficult to establish.

Is there identity or only analogy with a voodooistic crisis of possession? We are disposed toward the second hypothesis.

Judge for yourself:

The subject, in this case — most often, but not always — requires a special atmosphere, that of the worship ceremony which unfolds only in a setting where the mystères of the faith hover. The scene takes place in the approaches to the temple or the home of some devotee. In the open air or under a *tonelle* [thatched canopy] a space is reserved for the execution of the ceremony in which the dance is the most joyous episode. The high priest inaugurates the ritual of worship with the consecration of the premises. He offers libations to the gods, scatters wheaten flour on the ground, pours spiritous liquors as he pronounces the liturgical words. The deep and muffled voice of the drums prolongs the vibration of the chants and incantations. The *Hougan* invested by his insignia intones the liturgical *melopée* [recitative chant] that the whole audience

---

[108] Generic name used to designate confusion in the perception of colors, particularly the difficulty of recognizing slight variations.

takes up in chorus. Agile dancers, as if spirits, leap about the arena and increase the rhythm of pace to the cadence of nostalgic sounds and those evoking orgiastic frenzies. Abruptly the possessed one bursts out from the crowd where his attention was intensely concentrated on the movement of the ceremony and mixes with the dancers, or else dancing by himself, he is more and more intoxicated by the sounds and movements and dances, dances madly. But then he stops, dazed. He staggers, shrieks, sinks to the ground, prostrate or shaken by violent contortions. He rises again by himself or with the help of an assistant. His face assumes a tortured expression. Often the drums become silent at this moment. The audience is pensive and the possessed in an altered voice tremulous with the tumult of his mind improvises an air in honor of the god by which he is possessed and who identifies himself through the lips of the subject. And the possessed transmits a new momentum to the dance with an enhanced power that is irrepressible, inexpressible.

But outside the cermonial atmosphere, the crisis can arise in the most discreet fashion in the world, sometimes provoked by a serious question involving the honor, interests, even the life of the subject or of his entourage. In this case the possessed one, without passing through the convulsive phases, and according to the attributes of the god that dwells in him, vaticinates [predicts in chanting style], prophesies, commands, prescribes imperatively.

Finally, whether it is manifested amidst the cultic rites or the calm and serenity of the familial atmosphere, the voodooistic crisis presents for observation its *pathognomonic*[109] *sign which is the delirium of possession.* Here the delirium is constant. It may itself constitute the whole of the crisis. If it does not exist, all the rest vanishes. Interestingly, very often, it is not incompatible with the performance of customary acts of everyday life. We mean that the delirious person is able to engage in his usual pursuits, to devote himself to the exercise of his job without upsetting the order of his habits, with a regularity that reveals the influence of the automatisms of coordination and direction. After the crisis has passed, the subject retains no memory either of what he said or he did during the time that his second personality has lasted. This is how the phenomenon of possession is realized by the "servants" of Voodoo.[110]

[109] The pathognomonic sign is encountered only in a determined morbid state and suffices by itself to characterize this morbid state and to state symptoms.

[110] It is of course possible that an hysteric may also be a "servant." Then he joins the two psychoses in himself.

According to the schematic ideas of the two psychoses as we have attempted to explain them, it seems to us that though there is parallelism in their symptomatic conduct there are some essential differences between them. We have tried to demonstrate by our analysis that both participate in the same process which is rooted in the depths of the unconscious, but we also have come to the conclusion that their manifestations are at a given moment dissimilar to the point that each has formed its own particular manner, its special character. In our opinion, the difference between them is even deeper because it rests on specific tendencies. Hysterical morbidity seems particularly to be more of an imaginative disturbance. Hysteria is not an imaginary malady, it is a malady of the imagination, the suggestibility of the pathological.[111]

Now the *possessive state* is quite different, it develops on the mystical level. If it offers the spectacle of neurological phenomena such as the convulsion, it presents as well syndromes that are non-reducible by persuasion such as sensito-sensorial anesthesia which permits the voodooistic possessed one to plunge his hands without wincing into pots filled with cooking foods or to chew glasses and fragments of bottles with or without injury, to lick rods of red hot steel without appearing to suffer. Ah! undoubtedly, one may encounter hysterical and other mad advocates of automutilation acts. But they only accomplish them involuntarily in mental aberration or excitation, while our "servant" does it of his own will or more exactly in obedience to the will of his god with a happy heart. In short, according to us, the voodooistic crisis is a mystical state characterized by the delirium of theomaniac possession and the dual nature of the personality. It determnes automatic acts and is accompanied by disorders of Cenesthesia.[112]

And the mechanism of this delirium is expressed through a pathological exaggeration of an internal language, what Delacroix calls a hyperendophasia.[113] In his mental instability, the individual under the influence of an auditory hallucination believes he hears an internal voice in place of his own verbal-motor faculties. "It is automatism which overtakes him and directs his attention to the content of the discourse and

---

[111] B.J. Logre, *Etat mental des hystériques, loc. cit.*

[112] Cenesthesia: *Koinos,* common, *Esthesis,* sensibility. "Feeling that we have of our existence, due to a vague and weak perception of organic sensibility in the normal state, which is derived from all our organs and tissues, including the sense organs." (According to Deny and Camus)

[113] *Hyper,* that which is in excess, *Endon,* within, *Phasis,* word [speech, language] — *Hyperendophasia.* Delacroix, *Le langage et la pensée,* Paris, 1924.

alienates him from its form. The affected person is conscious of formulating often word for word and phrase by phrase a thought that is foreign to him. Somebody speaks inside him." And this inner word, exacerbating what is only an auditive, verbal hallucination, becomes so imperative, "incoercible and compulsive" that it transmits to the subject the attitude of the alien personality which seems to have invaded his field of consciousness. However the discourse which the individual delivers is most always chaotic, unintelligible in itself. He is persuaded that it is the Spirit who speaks through his lips. Sometimes in this confusion of words there is a rough meaning which becomes all the more mysterious since it is obscure. Other times the language is lively and colorful and the hyperdophasia of the subject becomes explicit in eloquent terms, well-balanced phrases, even strange dialects, and all of it contrasts oddly with the habitual ignorance of the individual. It is in fact the phenomenon of glossolalia [gift of tongues].[114] It is common to all religions, at least in their beginnings, and is perpetuated in the mystical theology of all the cults.[115] And it is because the voodooistic "servants" are mystics that we find again in them the self-same phenomenon just as it is revealed elsewhere.

We know how shocking this conclusion is to a great many good people. People in general consider mysticism in Haiti as only a function of Christian piety and as a means of rendering homage to those who have been touched by this manifestation of divine beatitude. Furthermore, they will ask, scandalized, can Voodoo, ferreted out by secular institutions, condemned by the Church, feared by all as the worst of superstition, engender acts and phenomena of mysticism?

"No," will be the response of most people.

Well, we who are not worried about pleasing or displeasing whomever this may be, we who pursue scientific inquiry with the serenity born of experience in the laboratory, we can neither propose nor accept complacent solutions.

It is of little importance that the conclusions we reach go against respectable convictions, reverse constructs built on ignorance and prejudice, intervene with the traditions of the Church and State. Undoubtedly, all these considerations are formidable, but what is all that compared to the little glimmer of truth in the darkness of Time?

If Christian mysticism, in its most authentic and noble manifesta-

[114] Cf. St. Paul, First Epistle to the Corinthians, Chap. XIV.
[115] Henry Delacroix, *La religion et la foi*, Paris, 1922.

tions, is for the faithful an emancipation from carnal attachments which leads him gradually by prayer and ecstasy to a state where he feels himself as one with the divine being, aglow with the presence of God in his heart, should we forget that the subject draws the substance of this transformation not only from his affective aggregate, enriched by the contributions of the social milieu and perhaps by the alleviating quality of the neuron, but especially from the religious atmosphere charged with idealism and spirituality in which he lives? If despite all these conditions favorable to the emergence of the highest religious expression, more than one Christian mystic presents for observation some phenomena of obsession, of catalepsy, of possession, of sensori-motor difficulties,[116] how could we deny to elementary forms of religious life the possibility of producing some cases of mysticism? Could we dare to say that here the religious phenomenon is incapable of realizing the same marvels of transfiguration as elsewhere? Well, here as elsewhere, the first sensation of the subject in the state of trance is to believe himself subjugated by forces external to his consciousness, as William James has expressed it. Here as elsewhere, "the believer is not only a man who sees, who knows things of which the nonbeliever is not conscious, he is a man who *can do more.*" Here as elsewhere, his powers of realization are raised higher by the "dynamogenous quality" of the spiritual incarnation with which he has been favored. The person possessed of Voodoo, the humble unskilled worker of yesterday who has become suddenly the temporary dwelling place of the Spirit, not only chides, reprimands, prophesizes, but what of the respect and the veneration by which he is heard, obeyed, feared by his entourage?

It is not to his person that they address such hommage, but rather to the mysterious transformation of which he is the object. It is in this second state that our analysis has found an analogous form of mysticism, a form which is perhaps inferior because it draws the substance of its elaboration from affective aggregates which are limited in possibilities, restricted in their horizons, overnourished by a perception and a representation of the external world which is of infinitely poor structure. But it is mysticism all the same, and of the type as that which has been described in the Mohammedan sect of the Dervishes.

[116] Cf. James H. Leuba *Psychologie du mysticisme religieux*, pp. 92, 103, 111 and following, French translation by Lucien Herr, Alcan. 1920; Durkheim, (1) *Les formes élémentaires de la vie religieuse*, [Since all notes in Durkheim begin with (1) on each page, it is unclear to which note Price-Mars is referring. Perhaps the *Conclusion* would be of aid to the reader.]; [Georges] Dwelshauvers, *L'inconscient*, Paris, [1916].

We know that this strange flowering of piety has grown tremendously in the Mohammedan religion since the twelfth century. Howling dervishes, whirling dervishes, dancing dervishes — all are believers who, anxious to intensify their faith, offer to Allah the homage of their life consecrated to prayer and to ritual exercises of penitence, tortures, and automutilation which are extremely impressive in their singularity and bizarreness.

Here is a moving episode of asceticism among the Sufi, reported by James H. Leuba in *Psychology of Religious Mysticism!*

"The entire ceremony is composed of five successive scenes; we can omit the description of the first three. After a pause the fourth scene begins. At this moment all the dervishes remove their turbans, form a circle by pressing arms and shoulders against each other, and thus make the circuit of the hall in a measured pace, stamping their feet at intervals, and all springing into the air as if one person. This dance is continued while the "Ilahees" are chanted alternately by the two elders to the left of the Sheikh. During the chant, the cries of "Ya Allah!" as well as "Ya Hou!" redouble and alternate with the frightful noisy howling of the dancing dervishes . . .

"The fourth scene leads to the fifth which is the most frightful of all; the complete exhaustion of the performers is transformed into a sort of ecstasy which they call *Halet*. It is during this abandonment of self, or rather this religious delirium, that they use red-hot irons. A certain number of cutlasses and other instruments of sharp pointed iron are on hooks in niches of the hall and on a part of the wall to the right of the sheikh. Near the end of the fourth scene, two of the dervishes take down eight or nine of these instruments, heat them red-hot, and present them to the sheikh.

"The sheikh, after reciting some prayers over them and invoking the founder of the order, Ahmed er Rufâ'ee, breathes over these implements by bringing them gently to his lips, then distributes them to the dervishes, who demand them with the utmost eagerness and desire. It is at this moment that these fanatics, overcome by their frenzy, seize these irons in their bare hands, gloat over them tenderly, lick them, bite them, hold them between their teeth, and end by cooling them in their mouths. Those who were unable to procure any furiously seize the cutlasses hanging on the wall and stick them into their sides, arms, and legs.

"Because of the paroxysm of their frenzy and of their amazing fortitude which they perceive as having merit in the eyes of the divinity, they all bear up quite stoically against the pain which they experience with every appearance of joy. If however some of them fall under their suffering they throw themselves into the arms of their confreres without a complaint or the least sign of pain.

"Some minutes later the sheikh walks around the hall, examines each of the performers in turn, breathes upon their wounds, rubs them with saliva, recites prayers over them, and promises them a speedy recovery. It is said that twenty-four hours afterward there will be no trace of these wounds."[117]

To this description, of some thirty years ago, one may add the recent testimony of an observer particularly interested in the study of the phenomena of mysticism. In the January and February 1927 issues of the American magazine *Asia*, W.E. Seabrook has submitted an article on his research among the whirling and howling Dervishes of Syria. He visited a Sufi monastery built in the mountains between Aleppo and Hama and was the troubled spectator of the same kind of scenes described above. His impression varies somewhat from that reported above in the interpretation of some of the acts of ecstasy that he witnessed. He dwells notably on the ulterior consequences of the automutilation scenes to which his hosts were devoted.

Seabrook, having been authorized to examine subjects — about twenty — who experienced ecstatic delirium during the preceding night, stated that the wounds had left no apparent traces, probably because the red-hot irons had had time to cool down during the frenetic whirling in which the subjects had engaged before applying these instruments of torture to their skin. He had occasion, however, to observe old burns that were perfectly healed.

It would be superfluous, we believe, to insist upon positive analogy between Moslem mysticism in the Sufi sect and the voodooistic manifestations which we have previous analyzed. It would seem unquestionable that both phenomena are products elaborated in the subconscious and which, by means of the dynamism of faith, emerge in the efflorescence of impressive, disconcerting acts. Moreover, superior religions, even the most advanced, have all been marked in their origins by this elementary process of possession by the divine, by these accounts of strangely

---

[117] James H. Leuba [pp. 14-15] borrowed this account from [J.P.] Brown, *Dervishes*, p. 218-222, cited by J.W. Powell, in the *Fourteenth Annual Report of the Bureau of Ethnology*, Part 2, Washington, D.C., 1896, pp. 948-952.

close relations between the god and his worshippers, and although they glory now in having attained a high state of spirituality they still retain these encumbrances which from time to time cause them to retrogress toward old forms of cultic worship. Thus Christianity offers us, in the development of innumerable sects born of the Reformation, many an example of bizarre and eccentric worship in which ecstasy and mysticism, provoked or not by artificial means — especially dance and music — play a preponderant role. We know how much Methodism, the essence of whose doctrine is creative of inspirational acts, favors the impetuosity of these great currents of mysticism.

But it would be more correct to say that the free interpretation of Biblical texts is the main source from which these movements flowed. This is why the remark of Bovet is so apt when he states that "in Christianity, the more a sect is Biblical, the more willingly it cultivates such phenomena as were frequently associated with the origins of Christianity."[118]

And we may also be evoking the memory of the inspired of the primitive Church when we analyze certain cultic manifestations incited by the famous religious enthusiasms of Revivalism.

Here, for example, is one from Halevy[119] which is of such a suggestive character that we cannot resist disclosing it to the reader. It concerns a very curious form of Neo-Christian piety. "The members of the sect of 'Jumpers,' " he says, "born of Methodist revivalism, throw themselves flat on their faces when the preacher begins to speak; then when they feel themselves inspired from on high they rise to their feet to jump in cadence for hours on end." This sect, which is not confined to the British Isles, has recruited some followers in the United States of America. James H. Leuba, in a marginal note of his *Psychology of Religious Mysticism* [p. 15] has noted its invasion of New York City. "As I write this," he remarks, "the 'Holy Jumpers' are preparing to leave their idyllic original settlement in western New Jersey to establish themselves in the worst neighborhoods of New York. They will take advantage in the intervals between their dances, which include the entire gamut of steps from the tourbillon [circular movement] of dervishes to the bourrée [fast French gavotte] of sailors — to warn the New Yorkers of the catastrophe which threatens them in the form of a pillar of fire. The

[118] Cited by H. Delacroix in *La religion et la foi*, [p. 298].
[119] [Elie] Halévy, *Le peuple anglais*, I, [Paris, 1912], p. 396, cited by H. Delacroix in *La religion et la foi*, [p. 72].

jumpers rely on extraordinary zeal to win the city with the magical evolutions to which they owe their name; if they succeed in this, they propose to found a colony and a school for missionaries here, similar to those they have in Denver, their city of origin.

"At any given moment in the meetings of the holy jumpers, there is always a chance that some of the participants will be filled with such inspiration as to be unable to resist dancing. A cry of joy and the person begins. It may happen that at first he will waltz alone around the place. Then a second joins him. They grasp each other by the shoulders and the waltz quickens into a *two step*. Then they stop face to face, and whirl themselves in the manner of dervishes, ending with a very high leap into the air and at times making a full half turn before falling to the ground. The dance, the songs, and the shouts induce others to do the same; women skip about like schoolgirls, seize each other and pull one another into the circle. Little by little, the entire assembly begins to whirl, to jump, and to shout but the men never dance with the women."

We would overburden our evidence beyond proportion if we were to strengthen these observations by other examples borrowed from undesirable parts of society where the zeal of the revived Christian is allied with orgiastic practices. However that may be, it is not superflous to add to the events already mentioned a phenomenon of the same category which we witnessed in 1910 in Washington, the capital of the American Union.

It was on a Sunday morning when our insatiable curiosity led us into a Baptist chapel filled with people of color, situated in the northwestern part of the city. At the moment that we entered the pastor was at the peak of predicting the most dire calamities for those of his flock who, by their reprehensible conduct, were drawing down the wrath of God upon their heads. Then, abruptly, he asked the following question, "My brothers, if Christ appeared before you, would you not crucify him also, ye Pharisees of today? Would you not also throw him to the hatred of the godless crowd, ye new Pontius Pilates? How do you answer, ye souls jaded by sin?"

"Oh! No!" a voice from the congregation answered quickly, "Be merciful! Have pity!"

The orator was silent. A moment of anguish followed for the audience.

Suddenly, the pastor with haggard eyes, earnest voice, pointed the right hand straight before him and cried out, "There is the Christ!"

And the entire congregation turned instinctively toward the imaginary spot where the apparition seemed to be.

Then one good woman got up, uttered plaints and lamentations, and danced and sang. Another followed her, another, still another. . . Soon more than two thirds of the congregation were leaping around in a state of extraordinary exaltation, shouting at the top of their voices, "Oh Lord, have mercy!" But the pastor, who was himself silent during this whole strange scene, signaled that he had something else to say, and little by little calm returned to the flock. Then he extended his hands, implored the forgiveness of Christ for his flock of repentant sheep and the scene ended with a particularly expressive prayer. This lasted a good half-hour.

At the time we were both scandalized and moved by this show of foolery that so severely tried us before some of our American friends. One of them said to us, smiling, "They were happy." We only understood much later that our Baptists had been in a state of mystical delirium.

The historian of religions will have difficulty disproving that such religious manifestations accept the oldest Christian traditions and practices as precedents although such an observation would cause much bewilderment among most Christians who do not know the history of Christianity very well.

But then the analyst who wishes to categorize these phenomena is quite obliged to class them with the crude productions of mysticism. Moreover he will find the explanation for them in the inability of the will to overcome emotional states under certain determined conditions, in the mental contagion provoked by certain gestures, certain words when an entire crowd is in a paroxysm of expectation of something indefinable and imminent, finally in the confusion of primitive thought unable to discriminate between the subjective and the objective and very frequently incapable because of the inferior quality of perception to distinguish cause from effect. This dullness of thought is reduced in the end to no more than a form of affectivity and envisions all problems of life with an aura of mystery. *Life is mystical.* How then would it be possible for us to comprehend the process of events of this category, to perceive the ultimate development of such a state of mind, of a mentality so heavily handicapped, without calling upon the most plausible, the clearest explanation supported of course by the best references and on patient observations?

This is where, in our opinion, the key "to the mystères" of Voodoo is to be found and this is why from all the explanations that have been proposed, none appear to us to give its true character except that which considers and classes them as mystical states, characterized by the delirium of theomaniac possession and dual personality.

6

Nevertheless our task has hardly been complete if, having assigned a place to the voodooistic crisis in the Hierarchy of psychoses, having studied the multiple and diverse causes which have conditioned its existence in the past and explain its survival in the present, we do not take time to examine its pathogenesis. In other words, we should investigate why, among the mass of the faithful, of adherents and simple believers, the phenomenon has affected only a small number of elect ones — the servants or "les serviteurs" of the "lois."

By the very fact that we have found elements characteristic of a psychosis in the crisis, we have immediately chosen one of the two large groups into which modern psychiatry classifies psychopathies. We know that mental maladies are recognized as either lesional or nonlesional. The former reveal, either through the naked eye or the microscope, alterations which affect the life of the cells and modify the structure of the tissues. These diverse alterations of the nervous system are exteriorized by temporary or permanent disorders. If they lead to the death of the subject, the autopsy picks up in the organism all the ill effects by which the nervous system has been stricken. Such are, for example, the effects of imbecility, idiocy, epilepsy, dementia praecox, senility, alcoholic intoxication, and so forth. These are all organic or toxic-infectious psychopathies. It has been observed that they are acquired either during fetal life or later.

To this large pathologic group is added another which completes the classification — the category of nonlesional maladies. These are known as maladies which are not discernable by analysis, at least by our present methods of investigation.[120]

If "the individual with his organs, his tissues, his masterly organization is only the anonymous and ephemeral servant of infinitely reproducing cells,"[121] we must acknowledge that the extreme structural delicacy of these microcosms demands such a fragile state of equilibrium that subtle

---

[120] Cf., [François] Achille-Delmas and Marcel Boll, *La personalité humaine*, Paris, 1922.

[121] [Hyacinthe] Guilleminot, *Les nouveaux horizons de la science* (La vie, ses fonctions, ses origines, sa fin), Paris, [1926].

alterations can break up their harmony without our having the means to discover how the tissues might have been affected. In any case, the characteristic of nonlesional psychopathies is that they are transmitted through heredity and last the life of the individual. They are in the proper sense constitutional. Far from provoking, as the first group, "contradictory, chaotic, and tumultuous" psychological manifestations, they are only the exaggeration, the enlargement, the hypertrophy [proliferation] of normal tendencies. The notion of nonlesional psychopathies has led psychiatrists in the past twenty years to establish the successful distinction of maladies, those in which the partial and anatomical destruction of the nervous system produces an enigma and those in which it is always easy to recognize a predisposition, an inner tendency of the individual. From this distinction has arisen a new classification of mental pathology and recently in their authoritative work, *La personnalité humaine*, Achille Delmas and Marcel Boll have drawn up "an astonishingly precise nomenclature of the faculties of the mind."[122]

Thus there exists a whole category of mental maladies which derive from psychic constitutions in which the total human personality is developed. Thanks to this "definitive acquisition," psychopathic constitutions are assembled in five groups:

1. The paranoiac constitution.[123]
2. The perverse constitution.
3. The mythomaniac constitution.
4. The cyclothymic constitution.[124]
5. The hyperemotive constitution.

Without pausing to define each of these — which would carry us far from our subject — we can say, from the point of view of the formation of character and temperament, that each of these diverse dispositions, which may moreover combine permitting the dominance of the principal tendency, gives its special mark to the mentality of the individual who is tributary to it. In order to illustrate our thesis we will take the mythomaniac constitution in which we classify the "serviteurs" of Voodoo. We know that Dupré supplied the initial definition of this in attributing

[122] The terms are from Maurice de Fleury, *L'angoisse humaine*, [Paris, 1924].

[123] *Para* — near, beside; *Anoia* — foolishness. A psychosis characterized by ecstatic schemes of persecution and grandeur (commonly called: persecution mania and delusions of grandeur), Achille Delmas and Marcel Boll.

[124] Cyclothymia: *Cuclos* — circle; *Tumos* — state of mind. A psychosis characterized by an absence of equilibrium in activity. The cyclothymiac is sometimes hyperactive and sometimes depressed to the point of melancholy.

an involuntary propensity for fabrication, for lying to the individuals afflicted by it.

But it also comprises "a set of physiological and psychological manifestations that one finds associated with the same patients and which are presented, for the first time, as realizations of abnormal attitudes, of paralysis, of contractions, and of nervous crises." In our opinion, if the dominant note among the serviteurs of Voodoo is this inner tendency to realize nervous crises, then it is also accompanied by the subjacent [underlying] action of extreme emotivity and inhibitory weakness of will. Under these conditions the constitutional mentality of the serviteurs of Voodoo would be a component force in which mythomania would hold first place and hyperemotivity the adjuvant [auxiliary] role.

The essentially hereditary nature of this constitution explains to us how and why the voodooistic crisis is transmitted from family to family. It equally indicates to us why at the age of puberty, a child hitherto protected from the influences of collective excitation — the ceremonial dance and the cultic meeting — and put in front of such contingencies finds himself abruptly overcome by the crisis because he bears its hereditary imprint within him. All the more so will this enable us in light of this classification to reject the opinion that makes this phenomenon an attribute of race. Any individual of any race, who would have the characteristics of the constitutional component which we have just discussed, would be susceptible to having a voodooistic crisis, especially if, as a spectator of cultic ceremonies, affected by "motorial excitation" of the possessed, he was placed in a state of obnubilation [mind or intellect in state of being cloudy or obscure] and of receptivity which would make him prey to collective suggestion. Moreover we have in reference to this all sorts of evidence of the phenomena of mental contagion. And the historiographer of the colony, Moreau de Saint-Méry, informs us that the magnetism exercised by the dance of Voodoo is such that Whites found watching the mysteries of this sect and touched by one of its members who had discovered them began to dance themselves . . .[15]

[15] Perhaps it would be wise at this point to remind the reader that the Price-Mars explanation of trance or possession reflects the views of the time at which the text was written. His dominant motives, we believe, are 1) to refute the prevailing racial explanations of behavior and 2) to deny that possession is an hysterical phenomenon. But the attribution by Price-Mars of part of trance or possession to hereditary factors (pp. 132-134) is questionable, especially in the light of present-day academic investigation. [Footnote continues on the following page.]

7

The Sacrifice . . .

Nevertheless the greatest, the most vibrant aspect of the voodooistic arrangement is not the ecstasy. One would be still less likely to search for it in majestic hommages rendered to deified natural Forces. It resides almost entirely in the imperative fulfillment of sacrifice. Worship can

[15] continued

In "Phenomena of 'Possession,' " (*Tomorrow*, Autumn, 1954) the social psychiatrist Dr. Louis Mars, son of Dr. Price-Mars, states ". . . Voodoo . . . must be viewed in juxtaposition with the problems of the anxiety-ridden Haitian, consumed by economic distress. Only in this light can we grasp the full impact of its cathartic role; and we will be bound to agree that, if only from the viewpoint of the mental health of a people waging a heroic struggle against the pitfalls of ignorance and misery, this catharsis is effective. The ethno-psychiatric evaluation of social and economic factors involved in the loa crisis, therefore, calls for the rejection of the charge of hysteria. I believe we can conclude that the phenomenon of possession in Voodoo, as it occurs with the aforementioned characteristics, and within the framework of Afro-Haitian mentality, may be accepted as a normal phenomenon." (An earlier exposition of Dr. Mars on Voodoo, 1946, has been translated into English, *The Crisis of Possession in Voodoo*, and published in 1977.)

This theme is echoed in the writings of Janheinz Jahn and particularly in those of the Haitian anthropologist Remy Bastien who emphasizes both the dynamic and the stagnating aspects of Voodoo. Most modern anthropologists from the 1930's onward, including Gardner Murphy, Herskovits, Ioan M. Lewis, J. Milton Yinger, George E. Simpson, Michael G. Smith, and Erika Bourguignon do not equate spirit possession with mental illness. As Smith says, spirit possession is accepted within the cultural context even when it approves actions which in other circumstances would be unacceptable or not even available. Bourguignon states that dissociation may divert the individual from a "realistic" solution to his problems but that these "altered states of consciousness" are kinds of dissociated behavior that permit persons to relieve their psychic tensions in new modes of expression that do not prove dangerous to himself or those about him and even enable him to function more adequately in the society. In essence, Bourguignon is saying that the altered state of consciousness, known as spirit possession in the Vaudou practiced by the majority of Haitian people, has been institutionalized and is culturally patterned and utilized in a specific way. "The people find it possible to play the requisite roles and to have the appropriate experiences . . . , not only because cultural learning of this behavior is available but also because they have the personality structure, resulting from their particular upbringing and life experience, that make them apt to engage in such behavior and to find it personally as well as socially rewarding." (*Possession*, 1976, p. 41. See also, *Religion, Altered States of Consciousness, and Social Change*, 1973, pp. 3-35; and George E. Simpson, *Black Religions in the New World*, 1978, pp. 51-70, 130-145.)

In recent years the Haitian anthropologist Michel S. Laguerre has perceived Voodoo and possession in Haiti in a political and socio-economic as well as a religious context. See *The Black Ghetto as an Internal Colony*, 1976; "Voodoo as Religious and Political Ideology," *Freeing the Spirit* III, 1974, pp. 23-28.

dispense with choreographic meetings, with orgiastic festivities, with the display of nocturnal and processional pageantry, but whatever the social or legal contention may be for holding it, it positively confirms itself through the ritual obligation of the sacrifice. But why is the sacrifice the mainstay of worship? To what does it correspond? What is its proper significance?

It is difficult to condense the complex ritual included in the term sacrifice into a formula. It would be necessary to comprehend therein the idea of oblation, of mystical communion, of reverential hommage, of participation of the faithful in the life of the god or intercommunication between the profane and the sacred worlds. Each of these aforesaid considerations envisage an aspect of the rite, and together they bring about a sacrifice so rich in content that it expresses the general sense and the perfect symbol of the ceremony.

That is why, concerning the question of rite in terms of a primitive religion, we will choose the definition which may be the most adequate, not only in the sentiment which the believer of Voodoo infuses into his gesture, but in the unconscious symbolism which this gesture truly expresses. Thus, from this point of view, no conception would be more suitable to convey our thought than that which Loisy states in the following words: "The Sacrifice," he writes, "is a ritual action — the destruction of a sentient object endowed with life or which is supposed to contain life, — by means of which one believed he could influence invisible forces, either to escape from their grasp when one assumed them to be harmful and dangerous, or in order to promote their work, to procure satisfaction and homage for them, to enter into communication and even into communion with them."[125]

In the cult of Voodoo, sacrifice assumes several forms. It is fulfilled in acts of thanksgiving to the gods for their attention, their benevolence toward the sacrificer, individual or group. It is an act of expiation to appease the wrath of the divinity irritated by some voluntary or unconscious offense the effects of which have been translated into calamities of all sorts: maladies, sorrows, unsuccessful enterprises, and so forth. It is manifested by annual hommage in compliance with family tradition which if overlooked could engender misdeeds against the individual or family. It is the communal feast in initiation ceremonies where consecrations to the Priesthood take place and where the sacrificer is accorded participation in mysterious forces through which he acquires

[125] A. Loisy, *Essai historique sur le sacrifice*, Paris, 1920, [Introduction, p. 5].

supernatural powers of invisibility, invulnerability, success in his affairs, and so forth. It is a pledge or a pact with the Invisibles in the fulfillment of which both sides find benefits and satisfactions. It is a duty toward the dead whose existence in the supraterrestrial world would be disturbed if people neglected to accord it to them and who, to avenge themselves, would return to the living the pains and torments that could have been spared them.

We do not claim to enumerate all the aspects of the voodooistic sacrifice. And moreover, though our brief presentation may be incomplete and our outline awkward it aspires only to be true to life about the variety of its differences and the gradation of its intonations. Yet, ought we not to be perturbed that the cultic traditions of voodooistic sacrifice are in such a state of tangled confusion that at times it is impossible to discriminate between the different types?

Historically, it seems that this rite was rare in the colonial era unless its esoteric character escaped the observation of the non-initiated. We will point out that Moreau de Saint-Méry, generally so well informed, has made no mention of it in his various publications, save the remark he makes on the feast of fowls on which occasion the slaves yielded to Voodoo dances, feasts that were so proper that it was believed they were intended to throw the maréchausée [mounted constabulary] off guard. Meanwhile as soon as the conspiracies of the Negroes ended in the revolutionary explosion of August 14, 1791, it was through an actual bloody sacrifice that the strife was inaugurated in their camp and assumed the mystical character which the chiefs steadfastly retained until victory was won. It is thus probable that the notion and the practice of rite dated back beyond colonial life to the country of Africa. But as authentic as this observation may be, it does nothing to simplify the data known about the problem. For there remains to be learned in which African region animism was most analagous to our Voodoo from the sacrificial point of view.

It would appear to us that in this fundamental area a syncretism took place whose principal factors are easily disclosed.

Just as Dahomey has supplied us till now with the most notorious structural elements of Voodoo, so we have also observed that the cult has made impressions elsewhere.

We find ourselves confronting an analagous situation as to the functional arrangement of the voodooistic sacrifice. Let us say immediately that this concerns a form of rite that has come directly to us from the

Guinean region and which quite specifically bears the Dahomean imprint. This is the agrarian sacrifice *du manger yam* [of eating yam] with a tradition that is slowly being corrupted and obliterated. It exists now as no more than a symbol with its meaning expressed by the annual obligation of Voodoo adherents to conduct some sort of ritual oblation under pain of severe penalty, immediately or in the future, directly or indirectly against responsible transgressors of the pact. To what should we attribute this modification of the very essence of the rite? Probably to the paradoxical expression peculiar to our tropical climate. For it is not synonymous with the same act of seasonal renewal, of harvest of a product which is of first importance in agricultural life. We must consider, in consequence, that the yam ranks very highly among the plants to which populations owe or have owed their existence in Dahomey and most countries of the Gulf of Guinea, and in general, all of the equatorial and subequatorial region. There it forms the principal nourishment and has considerable influence as a means of exchange. So, it is comprehensible to us when the shrewd explorer, Colonel Toutée,[126] explains to us that in Dahomey this plant was cultivated in a manner which would be admired by the most demanding agronomers. "Neither the sugar beet in the North, nor the vineyard around Béziers," he says, "nor the asparagus of Argenteuil, are worked as industriously as the yam at Ritchi [Kitchi] and Cayoman."

This is why the yam harvest is the occasion for a solemn celebration in these regions.

"Here is, for example, what takes place in the sanctuary of Angyba, the Earth Spirit (among the Ewe people of Togo). Before the feast, each of the chiefs bring to the priest two pieces of yam. The priest adds his own to these and presents the whole in the dwelling place of the spirit; he makes the offering, saying: 'Today the yam of life has come to the village. Here is your share, take and eat. Let none of those who will eat yam today meet unhappiness!' The priest leaves the offering there, and returns to his home; he cooks a new yam, mixes it with oil, and places pieces of it in his courtyard and in his house as a new offering evidently intended for all the gods or spirits of the home. After these rites are accomplished, everyone may eat the harvested yam."[127]

The symbolism of this rite is so apparent that there is no need for

[126] Colonel [George Joseph] Toutée, *Du Dahomey au Sahara* (la nature et l'homme), Paris, 1907, [quotation, p. 41].

[127] [Jakob] Spieth, *Die Religion des Ewer in Süd-Togo*, Leipzig, [1911, quotation, p. 60], cited by Loisy in *Essais historiques sur le sacrifice*.

explanation. It accepts the ancient, universal belief that the earth and its fruits, the seasons and their rhythm belong to the mystical cycle of things to which man owes reverence and hommage as a token of piety toward the Divinity who is the giver and creator of these movements.

Homage, for the primitive man, becomes concrete in an offering of the first fruits — the first fruits of the harvest and of the hunt, of the first-born of man and of beast, the improper consummation of which could be detrimental to the well-being of the individual or community. Let us recall the liturgical regulations prescribed by Yahweh for the people of Israel to perform this type of sacrifice. "You will bring without delay the first of your sons," says the Eternal,[128] "you will do the same with your oxen, your sheep; their first-born will remain seven days with the mother; on the eighth day you will give them to me. . ."

It does not seem, however, that our agrarian rite as we have recognized it in popular traditions, necessarily has its place of origin in the subequatorial regions, where it also sometimes took on a character of bloody oblation — especially among the Ashanti because they had to spread the blood of slaughtered slaves in the holes of the first yams to be harvested. Somewhat further toward the Northeast, on the shores of the Niger, the same rite assumed a truly communal form unlike what we have just observed.

There indeed the priest, in a solemn celebration, shreds the new yam to make a paste that is cooked with fish and Kola nuts. The aliment thus prepared is broken into two small parts, one of which is kept by the officiant and the other placed by him on the lips of the person who will eat the new tubercle.[129] This variant of the rite brings us a little closer to what was the Haitian practice, at a given moment.

Here, the sacrificing priest very discretely prescribes a meal composed of two dishes, one of which is specially made of maize flour, red beans, and gumbo — this is *calalou* — the other of bananas, of sweet potatoes, even of yams crushed and ground to a paste. This is *moussa*. Dried fish is added to these two principal dishes.

Should we perceive in this meal composed largely of vegetable produce, at the annual harvest, the memento of the African agrarian rite. It is difficult to decide this. The only clue we have is the symbolic name

[128] *Exodus* XXII, 28, 29. There are abundant texts which relate not only the custom of offering the first agricultural fruits to Yahweh but also those of the first-born of man. Cf., Loisy, *Essais hist.*, *loc. cit.*, p. 233; Cf., Loisy, *La religion d'Israël*, pp. 99 and 100.

[129] Frazer, *Le rameau d'or.* New translation of Lady Frazer. Abridged edition. Paris, 1924.

of "Manger yam" which it bears and whose origin indicates preoccupations unknown to our agricultural production.

8

We have shown that the economy [functional arrangement] of voodooistic sacrifice is syncretic, just as is the cult itself. Nothing would appear to substantiate this more than the very object of sacrifice, the animals that are proper to it and the ritual which honors it.

For example in Dahomey, from which Voodoo has drawn so many cultic elements, the highest sacrificial ceremonies are carried out in memory of deceased kings and their ancestors. To solemnize and sanctify this day, after the processional return from the temple, the principal dignitaries of the nobility take their places on a platform which has been erected in the courtyard of the Palace. From this spot a crier calls by name the executioners of all the kings of the dynasty. Those who represent them answer the summons and receive the beasts destined for sacrifice: fowl, sheep, goats, oxen. The executioneers sever the head of the victims, while the women collect the blood which they carry to the altars.[130]

Now, even in the commemorative ceremonies of Voodoo commonly called "services of the dead," the sacrifices assume a quite different ceremonial form.

Here is a good account of this by Antoine Innocent, who is particularly well-informed.[131]

It concerns a "service" celebrated by a believer who wanted to appease the angry spirit of his ancestor.

Close to the white-painted tomb of the ancestor, the hougan gathered all the objects appropriate to the ceremony: three white plates, a pot of coffee, maize flour, rice-milk, slices of melon, chocolate, bonbons, sugar-almonds, l'acassan,[132] acra,[133] a handful of roasted corn and pistachios, and phials of liquid. All were laid out on a white cloth spread

---

[130] Le Hérissé, op. loc. cit., [p. 187].

[131] Antoine Innocent, Minola ou l'histoire d'une cassette, Port-au-Prince, 1906.

[132] A special preparation of maize intended for immediate consumption. One should notice that the word which is of Dahomean origin signifies a sleeveless tunic in which the Princes and Cabécères [grand chiefs] of the Court of Abomey [ancient title of Dahomey] dressed when they accompanied the King in some grand ceremony.

[133] Flat pea-cake.

out before the sepulture. Three holes of equal depth were dug wherein three lighted candles were placed.

An assembly of the Ibo sect with its hounsis dressed in white beneath sacred trees where a liturgical service is being celebrated.
Collection of Dr. Arthur Holly

The sacrificer surrounded by hounsis[134] invested in white, shook his açon[135] and his small bell. Then, over heads bowed toward the earth he began an invocation to the dead in an unintelligible language. At that moment, his assistant, the *houguenicon* intoned in a plaintive and sad voice the *bohoun* or dirge which was interrupted by the hoarse cries of the initiated, the *hounsis*, who tapped their lips.

The *hougan*, continuing his task, made a cross over each hole with the maize flour and placed therein a little of all the aliments of the funeral meal, along with liqueur, alcohol, and water. At his order, the holy assistants imitated the same gesture. After that, he seized two white hens which had been made to peck at pieces of minced melon, parched pistachios and corn and, holding one in each hand, he passed them over the head, shoulders, and breast of some of the assistants and made them spin around with such force that their heads were detached from their bodies. Then he pulled out several feathers which he glued with coagulated blood to the edge of each hole and finally gave them to those

[134] Young women initiated and consecrated to the service of the gods.
[135] A calabash with a handle growth in which grains of coral and snake bones resound as in bells.

141

who had to prepare them for the cooking of an expiatory dish known as *le calalou des morts.* When the meal was ready, it was served on three white plates which were buried in the three holes.

In this manner the propitiatory sacrifice to the spirits of ancestors was accomplished.

As one may see, it differs from the Dahomean rite by its greater complexity, by the greater richness of the ceremonial theme, by the quality and nature of the offering, by the admittedly rather awkward utilization of more spiritualized elements — such as the signs of the cross drawn over the holes for the plates of offering, such as the psalm-like chant sung by the hounsis like a litany.

Besides, while it is found that in every primitive society, numbers have a mystical value independent of their mathematical value, while in any era, in any country, and in almost any religion, the number three assumes a singular power in regard to its mystical quality and that even in civilized societies metaphysical systems are impregnated with this mystical survival, it is curious all the same to ascertain in the description of the expiatory rite that we are considering, how much the number three plays a primary role: *Three white plates, three portions of offering buried in three holes.* No less curious is the use of color: *white plates, white cloth, white candles, white vestment of the hounsis, white plumage of the victims.*

Are there symbols hidden in the use of number as in that of color? And if such is the case, what would be their significance?

It seems that we would have to go back quite far into prehistoric times, and inquire into the origin of demographic movements that have populated Africa and particularly the Sudanese plateau in order to find the beginning and significance of these religious customs whose tradition has come down to us.

We have known for quite some time that it was possible — and perhaps in our day it will be realized — to identify to which tribe, to which demographic group that such and such African populations disseminated across the breadth of the continent belong and attach themselves by nothing other than their common observance of certain practices, their fidelity to certain customary traits, to certain prescriptions of religious piety as, for example, the adoption of the same animal totem, the same color-emblem, the respect for the same taboo. We also know how these indicators, as valuable guiding clues, permit us to go back to their very origins, by establishing analogies with other peoples living in other parts of the globe. Now, among the Habbès of the Sudanese plateau, the Hogon or high priest sacrifices only to the divine triad and the sacrificial material may only be a white animal, either a sheep or a chicken. The rite is performed, moreover, only to implore the protection of ancestors. In addition, it indicates the Asiatic influence of the *Theban triad*, which has left many a trace in the usages and traditions of the Sudanese peoples — such as the worship of stars, the division of cosmic Forces into male and female elements, the usage of three-pointed altars, the persistence of which denotes the imprint of Assyrian-Chaldean tradition on the religious thought of certain Negroes of Africa.[136] Should we not search there for the solution of the problem which interests us?

We believe that the filiation between this religious conception and the one whose vestiges we have found in the ceremony described above is incontestable in the measure that we have likewise established the ethnic filiation of our community with the Sudanese communities among the diversity of Negro types imported to Saint Domingue and amalgamating to form the Haitian people. These customs have certainly been altered because they are only preserved by oral traditions and, in addition, influenced in the new milieu by the inflow of multiple contingencies, they have been molded, fashioned in a form so disparate that they present themselves now under a character which is new in a good many ways. It is to this work of transformation that we have applied the term of ritual syncretism. Moreover, we will find it again at work in other sacrificial themes.

9

We have just stated that the ritual gift of sacrifice takes place for a variety of intentions. But whatever may be the cause which determines the course of the sacrificer, whatever the idea to which he is obedient — an action of thanksgiving or of expiation, reverential homage or conditional token of piety, solemn service of initiation or of renouncement — the rite is almost uniformly performed by the bloody oblation of a principal victim which is most often a male goat, sometimes a bull or the two together, and, in the *Pétro* sect by the slaughter of a pig. It will be sufficient to describe the most customary ceremony to typify the voodooistic sacrifices.

[136] Lieutenant Desplagnes, *op. loc. cit.,* [p. 269].

Antoine Innocent once more lends us the authority of his testimony.[137] It concerns a service in honor of *Legba*, the most obliging of the gods, the good papa whose benevolent role consists of watching over the well-being of his faithful ones by remaining invisible and powerful at all times on the threshold of dwelling places, at the "barrière" [entrance] to properties, at the crossroads, to defend his subjects against the malevolence of evil spirits. This is what the song expresses in its symbolism:

"Legba non hounfort moin!
(or he who wears a crown)
Nan Guinée, parez soleil pou moin." [Creole]

"Legba whom I venerate on my altar
You, who wear a crown, in Guinea,
Protect me from the sun."

The Hougan traced out some cabalistic signs in front of the altar with maize flour . . .

Collection of Dr. Arthur Holly.

[137] Antoine Innocent, *Mimola, loc. cit.*, [pp. 138 and following].

In this way the Hougan, having shaken the asson and the small bell, announced that the ceremony was about to begin. He invoked the protection of the gods by murmuring a prayer and traced some cabalistic signs in front of the altar with maize flour.

He especially implored *Legba, in parlance,* to manifest his presence by selecting some believer in the congregation in which he would become incarnate.

Suddenly the god granting the prayer possessed a female believer. The usual scene of a voodooistic crisis ensued. Then the hougan, taking the chickens one by one — of lesser value in the service — wrung their necks and heaped them before the altar. On the pile he drew the sign of the cross with the maize flour. After that the women removed them for cooking.

At this particular moment, people left the enclosure of the Temple to take their places under the peristyle where the male goat, the principal victim of the ceremony was to be sacrificed. The animal was tied with ribbons and draped with a red cloth. The person possessed by Legba mounted the goat like a horse and rode it around the enclosure, then returned it to the sacrificer. The latter offered the goat a green branch which he removed three times from its mouth as soon as the animal began to eat it. The moment had come for removing its ornamental clothing. A person bound his feet which were held two by two by assistants. The latter swung the goat in cadence with the sound of a recitative chant. Finally, the victim was laid on the ground with the head resting on a block. With a sharp blow the sacrificer cut it off. The blood was gathered in a vessel and placed on the altar where it would be used in the preparation of a special drink intended for the initiates and composed of maize, liqueur, and alcohol. In order to complete the ceremony, those assisting the hougan served the faithful ones the communal meal made of small pieces of cooked meat and grilled bananas coated with olive oil.

This is the basic voodooistic sacrifice in its entirety.

It is evident that the rite changes, becomes complicated or is simplified in countless variants, first of all according to the type of sacrifice and especially according to the officiating sect: Congo, Pétro, Voodoo, Arada, Nago. But the rites influence each other and, tempered by Christian infiltration, lead to a sacrificial synthesis such as is revealed in the model we have described.

We think that it is not necessary to dwell at length on the genealogy of the mode of operation of the voodooistic sacrifice. Was it born of a conception specifically Negro? Is it a part of this very common human tendency in all regions which leads the believer to consider himself indebted to the divinity for the goods of this world, of life itself, in consequence of which he should bear witness by offerings and gifts? How will we ever know this? Is it fortuitous coincidence, simple analogy, or direct filiation which leads us to find almost identical phenomena in a very large number of ceremonies of worship of different religions in Israelite and Greco-Roman antiquity? Is it a question, on the contrary, of a common foundation exploited by each community according to its own inclinations? Was there "in the beginning" a revelation made to all peoples which has been lost in the obscurity of time? Vain questions. Insoluble problems. Let us simply establish undeniably the universality of religious phenomena, the human specificity of mystical sentiment and its inevitable consequence, the sacrifice. Let us add further that the sacrificial matter itself, in the form of the victim, has scarcely changed from people to people, from religion to religion.

First of all, the bloody oblation.

Does not blood possess an intrinsic mystical quality? Let us see. If, in voodooistic practice, blood serves as drink for the faithful, does not Yahweh, in Leviticus,[138] likewise order "the sacrificer to sprinkle the blood of victims upon the altar . . . And to burn its fat in sweet odor to the Eternal?. . .

"I have given you blood, (he says to Moses)
As a means of expiation for your souls at my altar . . ."[139]

As for the victim, it is always chosen from the animal kingdom among the domestic animals: horse, bull, goat, sheep, fowl, pigeon, and so on . . . And if we restrict ourselves to the religion of Israel for which the Bible is an inexhaustible source of information, is it not in the time of the Kings that it was obligatory to offer to the Eternal a daily holocaust of two lambs, embellished on the day of the Sabbath with a fine wheat flour kneaded in olive oil.

Every month, was there not prescribed a holocaust of two young bulls, of a ram, of seven yearling sheep, and of a male goat?

Whether we found again the taste for similar sacrifices though with a smaller number of victims in the cult with which we are concerned, whether we found ourselves in the presence of similar phenomena, again with innumerable variants, in Greco-Roman paganism, in Egypt, Persia,

[138] *Leviticus*, XVIII, 6, 7 and following.
[139] *Numbers, XXVIII.*

China, Japan, India, Africa — such observations can only induce us to confirm what we have previously advanced, namely that everywhere man similarly employs the same behavior to attract supernatural grace for himself and that by hardly changing the quality of his offering he obeys the same psychological injunction of employing everywhere the sacrificial matter most to his liking in order to seal his pact with the divinity, except to insert in each ritual gift the mystical qualities which heighten their value in the eyes of the gods.

And it is by following the same rules and the same comparative method that we now approach, in the matter of sacrifice, the question which most deeply affects the Haitian sensibility and which excoriates each of us as soon as it is raised. We speak of the immolation of human victims in voodooistic ceremonies for which the Haitian people stand accused.

Truly, we do not comprehend anything more plainly stupid than the legend which makes Voodoo a cult of cannibalism, except perhaps the almost general Haitian belief in supernatural maladies. Such dispositions of mind incline inevitably toward considering death as the product of an evil spell which certain individuals can prescribe against other people. It is the terrible power that the less intelligent people of this country generally attribute to voodooistic members.

Given such a mentality, is it surprising that reporters of the foreign press newly arrived in Haiti issue sensational reports in their newspapers about . . . the barbarous Haitian practice of human sacrifices of which they have not seen a trace anywhere, since after all they have drawn the material for their stories, which were as absurd as they were improbable, from the credulity of the milieu. And what is so astonishing about the spread of wild and absurd tales in a milieu where the critical sense appears non-existent? Not a year, not even a month passes that we do not hear recounted authoritative details of the most bizarre stories about people who have been dead for a certain period and had been found living again in some place or another. Even in Port-au-Prince, within the past fifteen years, there was the sensational affair of a young girl known by hundreds of people to be dead and buried but who had been disinterred and brought back to life. In fact, long after the funeral ceremonies, the rumor spread one fine morning that the young person had been found somewhere by a priest through the information of a penitent. The ecclesiastical authorities had hidden her in a convent. There was an enormous scandal. An inquest was ordered. The sepulchral vault of the dead girl was opened. A skeleton was found which the father of the deceased did not recognize as that of his daughter, said the newspapers. In what way, by what signs? This is what no one was worried about. And the legend grew among the less intelligent that Miss X still lived as an idiot, not in Haiti but in a convent in France.

We should note that these legends are not new. Did not Père Labat long ago recount boldly that a female slave mysteriously made away with the life of five naval officers because they were molesting her and that she even presented the spectacle afar off of sucking on the pulp of a melon? The imagination of the good father was never at a loss.

Moreover, this imagination easily complements that of theologians, inquisitors, and public prosecutors of the Middle Ages and the Renaissance who have lent an authentic reality to the myth of the Sabbath.

Alas! Through how many official reports can we reckon thousands of confessions of sorcerers who, moving about on brooms, were in the heavens at night carousing with Satan at fantastic banquets, and thereafter copulated with the Prince of Darkness? Nothing was missing in these monstrous manifestations of Justice, neither the confessions of the guilty, nor the theological explanation of the crimes, nor the expiation at the stake. And now what has become of these incubi and succubi which so many people believed existed? What remains of all this heinous rubbish? The unique testimony of the mystical and theological mentality of the era!

It is the same with the dreaded power of the Voodoo members and their capacity to mete out death through magical charms.

So, the inquiry whose results we have given you here and which is supported by more than twenty years of research permits us to affirm without reservation that Voodoo is not a cannibalistic sect.

At the beginning of this study we established that there is a large share of magic in the modifications of voodooistic worship. Though the hougan, the papa-loi, exploits the credulity of the populace by taking advantage of the prestige he has obtained through his traditional knowledge of plants, and though he is the parsimonious distributor of chance and good fortune by which he cannot profit himself, this is the least intrigue that can befall a society where the mystical element holds the predominant role in social dynamics.

But all this is the seamy side of Voodoo. It is the superstitious side of it. We admit readily that it is extremely difficult to draw the line between the sincerely religious element and the superstitious element. It is a distinction that is not easily resolved. But does this objection address itself only to Voodoo? We would like to know what religion, even among the systems of salvation, is undamaged by the infiltration of magic.[140]

Now, even when we go back in time to the most distant origins of Africa, we find a distinction between the magician and the serviteur of the gods, the first being very much feared in these small communities owing to his social evil-doing. Indeed it is startling to think of the legal offenses being committed every day in these regions by an individual accused of magic. For the protection of the community, in the name of the law which is the expression of social custom and preservation, the accused was subjected to an ordeal which was most often a prompt sentence of death by hanging, or stoning, without burial for the body of the guilty.[141] There was perhaps nothing more tragic than the fate of the individual suspected of sorcery in the African communities and we must add that suspicion arose as a consequence of the mystical mentality being incapable of finding a natural cause for illness and death.

So if, even over there, sorcery and religion are distinct, so also in our fine country whose visage has been transformed by the more secular effort of western civilization, we do not confound elements which we have always considered as contrary to the other.

That at a given time, the Dahomean cult was imbued with an obligation to perform ritual murder under the form of human sacrifices, is an historical fact belonging to the period when Dahomean kings annually offered, and most often in celebration of victories of war, scores of prisoners to the spirits of their ancestors.

Besides, the sacrifice of prisoners is not an exclusively African custom; it is as old as war itself.

In this the rite complies with the norm of the great majority of religions which were originally based upon ritual murder. It is sufficient to cite in this regard the sacrifices for the founding of cities and the erection of edifices which, in Israelite antiquity, demanded the interment of human victims in places where the towns and homes had to be built.[142] In order to denote the universal character of this action, it is sufficient to cite the innumerable holocausts of the first-born claimed by Yahweh

[140] Loisy, *Le sacrifice*, p. 29.
[141] Delafosse, *Haut-Sénégal-Niger*, Third Volume, p. 183; L. Tauxier, *Le Soudan*, p. 182.
[142] I Kings, XVI, 34.

in recompense for the protection he granted to Israel, and, closer to us, it is sufficient to cite the custom of the Celts in Gaul who slaughtered their prisoners of war by removing their heads, the example of the Bretons who, in the time of Nero, according to Dion Cassius, sacrificed Romans in the sacred forests of their gods.[143]

It would not thus be surprising that the African cult had a share in the same structural formations at a certain time in its existence. But like other religions which have broken away from their original character, it relinquished stabilizing influences in the course of its evolution to the point that, in the historical period in which we find ourselves, human sacrifices were grave obligations of the State for which the king had sole ethical responsibility. Its share in the formation of Haitian Voodoo has not succeeded in bringing about an attachment to this form of sacrifice which has lost its ritual meaning. In fact, no one has observed it here. No one can produce evidence worth believing. It would be contrary to the scientific mind to rely upon the trial of intended witchcraft in 1864 against Jeanne and Congo Pellé and a dozen accomplices convicted of murder and condemned to death, in order to conclude that such is the norm in the system of voodooistic sacrifice.[144]

Such crimes are common in the lower classes of every country, tarnishing all religions and giving rise to calumnious legends which grapple with the avowed integrity of most civilized and respectable societies. Is it not true that in anti-Semitic centers the Jews sometimes witness the recrudescence of accusations leveled at them with such great violence that periodically they lead to scenes of vengeance and collective murder as in Czarist Russia which has acquired an unfortunate fame for such deeds.

Proof in our own twentieth century that gross superstition and shallow beliefs can engender the worst acts of aggression and even pro-

---

[143] Loisy, loc. cit., [pp. 110-111].

[144] Yet we should know how justice was served in this criminal case where the most atrocious torture was employed to induce the indicted persons to confess. What is the value of a confession when the accused makes the following declaration before the court: "I confess everything you assert, but do not forget how cruelly I was beaten before having said a word." Spenser St. John, Black Haiti, [1884]. Is this the exact translation of the declaration of the accused? There is room for doubt.

As for the testimony of Sir Spenser St. John, Minister Resident of Her Britannic Majesty, and that of his colleague, Minister to Her Majesty's Catholics in Port-au-Prince, in respect to sorcery in Haiti around 1864, the two diplomats reveal such a lack of critical sense in that one could impose the worst foolishness upon them without a doubt crossing their pitiful minds.

voke crimes is to be found in two recent cases that we will borrow from the judicial annals of France and Spain.

The first pertains to the trial argued before the Court of Bordeaux in 1920 and known by the name of "The Weeping Virgin."

Mrs. Mesmein, a cleaning woman and concierge in Bordeaux, had acquired a plaster statue of the Virgin in Lourdes during a trip in 1908. She placed it in the kitchen of her lodging and each day performed devotions before it. To her great amazement one day she noticed big tears falling from the eyes of the Virgin. She hastened to tell a priest who advised her not to spread the news of this mystery. For two years she was silent. The miracle recurred from time to time. Finally, unable to contain herself any longer, she told her friends about it and the news spread like a train of powder. A good many people were disturbed about the phenomenon and an official report was filed. But the miracle became more astonishing when the Virgin, substituting her immaterial form in place of the statue, appeared to Mrs. Mesmein and demanded that a chapel be dedicated to her on the very spot where her effigy was crying. Then the ecclesiastical authority intervened, carried off the statue, and placed it in a convent. Mrs. Mesmein could not console herself over this loss. Another statue had to be found for her which, placed in the same conditions, began to weep.

Meanwhile the owners of the property, upset at seeing their house besieged by a growing tide of the curious and of pilgrims, dismissed the concierge thus forcing her departure. Mrs. Mesmein took the Virgin and her devotions elsewhere. The crowd followed her. In the new building where she settled another phenomenon followed the first. In July 1913, on the eve of Corpus Christi, a sweet fragrance spread through her private chapel. Decidedly the marvel was becoming more and more extraordinary.

With France at war the following year, the devotion to the Virgin of Mrs. Mesmein increased in proportion to the general emotivity. It was at this time that the personality of a Syrian priest, the Monsignor Archimandrite Saboungi of the Order of St. Bazile, doctor of philosophy and theology in Rome, Vicar General of the diocese of Sidon, intervened in the affair. Mgr. Saboungi had come to take part in a Eucharistic Congress at Lourdes.

Having heard of Mrs. Mesmein, he went to see her and became interested in the question of the miraculous manifestations.

He did not hesitate to establish himself in her home, and he became her spiritual adviser. He gathered all the information necessary to study the issue from the theological point of view.

Mgr. Saboungi remained the guest of Mrs. Mesmein until 1917, at which time their relations cooled for obscure reasons. Then the prelate left his hostess and settled in Nantes, since his diocese had just become embroiled in the terrible conflict. Now, at this same time Mrs. Mesmein believed herself to be the object of occult persecutions the origin of which she attributed to her former spiritual adviser. Thenceforth Mgr. Saboungi became the devil incarnate who cast spells upon the unhappy woman. Her friends came to her defense. They resolved to avenge her by seizing from the prelate the paraphernalia of magical charms by which he was overpowering the poor Mrs. Mesmein, tormented now by the worst maladies. One day they organized a veritable expedition including a stockbroker, a police inspector, an insurance agent, and a violinist. After leaving Bordeaux, these gentlemen landed at Nantes, went to the home of Mgr. Saboungi, assaulted him, ransacked his apartment, and seized everything which firmly convinced them of his powers as an evil-doer. But what disappointment! They did not find the classic wax figure which is the chief part of casting spells.

After this premeditated aggression the Archimandrite brought action against them during which singular revelations were made about the mentality of a great number of witnesses — priests, lawyers, business men — who still believe in this twentieth century, in France, in the possibility of magical charms . . .[145]

And now what about the horrible crime carried out in 1910 in the village of Gador, in the province of Almeira, in Spain?

There, lived a sorcerer, Francisco Léona. On a neighboring farm dwelt a tubercular, Francisco Ortega. He consulted Léona about his ailment and the bone-setter ordered him to drink the warm blood of a child and to smear his breast with the fat of the victim. Only at this price would he be cured. In payment of his services, Léona demanded 2,000 pesetas, with 750 of them payable in advance. The sorcerer, assisted by a certain Fernandez, was forced to find a child to complete the sacrifice. They lured a youngster, Bernardo Gonzalès, who was bathing in a nearby river with his friends. They invited him to come with them to pick apricots in a neighboring woods. As soon as they were certain of not being disturbed in their criminal work, they seized the boy and after having bound

[145] All the details above were taken from an article published in the *Mercure de France*, August 1, 1920, No. 531, with the signature of Jules Mauris.

and gagged him, they put him in a sack and brought him to their house. Then a monstrous scene took place. Léona thrust a long knife into the armpit of the victim. The blood flowed forth and was gathered in a porcelain salad bowl by Ortega who sweetened it and drank it in great gulps and, then, the body was opened from sternum to pubis. The intestines were removed and their fat used for the prescribed unction.

This was the drama of sorcery judged by the Criminal Court of Almeira on the 29th and 30th of November, 1910. The criminals Ortega and Hernandez were condemned to death. As for Léona, already quite old, he died in prison before the case came before the Court.

10

But the ecstatic delirium, the ritual sacrifice, the liturgical dance express only a part of the Voodoo complex or at any rate the cultic expression of which they are the coordinated elements has given us so far only a modest figurative representation of the problem in its entirety according to the explanation we have given in the course of this study.

Its content is richer in psychological synthesis. It has assimilated other ideas, it has assumed disparate principles, it has undergone transformations, it has submitted to productive compromises in its historical evolution. This is what we will bring out while considering more closely the role played by the ideas, the ceremonial of the Catholic Church in the ascendancy of souls already shaped or simply moved by voodooistic dynamism.

For one of the most startling and certainly the most curious aspects of Voodoo, is its association with Catholicism in the present-day faith of the Haitian masses.

The confrontation of the two beliefs goes back quite far in the course of time dating from the remote period when the Portuguese planted the cross on the western coasts of Africa and catechised a good number of pagans on the shores of the Congo as far as the active period of the slave trade undertaken in the name of religious proselytism by His Very Christian Majesty. Is this not what Saint-Méry means to denounce when he speaks of the Catholicism of the Congolese mixed with idolatry and Islamism? In any case, at Saint Domingue, the justification of colonial enterprise implied total and obligatory conversion in the terms we have already precisely stated. Most certainly many elite spirits were transfigured by the Christian miracle and remained active proselytes in the recruitment of the new cult. We would need only to cite a Toussaint Louverture, whose aggressive devotion never gave way to the conquering piety of great commanders who were at the same time inflexible statesmen and scrupulous men of the Church, in order to demonstrate what the faith in Christian mysteries [mystères] could be among privileged natures.

But without any necessity to edify dogmatics, but rather through the simple phenomenon of endosmosis and through the pragmatism of social action, the beliefs slowly reacted upon each other, amalgamated into inextricable skeins, and generalized motives in the behavior of man in such a fashion that their Catholicism was no longer the doctrine of the Church and their Voodooism was no longer simple primitive animism. This was and still is something new that is rather unusual, rather embarrassing, rather disparate so that one experiences hesitation in expressing it in well-defined terms — since the phenomenon has not crystallized and sometimes manifests itself by an anarchical individualism. Whatever it may be — and paradox aside — the two beliefs have so many similarities that a confusion of principles results simply from their juxtoposition.

Do not the Catholic and the Voodooist believe in the existence of a supreme God? Do they not believe in his incessant intervention in the course of human life and in the order of universal phenomena? Do they not believe him sensitive to offense, terrible in vengeance and yet compassionate, responsive to prayer, accessible to offerings of his poor creatures lost in miseries and sinfulness? Do they not both believe that between man and his creator there exist supernatural beings, saints, angels, demons who are quite inclined to be involved in the affairs of this world? Do they not believe in the efficacious intercession of saints esteemed by the supreme divinity on behalf of wretched humanity? Do they not both come up against the impotence of reason to explain the most essential things of life — its origins and its end? Have they both not found almost the same term — mystère — to cover up their ignorance of any phenomenon which they cannot explain? Moreover, are they not overwhelmed by fear and obsession of the demon, of Satan? Though this is so, nevertheless there are salient differences which distinguish one belief from the other, differences which are manifested especially through the manner of cultic expression of the Catholic sentiment and of that of the Voodooist. They are accentuated in proportion as the Catholic belief becomes intellectualized and justifies its existence through dogmatic, codified doctrines whose purity and integrity are guarded by a spiritual authority anxious to preserve the tradition and supernatural character of the belief. Thereupon, when the voodooistic rite displays the emotional bareness of its symbols, unintelligible for that matter to those very persons who pay heed to them, the faithful Catholic has the power to establish the relationship of the smallest ritual of his cult to some kind of revelation coming straight from heaven. Hence it follows that the origin of his faith grants him considerable trust and authority over most religious manifestations. It follows equally that it exercises a paramount attraction upon unorganized cults whose secret ambition is to assimilate some of the elements that assure the prestige of the church. From thence comes the maladroit imitation by Voodooists of the more external features of Catholicism — the pomp, the magnificence of the ceremonial, the mystery of signs, the sumptuousness of the sacerdotal garb.

On the other hand, if the savage battles which inaugurated the demand for the rights of man at Saint Domingue were expressed in the explosion of 1791 by a wholly voodooistic ceremony — the oath of blood — if, during the thirteen years of violence, of privations, of torture, the Negroes drew from their faith in African gods the heroism which permitted them to confront death and achieve the miracle of 1804 — the creation of a Negro nation in the Antilles — it is strange indeed to note how vigorously the leaders, in the dawn of victory, declared war upon the old ancestral beliefs.

As early as 1801 Dessalines, inspector general of culture for the Department of the West, learning that there had been a voodooistic ceremony somewhere on the plain of the Cul de Sac, led a battalion from the eighth regiment to the place and put fifty of the followers to the sword. A rather harsh display of police action. This was the first official repression of creed as a misdemeanor. Later the Charter, having declared Catholicism as the official religion, assured it the official protection of the State. The Penal Code specified superstition as an offense. Since then, the secular authority has arrogated to itself the right to punish any action attacking the orthodoxy of the official form of worship. And so the old primitive religion of the Negro, outlawed, persecuted as the undesirable legacy of a shameful past and as inadequate for the new political status of the Haitian citizen, searched in the obscurity of consciences and in the darkness of the *hounforts* [Voodoo temples] to adapt itself to the new state of affairs. The traditions of the African cult became difficult to preserve in this conscious or unconscious effort to assimilate.

People began to search not only for ritual analogies between the two religions, but also to identify the deities of Voodoo with the principal saints of the Church. They went so far as to prescribe an identical practice of sacraments in the two cults in order to be entitled to the favor of the gods of Voodoo.

As for the minor devotions such as the wearing of scapulars, votive offerings, novenas, the use of candles, requiem masses, and so on, these were found to be functionally useful in the ritual ordinances prescribed by the *Hougan* to his followers because they harmonized readily with the most intimate tendencies of Voodoo. And a slow, subtle transformation began in the very foundations of the ancient belief. And now, it no longer rests alone on the latent or formal spiritual power that is in every being and phenomenon of our universe, it no longer implores the Natural Forces endowed with consciousness and will, rather *it teaches that the world is governed by a Supreme Being who delegates his power to intermediary spirits to whom it is necessary to pay hommages and reverences. It says that men are not merely made of flesh and bone, they are also composed of a soul, which, beyond death and in spite of its imponderability, has need of the assistance of the living to fulfill the other condition, unknown, unsuspected, of its supraterrestrial existence. If the living were to fail in this task, the souls would not only be tormented on high, but would descend down here to torment the living.*

Such are the two poles of the new belief. So, since they are in accordance with the Catholic orthodoxy on a great many points, it is not surprising that the festivals of the Roman calendar have been adopted and practiced as their own festivals by adherents of Voodoo who embellish the ritual of the church on those days with ceremonies according to the traditions and in the temple of the Voodoo gods. Also people, paradoxically, by their own inclination have simply confused the denomination of saints and their functions in the two cults — a natural translation from one liturgical language to another.

Thus far it does not seem that the process of assimilation has encountered insurmountable difficulties, at least in the choice of the proper times for the celebration of fêtes, [holidays, festivals, feast days, holy days].

We have stated previously that in the Voodoo cult the special festivals perpetuate memories and constitute symbols of agrarian and propitiatory ceremonies. And this is why they mark the rhythm of seasons: the festivals of sowing in spring, the festivals of harvest in autumn.

But is it not one of the definitive attainments of modern exegesis [critical interpretation of the Scriptures] to demonstrate that "Easter is the festival of springtime and renewal; Pentecost, the festival of harvest; the festival of Tabernacles, the festival of gathering fruits and the vintage. The spiritual interpretation came later."[146]

But then, how does one prevent what are perhaps involuntary actions such as these preestablished liaisons that emerge from the choice of Voodooists who put their two principal times for festivals at the two characteristic periods of the year: in spring, before or after the Christian Easter, festival of renewal, festival of sowing; in the autumn before or after All Souls' Day, festival of harvest-time, principal time of "manger yam," the time of propitiatory services to the souls of ancestors.

Well, it is not audacious to assert that no religious ceremony of the Church is more faithfully and more scrupulously observed from one end of the country to the other than that of the festival of the Dead, [All Souls' Day].

From the humblest individual to the most opulent personnage, from the poorest peasant to the wealthiest bourgeois, from the most modest hamlet to the most splendid cities, every one, on the day of the dead, obeys the universal idea of honoring the departed with fond recollection in order to render more effective, at least for a few hours, the mysterious and sacred solidarity that binds the living with the dead — a solidarity that nothing can destroy, neither the will of men and the display of their vanity, nor the infinity of time which disperses and divides, nor the poignant decay that time produces and which blurs the memory and dissipates it. But as the mind obeys the superior rhythm of abstractions or grows dull in rudimentary perceptions, each person solemnizes the day of the dead in his way.

The Catholic tends to retain only the spiritual form of the memory — a simple evocation of the tedious or rosy hours passed together in joy or suffering, while the Voodooist almost always concretizes it in ritual offerings. Nevertheless, both join in a community of sentiment which apparently has fostered dissimilar actions.

However, despite the unique place of the feast of the dead in the new Voodoo system, nothing makes more of a Catholic imprint on the

[146] A. Loisy, *La religion d'Israël*, p. 106. Cf., A. Loisy, *Le sacrifice*, p. 96; James George Frazer, *Adonis*: Etude de religions orientales comparées, [Paris, 1921], p. 174; Solomon Reinach, *Orpheus*, p. 271; Nathan Söderblom, *Manuel d'histoire des religions*, [Paris, 1925], p. 19.

evolution of the old cult than the solemnization of some parish festival where the faithful, hovering between both beliefs, mix with equal fervor.

In our opinion, two parishes contend for the favor of the populace: *Limonade* and *Ville Bonheur.*

Limonade, lying on the plain near Le Cap [Cap Haitien] is consecrated to Saint Anne and draws pilgrims from the populations of the north and northwest.

As for Ville Bonheur, it is perched high on the mountain range which stretches from the western sierra of Cibao [rugged range mostly in Dominican Republic] toward the Gulf of Gonave around Saint-Marc. Ville Bonheur is the gift of Saut d'Eau and Saut d'Eau, springing from the bare slope of Doscale [mountain] is, in its turn, a present of the *Tombe* [river]. The river, in its feverish haste to reach the valley of the Artibonite [river] falls in many cascades and, confined and compressed in the narrow clefts of the mountain, roars wildly and impatiently against the sides of the mountain peaks which turn away the foaming billows against the oncoming waters. Numerous rocks rise up in its path. It bursts over them in breathless masses on its way toward a small plateau where its limpid icy current spreads out in channels dug out of the grassy soil. But the plateau is only a thin strip of terrain carved from the flanks of the mountain which broke away from large fissures for hundreds of meters, leaving precipices. The *Tombe* caught in the net of channels, follows the path of the precipices and facing south pours its sparkling translucent sheets of water over the slopes of the valley.

It is this part of the course which forms "Saut d'Eau," the most beautiful, the highest, the most splendid waterfall which has been bequeathed us by prodigal nature. It has given its name to the region which surrounds it and that it dominates, whether one hears in the distance the sharp plaints of kinetic elements flung in furious saraband[16] beyond the thrust of mountain peaks into the hollow of little valleys or whether, far away, one discovers the exquisite waterfall with sunlit iridescent droplets, enchanting in the dazzling metallic shimmer of its streaming waters. Then it may appear immobile, congealed, very similar to an image of rock-crystal set in the dark green foliage of the mountain.

Meanwhile the plateau rises and falls gradually in slight gradations toward the east where the folds in the ground meet the gentle curves of the small hills of *Trianon.* But before reaching the largest bend of the *Tombe,* formed beyond the waterfall, the plateau offers the generous

[16] A stately court dance of Moorish origin with strongly accentuated triple rhythm.

hospitality of the humid soil to a group of small houses, rather capricious-
ly aligned, inhabited by a rural population of several hundred. Here is
where the blessed one of Mount Carmel appeared one day. And it is
there, in memory of this miracle, that Ville Bonheur arose.

A modest chapel is dedicated to the Virgin — very modest, truly,
in its primitive architecture of badly squared timbers, naves walled with
rough-hewn planks, roofs of corrugated iron where the heat of scorching
summers condenses as on any ceiling above a compact crowd of
worshipers.

In the transept, the statue of the Virgin is adorned by a large golden
neck-chain, her altar surrounded by various votive offerings.

Ville Bonheur attracts an improbable throng of pilgrims. It has
become celebrated since the day when, the Dominican Republic having
closed its frontiers to the multitude of believers who came every year
in adoration of the Alta Gracia in the famous grotto of Higuey, the devotion of Haitians overflowed toward the humble village where the blessed one of Mount Carmel appeared in a vision. The picturesqueness of
the place, the impressionable quaintness of the scenery, the magnificence
of the waterfall — all contributed to increasing the number of pilgrims
each year. But then its Catholic character became profoundly altered
by the proximity of the waterfall because Voodoo gods inhabit the
unspoiled space as well as the fathomless depths of the waters, because
the spirit, Maître de l'eau [Master of the Water], chooses his residence
wherever a spring gushes forth and wherever the power of water is in
evidence. Saut d'Eau could only be the resplendent palace of some divine
entity. Since that time a twofold mystical current guides the crowd toward
Ville Bonheur where miracles of all kinds multiply. They are particularly frequent in certain places marked by the piety of the faithful. Thus
not far from the humble chapel, in a palm grove which covers a few
small fresh springs with its ornamental shade, and for many, many years
about the 16th of July, miracles have occurred which mark this place
with a sacred aureole.

Here in fact, among the high branches in the plumed top of the royal
palm, appeared Our Lady of Mount Carmel, Queen of Heaven,
thenceforth The Virgin of Saut d'Eau. This first miracle led to other minor
miracles. The deaf heard, the blind saw, the paralytics walked. But here
also, at the foot of the trees among the candles of the Christian penitents,
other candles burned illuminating other customs and amidst the sparkling dew of the thick grass the offerings of food to the Voodoo gods

multiplied. No doubt the voices of Catholic pilgrims, in vehement utterances, invoked the blessings of the Virgin, but also amongst the liturgical chants arose hiccups, laments, snuffling, senseless reiterations which marked the crises of theomaniac possession, the ecstacism of voodooistic mysticism. And every person in this dense throng, with eyes raised to the heavens, was in turn in such a state of heavy anguish that it was sufficient for a more oppressed breast to let out the cry of "Miracle," so anxiously awaited by everyone that all eyes, at the same second, saw high above the image of the Virgin among the patterned branches of the sacred palms in the luminous brightness of the blue sky. And the miracle reverberated as breaking waves over the crowd which went off shrieking and bleating about the miracle. And the deaf heard and the blind saw and the paralytics walked.

And each time the slow moving crowd wound its way toward the chapel, mixing at the first rest-stop with the human tide which was climbing the same path toward the waterfall for another phase of devotion. Because here also, an obligatory pilgrimage of both piety and curiosity was fulfilled. Here too hundreds of faithful, exposed in the emaciation of flabby anatomies ravaged by the pitiless destruction of age or in the relief of youthful flesh with its ruddy tints revealing lines of beauty, here under the electric stimulus of forceful waters, trying to avoid the whirling spray and foam dashing down from above, hundreds of pilgrims are possessed, every year on the 16th of July, by the Voodoo gods who control them temporarily. Under the cascading waters the possessed stagger, fall, roll and their clamor mingles with the clamor of the noisy waters and their voices are inhuman so long as their benumbed flesh trembles under the power of the god:

Nec mortale sonans ...   [Her voice not human
... Jam propriore, dei.   at all, as the god's voice
                                  Drew nearer and took
                                  hold on her,
                                        Virgil, *Aenead* VI, 50-51]

Others burn candles at the foot of trees, hang small cords and handkerchiefs on the supple branches. Meanwhile offerings of food lie in innumerable utensils in the shade of the great trees. Saut d'Eau and Ville Bonheur share in the same devotion of thousands of pilgrims, some of which are pure Catholics, some of which are restless souls in which the pomp of Catholicism is supported by the faith of Voodoo, finally many of which are pure Voodooists. The union of the two beliefs is sometimes so shocking to the eyes of pure Catholics that they make known their anger with violence, sometimes against all pagans who disrespectfully profane the new sanctuary of the Christian faith.

And furthermore the religious authority, initially prudent in the matter of the authenticity of miraculous apparitions in the sacred palms, in the end took the course of formally repudiating them and, since the crowd despite everything stubbornly contrived miracles year after year in the same spot, it resolved to remove all uncertainty by setting fire to the trunks of some of the palm trees. The Abbé L . . . took the initiative in this operation and incurred the curses of the crowd. By odd coincidence, they say he lost his reason following this unusual experience.

And the pilgrims attributed his madness to the vengeance of the gods . . . or of the Virgin. But other palm trees, just as majestic, just as stately as the first, took their place. Obviously the crowd persisted in declaring new apparitions, perhaps more obvious, perhaps more beautiful than the preceding ones because of the very hostility of the Church. Abbé C . . . successor of Father L . . . was up in arms against the loyalty of its faithful, demanded the assistance of the secular authorities and cut down all the impostor trees. What an imprudent act, my Lord! What a challenge to all the unknown forces that the society of men fears and regards as the immanent source of the misfortunes that overwhelm it!

Against whom now will the divine anger turn, the frightened demanded of each other?

And this is why the crowd, thrown into a panic because of the sacrilege by Abbé C. . ., implored the forgiveness of the offended divinities by muffled lamentations in the rhythm of liturgical prayers as it went in procession to the chapel. Fervently they begged for the mercy of the Virgin. Why? It no longer knew. Perhaps it was to efface the outrage of the good pastor who had acted nevertheless within the latitude of his sacerdotal authority. Did they perhaps have a faint intuition that the Abbé C. . . had just the same gone beyond the limit of his rights? In any case the immediate action was to command a public and collective admission of guilt. And the crowd gave vent to all this in low lamentations, kneeling on the beaten earth of the humble sanctuary . . .

A new coincidence. The Abbé C. . . was struck soon after by anchylosis [stiffness in the joints] of the lower limbs. Was this not again a miracle?

In truth, we are not necessarily questioning the credulousness of men when we inquire about the state of the earlier health of the two priests. Were they not already unwell before the radical operation they undertook as priests to prune the impurities of a detested cult from their religion? Nobody gave any thought to scientific criticism as an explanation of what proved to be an impertinent shock to good sense and reason. The mystical mentality became master of the senseless act and gave it the interpretation of affective logic. And the notion of miracle became further engrained as the credulous crowd longed for the marvelous. But we should not conclude from this reflection that we deny "miracles" or at least that we reject the repercussion of a moral shock upon the organism. This would reduce the question to a schema that is too simple. It does not seem, on the contrary, that there was a phenomenon in this case of psychological complexity richer than that of the miracle. We are very certain that mysterious apparitions may be a product of the collective imagination determined by crowd psychosis as analyzed for us by psychologists. But we are also entirely certain that in this mystical milieu of Ville Bonheur that the sick who had given up hope recovered their health, particularly those with nervous ailments whose cause was unknown to them. We will therefore contemplate the account of the two priests with only the strictest caution.

Not that we would consider it impossible for any relationship to exist between the accidents of which they were the victims and the action which they instigated.

But in this order of events it would be foolish for us to abide by the testimony of others. It would be necessary to screen the cases in question with the most rigorous examination. Even then many of the facts would escape us and we know the extent of the raillery, anger, even disdain that we would incur if we were to push a rigorously scientific inquiry in this direction. We should be able to concede à priori that the same laws govern psychological phenomena which perplex our poor judgment as when following an emotional shock our organism is so disordered that it is in a state of static equilibrium which impairs rational thinking. In addition, each believer admits the miracle readily in what concerns the supernatural possibilities of his cult and he contests those of the next. For very strong reasons the Church would consider as mad presumption the claim of the observer who would establish a relation of cause and effect between the fortuitous events — if there were any — which befell the priests and the action that they undertook against the popular faith. On the other hand, whatever was said or seen, the Church knows well that she does not have a monopoly of miracles in the category of celebrated, unexpected, and inexplicable recoveries. Without introducing the practices of animal magnetism about which numerous observations have been recorded but excluding hypnotic acts of which we are well informed, it is interesting to recall according to Charcot and Pierre Janet,[147] that miraculous recoveries were known in antiquity as having more or less the same authentic character as in our days at Lourdes. Thus, in Greece at Epidarus, the sanctuary of Asclepius was celebrated for the considerable number of pilgrims that it attracted and for the marvelous cures that were perpetrated there. A statue of the god placed in the center of the temple received the pious homages of believers from everywhere. A body of officials assisted in the order of ceremonies during which the miracles occurred and priests were in charge of interpreting the signs, the responses by which the divinity conveyed his oracles. Physicians were placed in the proper places to attest to the authenticity of the cures. On all sides there were, in addition, votive offerings as witness of the gratitude of the miraculously healed.

Other inscriptions have been preserved which reveal certain details of cures obtained just as in the most famous grottos of the present time.

Here is one of them: "A blind man named Volérius Aper, having consulted the oracle, received the response that he must mix the blood of a white cock with honey into an ointment with which to rub his eye for three days. In this way he recovered his sight and gave thanks to the god before everyone. [And] Lucius, a consumptive, took ashes from the altar, blended them with wine and rubbed his breast, immediately he recovered from his consumption and the multitude rejoiced with him."

It seems that these two examples, which could be multiplied by many others, prove that we cannot flatter ourselves that we understand the mechanism by which complex psychological elements enter into this order of occurrences. In every case it would appear that there are some parallel conditions that have made the occurrence of the phenomenon possible. First, there is a certain state of psychological tension, the anticipation of an indescribable something that surpasses the normal and the natural; and even though one seems to question it, just the same one experiences no less fear and obsession when that has not happened; next the ascendancy of the human milieu, that is to say the tension that the anxious belief of the multitude exercises upon you through the satiating repeti-

[147] Pierre Janet, *Les médications psychologiques*, 1st volume, [Paris, 1919], p. 13.

tion of the most fantastic accounts of marvels that have been performed or are about to be performed, the moral and physical fatigue brought about by the long trips, the acts of penitence, the fasting, the prayers. All this constitutes a mental state, a special preparation, a specific field of action very peculiar to the accomplishment of the extraordinary phenomena of miraculous cures.

Are these conditions found not long ago at Saut d'Eau in the sacred shade of the palm trees not repeated again completely today in the purifying spring-waters of St. John, always in the marvellous surroundings of waterfalls amidst the faith of the multitude overcome by terror, throbbing with enthusiasm, anguished by hope?

Ah! One must see as we have the sight of these multitudes thirsty for promises, anxious in the anticipation of miracles in order to understand the release of such phenomena. We have preserved as snapshots, recorded notes on the life of the region which we would like to reproduce here.

Ville Bonheur, July 16, 1926

Today is the glorification of the Virgin of Saut d'Eau. It is also the greatest festival of the fountains of St. John and it is above all the pilgrimage to the wonders of the waterfall. The crowd, as heterogeneous as one could wish, swarms in the street that leads to the Chapel and to the Saut. It huddles and presses together in a constant, eager, seething mass. It is singularly composite and yet very much the same in its psychological and miracular unity. One might compare it to foaming waves in which the bright sunlight catches the glint of many-colored grains of sand. Pilgrims, the curious, gallivants, the pious, peddlers, peasants in their Sunday best, superstitious bourgeois, they are all there jostling, pushing, impatient with each other, but resolved to advance toward whatever is on the other side of the street — completely to the other end of the path — to the chapel or the falls. And there they all are with the awe-inspiring gregarious instinct which forms the crowd. See there the pitiful sick, emaciated with suffering, out of breath from the clutches of syphilis or tuberculosis, there the professional beggars, haggard from misery, infected by the rags they wear and their skin ulcerated by vermin. Here come a group of prostitutes, unbecoming for their age, worn out by greedy, moneyed debauchery, then the peasants gripped by devotion in motley colored blouses, — in *sapates* of penitence — every one a pilgrim of woe on the point of redemption. A little farther there are some peasant women in votive robes of blue, white, or gray cotton, small cords crosswise over the shoulders. Some, dressed in flowing garments made of many pieces of various colors fitted one to the other with a subtle and singular artfulness, resemble nuns escaped from some outlandish convent. But notice how, challenging attention above everyone in the tumult and disorder, the young people stand out conspicuously: occasional defectors from Port-au-Princian dance halls that debauched dissolute living transfers into the patronage of cheap public dances, revellers whose sunken eyes express the senseless effects of sleepless nights, young fellows experimenting with venal passion and who find in this unique day of the 16th of July the long-awaited occasion to sow their wild oats in exhaustive and lascivious extravagance. And how shall we describe the distress of the very young, the bawling of small children perched on their mother's shoulders amidst the vast surge of people, carried there in homages of gratitude toward the divinity who was compassionate toward the prayers of sterile couples, how to describe the wailing music of their voices lost in the plaintive cries of the human crowd?

The crowd is so dense that it gives the impression of trampling others underfoot. But in the apparent disorder, the shifting of people brings about discipline. The tide reveals a movement of ebb and flow: those who are climbing toward the waterfall or the Chapel and those who are returning. In the street where the geometric line roughens out into shapeless patterns, the assembly chortles, shrills, or laughs excitedly while cascades of oaths, words of joy or anger, and the roar of a thousand voices, mixed with the rhythmical sharp beat of dance-hall drums, join in like an echo of the distant thunder under the low sky streaked with flashes of lightning. It is true that heavy showers are approaching from every direction. The suffocating heat rouses apprehension of impending disaster. And here in the lake district clouds rise up in heavy black masses around the ridge of mountains and roll with amazing swiftness toward Ville Bonheur where the storm finally breaks.

Then the crowd, like startled cattle frightened into a stampede, rushes for the small houses, too few to contain it. And it became a bewildered melee amidst cries, laughter, and oaths under the pressure of the heavy downpour. And the quick, vigorous torrential shower enveloped the countryside with a thick and heavy mist. And that also was a miracle, a rain of benedictions, said the good women. Nevertheless, though night was approaching swiftly and prematurely, the torches in the indistinct shadows and the sound of worn copper indicated that the peasants were continuing the pagan orgy of the fête of Saut d'Eau.

Are the stirring details that we have just described characteristic of the Haitian milieu and exclusive to Voodoo? Who would venture to think so. It seems, on the contrary, that one is warranted in principle to state that whatever may be the milieu in which two or more religions exist side by side, it is inevitable that they will pervade each other and react upon each other independently of the desire of men. And the phenomenon is especially evident wherever the milieu is more primitive and wherever the State interferes to protect one religion at the expense of the others. The history of religions is full of teachings that confirm the accuracy of this proposition. And if examples are necessary, we will borrow from the history of Christianity which is more familiar to us.

What spectacle did the ancient world offer us in the third and fourth centuries at the moment when triumphant Christianity was absorbing dying paganism? Did Christianity rise according to the purity and integrity of its original doctrine?

Did it not, on the contrary, assimilate some of the ideas, notions of enlightened ancient thought?[148] In its conquest of the Roman empire, did it not concede that it owed some of its moral transcendency to paganism and, in order to accommodate the newly converted belonging to the upper classes of society, did not the effort of the theologians consist of reconciling the doctrines of the Church with speculative philosophy? And this effort of adaptation, this transition from one faith to another has been such that one is able to discover in the works of Christian apologetics how the scholars of the Church, issuing from the schools of Greek philosophy, have kept the forms of thought, the mode of reasoning, the tendencies of mind acquired in the intellectual milieu which they had conquered. On becoming Christians they put all the resources of Greek dialectics to the service of Christian metaphysics. And the observation is still of more striking and immediate interest if we consider the conversion of pagan masses to Christianity. Here, the conflict of beliefs does not linger over the subtlety of intellectual compromises. The stress of adaptation is demonstrated in the unconcealed juxtaposition of the two beliefs in the ritual scheme where pagan survivals persist in the celebration of certain Christian ceremonies. Such is the very curious case reported by Gaston Boissier in his study of Saint Paulinus of Nola.[149] Paulinus, who belonged to a very old and rich family of Roman Gaul,

---

[148] Cf., Ch[arles] Guignebert, *Le Christianisme antique*, [Paris, 1922].

[149] Gaston Boissier, *La fin du pagamisme*, Volume II, [Paris], pages 95 and following.

had acquired the taste for the humanities before his conversion to Christianity. But when he was enlightened by the truths of his new faith, he searched for isolation, left the shores of the Garonne [river] where he was born, took refuge first in Spain, then at Nola in Roman Campania in which is to be found the tomb of Saint Felix, whose fête we celebrate every year on the 14th of January.

There Paulinus led a life of an ascetic, no longer left the little community of which he became bishop, and drew up in verse the life of the fortunate ones for whom the fête worked so many wonders each year. The devotion at the tomb of Saint Felix was highly popular. The Saint was considered to be understanding of the prayer of the lowly. Thousands of poor people from all parts of Italy went to Nola. Saint Felix performed miracles particularly upon the possessed whom he freed from their obsession. Paulinus has left us an excellent description of the condition in which these unfortunate ones approached the basilica of Nola. "Their teeth grind," he says, "their hair bristles, their lips are white with foam, their bodies tremble, their heads shake dizzily. Sometimes they take themselves by the hair and pull themselves up, sometimes they suspend themselves by their feet." It was sufficient for the possessed to draw near to the tomb of Saint Felix in order to be cured despite the persistence with which the emotional disturbance sometimes took hold of them. But the most curious aspect of this popular fête was the attitude of the crowd. "It was composed," it is said, "especially of peasants, that is to say, of the last to have come to Christianity, of those who parted with the most reluctance and after all the others from the old mythology. Also they were still only half Christian. They stubbornly retained many of the practices of their ancient cult that through long custom had become dear to them. They were coming to Nola with families, with their wives, their children, and sometimes their livestock. They continued to believe that there was no better way to gain the favor of the divinity than to make bloody sacrifices to him, and they were eager to offer to Saint Felix the sheep or the ox that they immolated formerly for Jupiter or Mars. As they came from a distance, they arrived in the evening and spent the night without sleeping so as to prepare for the festival on the next day. This was in remembrance of the *pervigilia* or old sacred vigils which had preceded the grand pagan ceremonies; they did not consecrate these vigils to prayer and to fasting as was considered proper, but spent them in joyous feasting; this was as yet an ancient tradition that the Church had tolerated without saying anything for two centuries . . ."

It appears that it has been paradoxical to question the analogy between the celebration of the festival of the Virgin of Saut d'Eau and that of Saint Felix of Nola. Moreover one may find in the mechanism of the two devotions the same tendencies of the human mind, no matter what the locality or the beliefs in question, to accommodate slowly to the most incompatible conditions of faith in different divinities so long as these conditions do not violate any customs of thought, time-honored approaches of affective logic, certain cultural routines, until the slow transformation of ideas eliminates little by little the aggregates of the most ancient beliefs and common ground sets up reliance in new beliefs. It is this transitory course, this hesitant approach of popular Haitian thought that we wanted to grasp and put forward. It will become more evident in a quite suggestive form through the attempt that has been made to identify Voodoo gods with Catholic saints. Does not this propensity of the popular sentiment give an elevating sense to present-day tendencies of Voodoo?

But first, let us make a reservation. The designations that we are about to mention are not absolute. It is said that they can vary somewhat from one part of the country to another. It is only the principal voodooistic divinities that have found an intangible Christian incarnation in the Catholic paradise. In all cases, our denominations hold true for the North of the country where they have been carefully recorded.

The first incarnation is that of:

Legba, the grand master, the father, the familiar god of the Dahomeans who has become *Saint Anthony* (probably Saint Anthony the Hermit because the Saint is no longer represented by a pig but with a black cock as his faithful companion).

Next there are:

Ougou Balindjo who became *Saint James the Major;*

Agomme Tonnerre who became *Saint John the Baptist;*

Daguy Bologuay who became *Saint Joseph,* to whom one addresses the following prayer: "Saint Joseph, lead me if you please as you led Mary into Egypt. I do not deserve this favor, it is true, but I am your child."

The *Roi d'Aouèseau* who became *Saint Louis* (King of France);

Grande Mambo Batala who became *Saint Anne;*

Maîtresse Erzulie who became the *Holy Virgin* (more specifically the Holy Virgin of the Nativity);

The *Sirène* who became *the Assumption;*

Pierre d'Ambala who became *Saint Peter.*

An altar of Voodoo gods adorned with a cross.
Collection of Dr. Arthur Holly.

It is obvious that the voodooistic Olympiad is filled with a great many deities. We have only wished to cite here those gods whose attributes and names have been identified with saints of the Roman calendar.

There are others, minor gods so to speak, who have found their correspondents among the blessed of the Church. Those we have designated are the greatest and occupy the first rank in voodooistic syncretism. On the other hand, the practice of misleading identification has given rise to a literature of inferior worth which produces *Oraisons populaires* [popular prayers] of the most dubious nature. What is in these prayers?

Some are composed of pious phrases that were approved by ecclesiastical authority and inscribed in the best of the rituals. Others borrow the general tone of authorized forms, invoke the intercession of saints whose names are nowhere to be found, and accumulate a web of commonplace and grotesque discourse that are the worst caricatures of prayer. Almost all are addressed, in addition, to true Saints of the Church with pleasing expressions of promises which indicate the crudest conception of the divinity: *Do ut des.* [I give that you may give.]

Would you like some examples?

Listen to the Prayer of Saint Roi Degonde (Saint Radegonde). [Not only does the spelling change but the Saint changes from male to female.]

"Recipe."

"The day of the Good One is Monday and Saturday you will go to the cemetery to light candles and say your prayer. Good One, I put myself in your hand, Dear Good One, all is said."

"Prayer."

"Good Saint Radegonde and Good Baron Samedi, guardian of the cemetery, Grand Saint, you have had the powers to pass through purgatory, give to my enemies some kind of job so that they can leave me in peace. Jesus who is master of all, who judges the living and the dead, judge in my favor, turn the conspiracy of enemy spirits back on themselves. Cross, Holy Cross, sanctify the Judges, convert sinners. Grand Saint Radegonde, Queen of the souls of Purgatory, who has delivered from purgatory, deliver me from those who pursue me. I promise you an Our Father. Please deliver me."

The accumulation of nonsensical phrases, the triviality of the language, the clumsy inaccuracies of the wording indicate the milieu in which and for which it has been written. By contrast the extraordinary vogue which these prayers enjoy shows eloquently how much the popular masses believe in their effectiveness. And when, by chance, one meets a good woman somewhere in the church, at the cemetery murmuring a prayer, we are quite right in saying that her lips are eagerly moving in the peculiar garble of prayers to Saint Joseph "asking of him the favor of a good marriage since he was a good husband of the holy mother of God," to Saint Bartolo who "as soon as the cocks crow, wakes from deep slumber, puts on his shoes, after having washed his eyes dons his cap as is his habit then, armed with his mabial staff, [type of West Indian wood] goes out and profits on the highway." Saint Bartolo is gracious to those who must hide from the police.

But the piece which seems to us to contain the quintessence of this vernacular literature is the prayer to *Saint Bouleversé.* It is unnecessary to note that this personnage has been wholly invented by the superstition of the lower classes and that the powers that are recognized as his are closely connected to the very meaning of the name he bears [the Saint who can turn things around]. Furthermore, it is not inappropriate to point out that the infatuation for prayers is more pronounced in the plebian of the cities than in the peasants. The reason for this is probably because the clientele recruited in the cities has an elementary culture consisting of a mere attraction to knowledge. The magic of the written word, however incomprehensible it may be, is infallible for these almost un-civilized minds, whereas in the country where the people are totally il-literate, the oral traditions by themselves maintain their inviolable authority, and because the literature of prayers is fairly new it is in con-sequence more prevalent among the plebian of the cities than the rural masses.

But let us take a look at the prayer to *Saint Bouleversé.*

"Saint Bouleversé! You who have the power to disrupt the world, you are a saint and I am a sinner; I call upon you and take you henceforth as my patron. I send you to search for so and so, to disrupt his head, his memory, his mind, his house, disrupt for me all my enemies visible and invisible, bring the thunderbolt and the tempest upon them. In honor of Saint Bouleversé, three Our Fathers.

"Satan, I renounce you, if you come on behalf of the demon, let the demon carry you away and throw you into the abyss and into everlasting inferno.

"Wicked beast, viperish tongue, pernicious tongue, if you come in behalf of God to deceive me, you shall walk from land to land, corner to corner, village to village, house to house, job to job, as an errant Jew, reviler of Jesus Christ. Lord, my God, come search to get rid of such a one, so that he may disappear before me as the thunderbolt and the tempest."

The state of mind that expresses these lamentable words published as tracts is not far from the voodooistic mentality. It holds the stage between one faith and the other. It indicates this transitory period, singularly troubled, in which the blend of the beliefs occurs. It is the unerring mark of the anarchy of beliefs.

The individual attracted by both poles of belief swings from one side to the other as the balance of incentives inclines in search of assistance toward one side rather than the other. However, to be more certain of success in his application he sometimes associates the two divinities in his prayers, being persuaded moreover that they are considerably above his poor intellect and that in case of need they can verify the purity of his intentions and excuse the weakness of his heart. So thus, such as they are, the prayers indicate a momentary elaboration of the religious thought of the popular masses which is closer to superstition than to any religion by their puerility but as ardent as any other kind of demonstration by those who find the way of God through obvious naivité and unyielding good faith.

This is all that we have wished to demonstrate.

A day will come when this transitory form will have disappeared to the great regret of philosophers and ethnographers. For none of this which was for a while the thought and conscience of a people can perish without loss to the history of human thought. We have written these essays in order to save these manifestations of the popular consciousness from the destruction of Time. And it is because we found a beautiful literary cultivation of such traditions in the *Esquisses Martiniquaises* of Lafcadio Hearn that we are going to question the Haitian literature on how it has made use of the themes of our folk-lore.

Chapter VII

Folk-Lore and Literature

1

Having reached the end of our inquiry, we can take a glance at our research as a whole and from it draw some information useful to the way of life and character of our social group.

To begin with, the demonstration has not contradicted the premises posed at the beginning of these studies when we suggested that our folk-lore was rich in diversified materials.

Tales, legends, riddles, songs, proverbs, beliefs thrive with an extraordinary exuberance, magnanimity, and ingenuity. These are the superb human materials from which are molded the warm heart, the multi-consciousness, the collective mind of the Haitian people! Better than the accounts of great battles, better than the recital of the great events of official history always formed under the constraint of expressing but a part of elusive Truth, better than the theatrical affectations of statesmen in postures of authority, better than the laws which are but borrowed finery ill-designed for our social state in which short-lived retainers of power concentrate their hates, prejudices, dreams, or hopes, better than all these things which are more often than not the result of chance imposed by contingencies and adopted by only a part of the nation — the tales, the songs, the legends, the proverbs, the beliefs are the works or products spontaneously springing at a given moment from an indigenous conception, adopted by all because of being faithful expositors of a common sentiment grown dear to everyone and, in the end, cast into original creations through the obscure process of the subconscious.

If a childish roundelay which comes unspoiled from the lips of the feminine patrician puffed up with nobiliary pride is the same heard in the touching voice of tenderness of the peasant woman bent over her sleeping child; if a legend which thrills a dandy filled with the latest theories of art or science, equally delights a craftsman in the workrooms of large industrial firms; if the belief ostentatiously denied by the important man seated at his counting-table compels him to question the natural course of things when his affairs go badly and impels him to search for justification of his doubt in the bitter words of the Shakespearean character: "There are more things on the earth and in the heavens, than our philosophy can dream of"; if the same belief leads the bourgeois little by little to communion with his servant in the same fear of the unknown, because unusual things as grilled corn, blighted leaves, and other ingredients have been gathered in his courtyard whilst someone in his entourage is stricken by illness or death; if the same imperturbable optimism galvanizes the energy of everyone in the gloomy moments of discouragement because with each of us, in the elite as in the plebian, confidence in the correction of things here below by some providential intervention forms the potential for action; finally, if this miracular thinking which is at the base of Haitian life and confers upon it its own identity — the mystical tonality — if all of that is drawn from the common reservoir of ideas, sentiments, acts, gestures which constitute the moral patrimony of the Haitian society, then it will be in vain for the arrogant among elite and plebian to jibe at the joint responsibility for faults and transgressions, for dilettantist bovaryism to dictate to both acts of cowardice and falsehood, for imbecilic class egotisms to trigger attitudes of antipathy and measures of ostracism — nothing will know how to prevent tales, legends, songs received from the past or created and transformed by us from being a part of ourselves, revealed as an exteriorization of our collective ego, no one can hinder latent or formal beliefs from the past that have been transformed, recreated by us from having been the driving elements of our conduct and having conditioned the irresistible heroism of the throng which was slaughtered in the days of glory and sacrifices for the sake of implanting Negro freedom and independence on our soil; nothing in fact can prevent, in the period of transition and uncertainty that we endure at this moment, these same imponderable elements from being the mirror which reflects most accurately the restless countenance of the nation. They constitute in an unexpected and breathtaking fashion the materials of our spiritual unity. Therefore where could one find a more genuine image of our society?

What else has ever expressed the Haitian mind more completely?

But then does not one have the right to wonder how art and literature have used our folk-lore? And at first sight is there a Haitian art, a Haitian literature?

This last question periodically preoccupies the press and, from time to time, an interview with a man of letters resolves the matter in the affirmative or negative. It is a game of princes. One will pardon us for finding this preoccupation a bit useless. Probably the reasons provoking publication of the matter lie not only in the scarcity of works but in their mode of expression. Because the cultivated Haitian will use only one borrowed language — French — because he sustains his thought with French works, because he concerns himself, owing to the language, with all that affects French life and civilization, one concludes from this that his literary productions can only be French productions. Though these reasons have some apparent justification, they are insufficient to keep us from having an indigenous art and literature.

Certainly, whether the language is the vehicle of thought and the winged messenger that supports the principal attribute of social life — intercommunication between the members of the same group — it does not create the thought itself and it is not its exclusive mode of expression at all. It is only an artifice to translate emotions, sensations, all of inner life. Yet in its many modalities it is often subordinate and always subsequent to behavior which is itself the most elementary expression of the needs of the mind.

Language is the function of psycho-biological and sociological[150] factors which explain its genesis, condition its existence, determine its evolution, and engender its richness or its poorness. It is, among institutions, that which adapts itself the most to the mentality of the group which uses it as the most versatile instrument of social life. Yet it is interchangeable. This is why various peoples sometimes speak the same language but do not have identical sentiments and beliefs, common tastes and ideals. Are not the Spanish states of America far from being simple imitations of the Iberian peninsula? Has anyone ever confused Anglo-Saxon literature from abroad with the literary productions of Ireland or Scotland? Who has ever disputed the existence of Swiss, Belgian, Canadian literature expressed in French? Who has ever opposed the use of the English language to express the state of mind of American Negroes in the works of James Weldon Johnson, Du Bois, Booker T. Washington, Chesnutt?[17] And why would language be an obstacle for Haitians to

---

[150] Here we choose to make no distinction between *langue* and *langage*. [*La langue* signifies tongue, language; *le langage* refers to language, speech, diction.]

[17] *James Weldon Johnson* (1871-1938), was a lawyer, U.S. Consul, Professor of Creative

bring to the world an idea of art, an expression of mind which may be altogether very human and very Haitian?

Without doubt, our greatest man of letters of the last century, [Demesvar] Delorme, in intelligible works that he has left for our ad-

Literature, and Secretary of the National Association for the Advancement of Colored People. Johnson was part of the Negro Renaissance movement of the early twentieth century. Two of his literary contributions are *Black Manhattan* (1930) and *Along this Way: the autobiography of James Weldon Johnson* (1933). He also wrote a series of articles for *The Nation* entitled "Self-determining Haiti" in 1920 which were translated into French and published in Haiti the following year. Johnson attacked the policies of the American Occupation.

William Edward Burghardt Du Bois (1868-1963), well-known black spokesman, sociologist, and writer, lived during almost the same years as Price-Mars. He was opposed to the accommodation and compromise policies of Booker T. Washington. In a direct and militant approach to win civil rights rather than economic opportunites for black Americans he advocated the training of Negroes on an intellectual level rather than emphasizing vocational education. He believed that the burden to uplift the Negro lay not with the blacks themselves but belonged to the nation which had instigated a system of slavery and of racism which had brought about Negro degradation. One of his great books is *The Souls of Black Folk* (1903) in which he indicts Washington for his policies, especially the compromise attitudes which seemed to accept the inferior status of Negroes. Today sociologists are again taking a look at *The Philadelphia Negro* (1899), a systematic study of Negro socio-economic life in Philadelphia, because Du Bois had said that scientific attention to the problems of a people were a necessary adjunct to the development of action programs.

Booker T. Washington (1856-1915), Negro leader and educator, believed that the Negroes should fit into American society through a program of self-help and industrial education. In his famous speech at the Atlantic Exposition in 1895 he told them to "Cast down your bucket where you are . . . in agriculture, mechanics, in commerce, in domestic service, and in the professions." He himself built, with the aid of his students, and established the Tuskeegee Normal and Industrial Institute as the center of industrial education. Though he himself did not stress political development, nor did he press for social relationships with whites, he exercised powerful political influence behind the scenes with northern financial and industrial leaders and with Presidents Theodore Roosevelt and William H. Taft. He was the single most influential spokesman for the Negroes until his death in 1915. Dr. Price-Mars was his guest for several weeks in 1904. Probably the best known of his literary efforts is *Up From Slavery* (1901).

Charles Waddell Chesnutt (1858-1932), is considered the "first American Negro novelist." More importantly he was the first to be acclaimed nationally for his artistic abilities above his technical brilliance, and for his commitment as a social spokesman in attacking the problems of "discrimination, insensitivity, hatred, and violence on a higher, moral, universally human level." One of his novels, *The House Behind the Cedars* (1900) was the first in the United States to take up the moral and social difficulties of Negroes who are able to "pass" for whites, while another, *The Colonel's Dream* (1905), castigated the convict lease system in the South.

miration as much for purity of style as clarity of composition, has put nothing there that might suggest, not even remotely, that they have been written by a Haitian pen. Without doubt, the novels of Delorme borrow the setting of their action as well as the characters from Turkey, Italy, France, but never from Haiti, and one is eager to scrutinize the reasons which justify such disdain or such reserve. And without infringing on the liberty or the right of the artist to seek the meaning or the inspiration of his work according to his own imagination, one is disposed to ask whether Delorme succumbed to a certain snobbishness in failing to recognize the literary possibilities of the Haitian milieu. Did he yield to the fashion of romanticism by looking into the past in the style of Alexander Dumas, an early compatriot, for the subjects of his books? Had he perhaps understood also that success and glory would reward his talent only if he wrote for a foreign public that was more apt to appreciate him than a Haitian public? There is a little of all this in the posture of the great writer. But there is something else. In our opinion, Delorme has conformed to one of the most senseless, the most pointless prejudices that strangle Haitian activity, that is to say that our society in its past as well as present existence has offered no attraction to the art of the novelist. Thus he has passed by a thousand and one stirring dramas, by the troubling vicissitudes of tragicomedy with which Haitian life is woven; he has skirted this baffling humanity in which collective or individual vanity, social hypocrisy, pompous stupidity indulge in the wildest assaults on sincerity, on serene self-sacrifice, on genuine cultivation of intelligence and moral sense; and he does not even notice that these things exist. He who was the orator whose charmed voice nursed the political dreams of his contemporaries; he who was the idol of youth avid to learn and smitten with beauty and for whom they threw open their salons in which all the questions of art and literature were discussed; he who understood the precarious triumphs and the sudden defeats of politics; he who was the representative of his people similar to the Victor Hugos, the Alphonse de Lamartines, left nothing in his work which shows a shred of perception in response to the action of its milieu, nothing that gives us an idea of the mores of his time or of any other period of Haitian life. And this distinguished man who could have been a great French author is not known in the French literature and almost does not exist in Haitian literature. In truth, the case of Delorme is an illustration of our mentality which grants distinction to the intellectual character of a writer only if it is projected on the dubious screen of foreign glory.

It is a good thing that a belated reaction led our writers, poets, and prose-writers to draw the material of their works from the milieu where they live and this new conception of art has gained for us, in the past thirty years, an efflorescence of works that is interesting from the Haitian point of view.

We would need only to collect bit by bit from the works of George Sylvain, Frédéric Marcelin, Fernand Hibbert, Justin Lhérisson, Massillon Coicou, Burr-Reynaud, [Dantès] Rey, Carolus, and so many others whom we could cite if we made a list of Haitian literature, to demonstrate the concern, more and more evident, of our writers to search about them for sources of inspiration, characteristics of mores, studies of character and social behavior which are very appropriate to our manner of love, hate, belief, in short to our way of living. And in that case how can one deny the national character of this literary production? Are not *Séna Chacha*, *Epaminondas Labasterre*, *Féfé candidate*, *Eliézer Pititecaille*, *Boutenégue* typical Haitian characters? It would not be bold for us to add that a foreign writer who would try to present them might succeed only halfway whatever his talent because in order to make them live it is first necessary to penetrate the mysterious motives activating all of the paladins of vice, of debauchery, and of falsehood which are everywhere in our society. Better than that, in order to take an interest in the buffoonery of their gestures and to savor the absurdity of their behavior one has to be a Haitian. In a word, there is consequently a Haitian literature. We do not mean, let us repeat, to strangle the liberty of the writer, still less do we pretend to intimate that the qualities ennumerated above are the sole qualifications stamping literary works as Haitian. It would seem that a certain sensitiveness common to the race, truly a certain turn of language, a certain conception of life very peculiar to our country by which a talented writer would mark his works without employing Haitian characters, could give them the indigenous character that our critique demands. But, aside from all this, something else is necessary that is greater, more faithful to Haitian and human verities; it is necessary to draw the substance of our works sometimes from this immense reservoir of folk-lore in which the motives for our decisions are compressed after centuries, in which the elements of our sensibility are elaborated, in which the fabric of our popular character, our national mind, is structured.

Is our literature inspired by this?

Timidly, so timidly, except in the *Mimola* of Antoine Innocent where fiction is enmeshed with painstaking apologetics, that it takes a magnifying glass to discern here and there some motifs, some themes of folklore. Would you like some examples?

Why should we hestitate to begin with one of the works of Georges Sylvain? In reality, no writer can justly claim in all of his works a more authentically French derivation in respect to classical style of language and beautiful diction. Georges Sylvain, taken too soon from literature and from the Haitian homeland which were the two great passions of his life, left in his *Cric-Crac* the evidence of the most formidable odds to which a man of talent may commit himself. The effort that he realized was to transpose the fables which have immortalized La Fontaine into patois and into Creole verse. And through the language which he has his characters, animals and people, use even when they are not Haitian, he succeeds so much in giving to them the intonation and the mimic art of the people among us that one asks why did he need to pattern his thought on that of the ingenious fabulist?

Note how Georges Sylvain could have achieved a magnificent original creation if he had forgotten La Fontaine and instead drawn his subjects entirely from the legends and tales of Haiti. Is it not regrettable that we have lost the finest opportunity to have a masterpiece of folkloric literature?

The racy and lively local fables of Carolus[151] are born of the same humorous and broadly comical vein. Written in French, they bring the reader to the moral conclusion which in every instance is a Haitian proverb.

Of another genre, and based on a pedagogical concern is the daring attempt of Frédéric Doret who has published an opuscule, [small work] *Pour amuser nos tout petits*, [To Amuse Our Little Ones] in which he has transferred the principal fables of La Fontaine from French into Creole. The purpose of Doret, very commendable, is to adapt to education the famous precept of Pestalozzi that we must proceed from the known to the unknown. This would bear no relationship to our subject if we had not found some aphorisms, some proverbs which are the materials of folk-lore in the Creole prose of the small opuscule.

Moreover, each part of the *Petite Revue* which Doret directs with so much tact and authority contains a tale taken from our oral tradi-

---

[151] Carolus is the pseudonym of a retired writer in seclusion who follows all the intellectual life of the country. [Price-Mars is referring to Carl Wolff (1864-1934).]

tions. One can hardly over-compliment the clairvoyance of this fine Haitian who in many an article and booklet commends the use of Creole as the starting point for the instruction of French, so that the Haitian primary school may no longer be a temptation for psittacism [mere parrotry], an outrage to good sense, but give a solid instruction, substantial and more profitable, to the popular clientele for which it has been created. We should want all our thinkers to be free of prejudices that bind and constrain them to pointless imitations of the foreigner, to make use of subject matter which is within their reach so that from their works emerges, simultaneously with a great human inspiration, this eager and warm fragrance of our soil, the overwhelming luminosity of our sky, and the indescribable something of the confident, of the candid, and of the positive which is one of the particular traits of our race.

Almost the same thought has engaged the attention of Dominique Hippolyte whose persevering labor has added a new volume of poetry, *La route ensoleillée*, to the Haitian collection.

Many are the notes of folk-lore from which his inspiration has modulated simple and touching harmonies. And it can only be a pleasure to encounter in our young men the concern for translating into works of art that which they are conscious of owing to the ancestral soil. Did not Hippolyte express the depth of feeling when he inscribed his poems with this thought of Charles Maurras: "I have received everything from my native soil . . ."

We can say that the same sympathy for things and beliefs of the past has marked the work of Burr-Reynaud very strongly. All of his plays and his poetry are impregnated with this. He has said that:
"In the large shady forest, when midnight is sounding,
   Under the cascade white with notes crystalline,
   One can see rise, silently and caressing
   A woman with breasts uncovered, a sister ondine:
   The mistress of the Water . . ."
Woe to the passerby who stops, fascinated, to contemplate the beauty of the immortal! He will fall fatally in love with her. For, it is the destiny of this cruel sovereign to be insensible to the desires of men. The more wild and ungovernable is the love that she inspires, the less possible is it to win her heart. And it is to accomplish her work of cruelty that she appears to men.

"Under the cascade white with notes crystalline" she is ready to snare the imprudent in the depths of her shifting empire.

With equal delight, the poet speaks to us of the flower of the bamboo which blooms only once a year at Christmas. All those whom love holds in bondage and are besieged by dread and desire must be alert to go into the depths of the forest to gather the petals of the rare flower at Christmas at the hour of midnight. If by chance the holy night catches them under the tree before the mysterious flowering has taken place, they are enveloped by it as though it were their shroud.

What a fine theme the poet has evoked in delicate and subtle verse.

Long before Burr-Reynaud, in many a page colored by humor and roguishness, Frédéric Marcelin has laughed at the superstitions of *Marilisse* upset by the card-predictions of the lady fortune teller, has brooded over the tragic adventures of *Jan Jan* too naively faithful to ancestral customs, and inspired by these popular beliefs, his pen leads us in *Mama* to the Hougan, the preparer of the poison intended for Télémaque, who is the assassin of the fiancé for whom the mad heroine mourned. *Mama* had gone on the road, alone, at night: "With a bewitching melancholic sadness hostile to profuse brightness and evocative of somnolent thoughts easily assimilated, the moon cast its bleak face over the already sleeping woods." The young girl had cleared the gate of the premises where the consultant resided and was feeling her way across the garden. Suddenly she heard a low, mournful, sad wail which seemed to come from the depths of the earth. She trembled, almost fainting. And the wail continued on and stretched into the silence of the night, ominously and indefinitely.

Bewitched, *Mama* rushed toward the doorway of the Hougan and begged for some explanation of the source of this odd sound.

Then the old man, knowledgeable in the things of earth, said to her:

"What has made you fearful is the cry of the yam, swelling under the ground. It is the effort it makes to break out of its crust, it is its time, it is this which wrenched the groan from it . . ."

And who then has found a way before Marcelin to gather these bits of popular beliefs in order to lend realistic and picturesque action to some of his books?

The author has another ability which he shares with Fernand Hibbert. From the forty works which compose the whole of their production — novels, critical tales, political works — not one, not the smallest opuscule treats a matter which is not closely attached to Haitian things and life, although Frédéric Marcelin and Fernand Hibbert lived in Paris for quite a long time and have been very involved in Parisian life by preference, education, talent, or fortune. It is this inflexible desire to make the best of Haitian themes for edification in a work of art which gives them the privileged place that they occupy in Haitian letters.

They appear to us to embody the most serious effort that has been made up to this time to work out a literature that is properly indigenous. We do not mean at all — once more — to reject those of our writers who search for their inspiration elsewhere than in our milieu. This would, truthfully, show a pitiable narrowness of mind, and we know of no invincible tenet by which we would forbid a Democlés Vieux, an Etzer Vilaire, a Charles Moravia, who are among the best known writers of our time, or a Léon Laleau whose talent is rich and diverse and so many others whose literary productions augur abundant laurels and sterling quality. What we felt necessary to state was that the work of the writers in question places them outside the preoccupations which are the concern of these essays.

2

And now how can we venture an opinion upon Haitian art without being self-contradictory.

Do a few sporadic demonstrations of painting and sculpture suffice to characterize an artistic production? Is it true that Normil Charles lives and molds in clay the dreams of glory that daily haunted the mind of our heroic ancestors?

But one swallow does not make spring . . .

Perhaps it is not improper to simply mention the aesthetics of music that are attached in some way to the subject that concerns us.

Our popular dances — vaudou, yanvalou, pétro, ibo, méringue — all have their rhythm and this rhythm is heard in the cadence of the melodic measure.

All the voodooistic ceremonies — evocations, initiations, exorcisms, expiatory rites, and so forth — are only fulfilled by the plaintive rhythm of liturgical chants composed of a line as simple as the plain chant. It seems to us that there would be reason to study these themes and to produce from them poems, dramatic pieces that are of an original and new vein. Although we may not be qualified to speak in a technical sense, we have not found a single decisive work in all this mass of production that in recent times may be designated: "Voodoo music."

It has even appeared to us that popular dances are quite readily mixed with voodooistic themes. Meanwhile the subject is in its conceptive stage. Many artists are undertaking the task. An Occide Jeanty already in his prime but with a head still brushed by the wing of the Muse, a Lamothe whose perceptivity is an inexhaustible reserve of dreams and hopes, a Justin Elie with a talent ripened by so many auspicious essays that promises us a great work, a Franck Lassegue who, from the banks of the Seine, gives vent to the nostalgia of his vagabond soul in plaintive notes, and all the others who are obsessed with the problem of creating an original Haitian music, sensual and melancholic, all are guarantors who in the matrix of Time are preparing the work which will mark the capacity of the race for an individual art generating ideas and emotions.

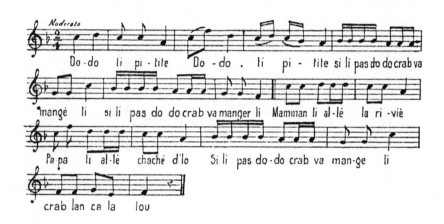

Chapter VIII

Postface

Address Given at Primavera

April, 1922

Ladies and Gentlemen,

On a certain day of last November one of my friends, having just come back from "a trip to a remote country" fatigued by very exacting scientific exertions, proposed that we take an excursion for a few days into the high altitudes of the Sourçailles where one can see the summits of the peaks of La Selle outlined in solitary majesty over a jumble of valleys, hills, and knolls. I was accepting the offer with enthusiasm not so much because I, myself, had need for intellectual relaxation or even was anxious for carefree diversion after having been riveted for three years to a professorship of education, but because nothing could give me more eager delight than to be in the closest association with an affectionate friend whose keen and singular spirit offered pleasing conversation that forced me to be on the alert and to reply in kind.

Because it would be just us, I was accepting the offer enthusiastically: "because it was him, because it was me."

But please pardon me for being so intimate with you about these delightful hours. It is not in order to demonstrate how warmly and sympathetically we agreed with each other. I am certain however that when I tell you that my companion on the trip was the attentive and clairvoyant critic of the ideas that I am about to impart to you that your understanding of the situation will be less influenced by any indiscreet remark upon my part.

Together, we collected the hesitant words of our hosts in peasant habitations; together, we broke through their reserve, urged the legitimacy of doubts, disarmed sensitive feelings which are only weapons of defense. Together, we appeased the uneasiness born of our searching inquisitiveness. Together, we induced the most devious person to confide little by little to us the treasures of a life flavored by absurd legends and superannuated beliefs.

Thus, we linked bit by bit a ponderous set of oral traditions into what one can distinguish as survivals of the land of Africa, the contributions of European colonization, the ephemeral shadow of aboriginal memories, and finally the continuous exertions of local transformations under the dual pressure of a still unsettled civilization and the resistance of a mentality that has never been touched by doubt.

So, in recapitulating my investigation of folk-lore, I bring you now the result of my procedure whatever its value, and above all whatever you may think of a method which is not rigorously scientific, I would really be inconsiderate if I did not acknowledge in some way the collaborative efforts of all these anonymous people who have assisted me, still less could I be silent as to the cooperation of a comrade whose interest in the work that I pursue will be the principal, the conditional element for success . . .

Ladies and Gentlemen,

I am quite positive that you were somewhat uneasy, indeed were seriously upset when you learned that I intended to examine the peasant family openly with you.

Peasant family! What is this ambiguous expression of contradictory terms? Is not a family, according to the most elementary conception you have conceived, the starting point, the embryonic nucleus of every society by virtue of Christian doctrine and according to the ritual that your catechism teaches when it raises marriage to the height *of a sacrament which sanctifies the legitimate union of man and woman and gives them the privilege of fulfilling their obligations?*

Thus, strictly defined, the union of man and woman, even when it is consecrated in conformity with the obligations of Civil Law, has no moral worth if it has not received the sanction of the Church. And since *in our Christian society* the Curé [priest], at the height of his sermon, denounces the fantastic proportion of baptisms of natural [illegitimate] babies, four-fifths of which as registered in the village come from rural populations, is there not some paradox in linking these two terms: *peasant family?*

Ah! Of course not. For the contrariety of terms is quite easily understood or at any rate it discloses to the attentive observer one of the most striking forms of conflict of beliefs and mores upon which our society is constructed.

Most certainly, he who deludes himself through vanity, illusion, or foolishness can end up believing that we live the Christian life fully, but he who has no fear of confronting the Phariseeism of our conventional falsehoods, who unmercifully denounces the inelegant gestures of social indifference and is perceptive about the problems of our ethnic past, that person will discern that our society is in the full tide of evolution.

Just as the geologist through the study of fossils and superimposed strata calculates the age of the terrain, just as the naturalist demonstrates the originality of the present form by uncovering the vestiges of old forms which reveal the series of mutations that the being has undergone during prehistoric periods, so in the same way the survival of ancient customs, beliefs, and mores in a contemporary society which has accepted Western Civilization as the standard of progress, the triumph or the recession, the compromise or the apparent repudiation of these mores, customs, and beliefs are the surest evidence of stages traversed from the starting point to the point of arrival of this society; they are the most veracious evidences of its aptitude to accomplish its destiny, of the potentialities of the society to realize the ambitions which stimulate its vitality. To capture some of the details of this process of transformation is such an exhiliarating pleasure to me that I am not afraid of provoking you in urging you to share it.

*

*   *

So the Church made the establishment of the family an act of faith. I accept the rigor of its doctrine. But then I will say that the conformity of the peasant himself in establishing a home according to Christian ritual depends upon the state of his sincerity or of his compliance with the Credo of the Church. Better than that! If his life continues to be dependent upon other religious beliefs and if the family temperament accepts the influence of these beliefs, it will be interesting to discover in what measure he remained faithful to them, in what measure he made his concession to the new divinity which has been revealed to him, to what disparate compromise and conciliation his pride has led him to appear in no way to stray through any action or inner desire into violating prohibitions which may be prejudicial to him.

But I am musing now. Such a study would embrace nothing more or less than the whole of peasant life: habitation, clothing, sustenance, work, in fact all of the manifestations which comprise the existence of the campagnard [one living in the country] from birth to death.

Despite the desire for such a study it would comprehend nothing less than an important monograph, and in this genre, the *conférence* [formal address], which cannnot be as precise — time being curtailed — we must limit our selections.

Shall we simply take a look at the establishment of a family in the district of Kenscoff?

*
*   *

Kenscoff? Perhaps many present here have some close friends in this delightful region?

Over there is a mountainous section set in the cluster of peaks form- ing a sinuous chain that blends with the massive formations stretching to the far end of the peninsula.

The Black Mountains which form a unit to the southeast of Port- au-Prince extend toward the low plain to the northwest in a continua- tion of mountain divisions broken by gorges and valleys. One of these divisions thrusts a spur of clayed rock scattered with pines toward the sea. The rest of it is whipped by raw winds. It is this high point so often lashed by storms that forms the plateau of Furcy.

To the East — quite close — another division contained by the counterforts of La Selle exposes its undulating backside toward the West where there seems to be more space, then as if exhausted by the effort deviates and sinks into the valley of Grands Fonds. Huddled in this sud- den depression, similar to a washbowl with a dented bottom, are the little houses of Kenscoff. Here we are at a height of 1,200 meters [3937 feet]. On the steep sides of the basin grow dense clumps of bushes that the inhabitants call "wild tobacco," and also on the slope, steep or gen- tle, in the less craggy spots, a short grass, thick and vigorous, covers the ground with a green, velvety, soft carpet.

Kenscoff is a cool pasture land. Cattle grown here are sound and sturdy. Likewise because of its bowl-like shape and high altitude the land of Kenscoff, sheltered from violent windstorms, retains a very high degree

Ti Jean, peasant of Kenscoff.

of humidity whether the cloud brings fine or torrential rain, whether the daily fog clings to the flank of the hills and trails its robe of white mousseline into the smallest recess of the valleys. What is more, a clear brook falls in small cascades watering the region. Ah! this distinctive water of Kenscoff. One is no longer aware in refreshing himself whether it is tasty because of having inhaled the sweet-smelling scent of the nearby *petit baume* [a small balsam] or because of having gathered up, absorbed, filtered through the century-old humus from the generous and fertile ground of the watercress beds.

But still, from this hasty sketch, it seems possible to me to draw various conclusions as to the abilities of Kenscoff to maintain a human community.

First, the country offers the greatest facilities for the establishment of agricultural habitations. With the system of small parcels of land ownership which prevails in our rural economy, each family in Kenscoff owns its plot of ground and possesses one or several cows through which it derives an appreciable supplement for balancing the budget.

In each family it is the little girl or young daughter, very rarely the youth, who on foot carries the milk, five to ten litres, from Kenscoff to Petionville and to Port-au-Prince. Our milkmaiden thus daily covers a distance of ten to twelve hours of walking[152] often over paths that are frequently slippery, rocky and rough . . . To the milk trade, the peasant of Kenscoff adds the cultivation of market gardens and horticultural plants. And because of the altitude and fertility of the soil it is a pleasure to see how the vegetables and fruit trees native to temperate countries grow so exuberantly. Peaches, strawberries, apples, vegetables, and other succulent things are to be found there. Upon the whole here rural life takes on an aspect of ease that is quite remarkable, and this is due as much to the richness of the terrain as to the exceptional coolness of the climate.

And now in what manner will these magnificent gifts of the physical milieu influence the development of the human being?

But first what type of human being is he? And to what variety of specie or race does he belong?

*
*   *

It is difficult to determine, even in an imperfect fashion, the respective portion of the various human groups who have contributed to the physical formation of the contemporary Haitian type. We have said this elsewhere, but please excuse us for repeating it. This type is the result of races amalgamated in other continents for thousands of years, and here in this country of the elements of a race historic in the process of evolution, consolidating, condensing, and aggregating for almost two centuries. But as far as hypotheses of a general nature can be indicative it appears to us that the community of Kenscoff has preserved rather remarkable physical resemblances to the Congolese type which — we recall — appertains to the largest of the African tribes imported to Saint Domingue. In any case, at the present time, the peasant of Kenscoff is generally a man of medium height, cheerful and energetic; although he may be neither tall and sturdy nor short and stocky this mountain man

[152] Fifteen to twenty kilometers [approximately ten to fifteen miles].

who with bare torso tolerates temperatures of four or five degrees above zero [39° to 41° F.] is all told a solid fellow, well balanced on his somewhat slender legs and much more ingenious than one thinks from the accentuated characteristics he projects, with his slow gestures and his immoderate style of speaking. At the age of twenty-one he is ready for serious enterprises and for the most important of them all, the establishment of a family home; at this age he may, if he is well-organized, have landed property. Let us suppose that the alternating seasons have been favorable to his labor: neither too rainy, nor too dry. With a lively *coumbite*,[153] he has garnered a respectable supply of red beans. The maize seed has quintupled the normal harvest. On the best avocado trees which surround his father's dwelling he displays six or seven bunches of well-filled ears of maize, the heavy pyramids attesting to everyone the vigor of his labor. There has been a good stock of vegetables for the village market. For more than six months his cow has daily supplied full measures of milk that he sold on the premises to peddlers. Though he has even been lucky more than once at the *gaghière*[154] why is *Ti Jean Pierre Jean* not entirely happy? What is missing? Why, of course! It is because he does not have his own home, his own wife, and his own children which signifies to everyone that he is a married man, a father of a family, a *habitant notable* [person of standing]. Well! Without doubt, as with all the young men of the region, he has had his share of disappointing adventures with easy-going young maidens. But then, never has his heart beaten more strongly and his temples throbbed from the quickening of his pulse than when by chance he meets *Dorismène*, the milkmaiden from Guibert,[155] on the road returning from the city with her loaded basket, her bosom swelling strongly under the pressure of her tight bodice, her hips arched, and the plump calves of her legs exposed under the rolled-up hem of her blue dress.

Then frozen by emotion, the sickle under his arms, he gazes at her intently, permits her to pass, then remarks quite loudly:

"Well! *Mainmainne* ou t'a capab' dit m'bon jou!"[156]

She beams. And in the luminous daylight there is a cascade of laughter which sounds like a call of springtime.

---

[153] *Coumbite:* An agricultural get-together where people aid one another in clearing the land, sowing the seed, and gathering the harvest.

[154] *Gaghière:* place where people assemble for cockfights.

[155] *Guibert:* rural community close to Kenscoff.

[156] Well! *Mainmainne*, couldn't you say hello to me?

"No! *pas possible, ou gangnin l'air ou soude . . .*[157]

It is true that *Ti Jean* is acting a little crazy though he is not deaf. He is smitten with ecstasy, the restlessness of love, and the ardent desire to share it, as any young man of twenty years. But he is bashful. Has he not resolved many times to speak freely with the beautiful girl, to win some approval in order to finish the matter? Each time he has stammered a few unintelligible words and stopped silent, although so jealous he is ready to fight with any one of the boys who might speak too freely about *Mainmainne*. Meanwhile he works hard and hoards sou after sou.

Mainmainne, the milkmaiden.

At last, one evening, the opportunity came.

It was at Corail, at the home of *Lapointe*, the most prestigious

[157] No! It was impossible, you looked as if you wouldn't hear me.

hougan in the vicinity. A *service*[158] was to be celebrated in which everyone had been preparing to participate for days in advance. The most charming young girls of *Viard*, of *Godet*, of *Robin*, of *Kenscoff* rubbed elbows with the young men who came from several places around.

The *service* was "gras"[159]: the food plentiful, the tafia [unrefined rum] abundant. The drummers, the chant leader, and the chorus tormented the audience with intoxicating deep bass sounds that gave rhythm to the raucous plaint of the *Assôtor*.[160] Meanwhile female and male dancers, covered with dust, were turning and spinning around vigorously and continuously, as they stamped the earth with a supple cadence.

In the front ranks *Ti Jean* and *Mainmainne* were together, carefree, gay and lighthearted. Suddenly a signal, a very strong drumbeat upon the *Assôtor*, arrests the momentum of the audience.

Now the chant leader improvises an air in honor of *Ogou Ferraille*.

The audience is pensive. It is also midnight, the hour propitious for ritual incantations [ritual recitation to produce a magical effect] . . .

Ti Jean takes advantage of the interruption to drag his partner to the rear of the place. He has to talk with her. About what? He does not know himself but he feels a need to say something to her. His chest contracts, he clenches his teeth. Alas! His limited vocabulary holds him silent. Then, without any further ceremony, in the darkness of the night and in the cool wind that whispers under the stars, he seizes her abruptly and, in a fierce embrace, kisses her madly upon the neck. Evidently he is overcome by the excitement of the dancing . . .

But she, astonished, bewildered, remained for a short moment as if stunned by the impromptu action. Then with a sob, whether of apprehensive joy or of inexpressible sorrow one does not know, with a sob she could not hold back, she cried out:

Oh! Oh! Mèz zamis. Oh! Oua vlé coué Ti-Jean radi, mes zamis Ti-Jean horde débordé. Parole ça trop fort. Faut m'dit papa m'ça.[161]

Ti Jean himself, was happy. At last he had made his intentions known. He is or believes himself to be engaged.

But why, then, for such a long time after the event did the beautiful girl refuse to greet him and even avoid meeting him? Had she been forever

---

[158] The service consists of a liturgical ceremony offered to the gods according to the rites of a particular cult.

[159] An expression which means that it was an important ceremony.

[160] *Assôtor:* the largest of the sacred drums.

[161] *Oh! Oh! My friends, do you believe Ti Jean is impertinent? He has definitely overstepped the limits. It's really too bad. I must tell my father.*

offended or might this be merely the capriciousness of a woman? Still
no member of Dorismène's family has reproached Ti Jean. This is proof
that she has kept silent about what has passed between them. Herein
lay an enigma which the lover intended to resolve. Slyly and timidly,
he started more than once on the path which led *à la Cour* [to the court-
yard] where Dorismène lived to get a positive understanding. To no
avail. Some pretext or another always stopped him on the way. And
he had to content himself with gazing at the house where the beautiful
girl lived from the top of the hill.

One day, come what might, he resolved to take a supreme step to
approach the young girl.

He got into his newest pants, put on his blue cotton shirt with the
buttons of gilded *corozo* [ivory-nut], the special one on which the skillful
artist has stitched the most fantastic original designs with a needle; with
sapattes[162] on his feet, with a *halefort*[163] made of latania [a type of palm]
painted with motifs in anilin dye slung debonairely across his back, Ti
Jean goes to speak about love. The *halefort* is bulging with little gifts
of spicy cakes and breads, barley-sugar and bonbons from the city, with
four or five of the finest ears of maize from his garden. But this is simply the beginning. On the way he loiters, exchanging joyful greetings with
passing friends. But as he emerges from the valley he bruises his left foot
on a sharp pebble just as a flock of cawing crows circle overhead.

"Unbelievable! Did I misstep?" he muttered.

What a nasty warning! He hesitated an instant then resumed his
way. Alas! What did he see just as he passed the banana plantation which
ran along the adjoining slope? It was Dorismène in person having a tête-à-
tête with a suitor, his cousin Florvil.

Misfortune of misfortunes! Was it for this that he had worked so
hard, put so much money aside? Was it to be made ridiculous by a
woman? Of course not, he will be avenged, he will take up the challenge.

Then he ran posthaste to tell his disappointment to *Lapointe*, the
most renowned *hougan* of Corail, and to solicit his aid. Lapointe
meditated gravely, threw sacred shells on the ground, interpreted the
response of the gods, and gave the decision:

"*Ti Jean* neglects the *Esprits* who are upset by such culpable indifference. That which has happened is only a warning. A greater misfor-

---

[162] *Sapattes:* a kind of sandal.
[163] *Halefort:* a straw bag.

tune was about to befall him. Fortunately Maîtresse Erzilie[164] is there protecting him. The *Esprits* will be propitious to his wishes if he no longer forgets his duties. Let him sacrifice a *white cock* and a *black chicken* at the crossroads of *Rendez-vous*, the third Wednesday before the cocks crow at midnight. Then he will recite the phrase: *Loco Louéba Yanzi cé Yanzi*[18] as he strikes his chest three times.

"With the ceremony which will be arranged in her honor, at the same hour, in the hounfort ["temple" of a Voodoo priest], he can be certain that not only will the heart of *Mainmainne* belong to him but henceforth she will follow him wherever he will wish to go."

Ti Jean smiled, and having recovered his spirits at this revelation, had himself repeat the order several times, muttered it all the way home, and re-entered his home much more tranquil than when he had left it. So when the time for carrying out the order came he was faithful and punctual in fulfilling the stipulated promise and awaited the sequel of events.

Definitely the *Hougan* of *Corail* is a powerful man:

For emboldened by the assurance of promised success, according to the will of the gods, in the months which followed the sacrifice, Ti Jean paid a visit to the home of *Fré Charles*, the father of Dorismène, where he was cordially welcomed and it was arranged that within the week *Captainn Cazeau Jean Pierre* would personally bring the letter of request for the marriage of his son. And the letter came.

Ah! As to this letter, nobody in Kenscoff was able to write it. A clerk was discovered in Petionville who, for a stipend, about twenty gourdes, set the sentiment of the suitor in traditional style.

This letter? But I assure you that none of us present here could have drawn up this letter. This letter? It is the faint echo of a very old custom going back to that early period in which the scribe [official writer] was the oracle [source of wise counsel or prophetic opinions] of the Cité, no matter whether his obscure language made sense or not. A letter of request in marriage must always contain the avowal of love of the suitor, his promise of good conduct toward his future companion, and the

---

[164] *Erzilie gé rouge:* [the red-eyed Erzilie]: Voodoo Divinity who is accepted as representing the Holy Virgin.

[18] This phrase seems to be an appeal to the loa *Loco (Loko)* of the Rada cult whose domain is in the earth. He is a part of the African past; he is well-loved and one often converses with him as "Papa Loko." See J.B. Romain, "Introduction au vodou haitien," *Conjonction,* 112 (1970), p. 9; Harold Courlander, *The Drum and the Hoe,* 1960, pp. 22, 50-51.

guarantee given by his family and friends that he is of good character. It is signed not only by the suitor himself but also by his natural parents and his spiritual parents, his godfather and godmother, if it be possible. And particularly it must be written on special paper, embossed, embellished, and ornamented with colored designs, and sealed in an envelope of the same pattern as the paper. In addition, it must be brought to the parents of the young maiden by the oldest man of the other family carefully wrapped up in a handkerchief of red silk and the whole, letter and kerchief, is to be delivered to the head of the family from which the alliance is being requested. The response is carried out with the same formality. The date of the marriage is then fixed.

Perhaps you do not believe me. Let me read you one of these documents drawn up in Dame Marie which has an authenticity guaranteed by the patina of time and by the honorable character of the person who gave it to me, my friend Doctor Fouron.

Facsimile of a letter of request in marriage:

"Second rural section of Dame Marie, December 5, 1905

To

"Mr. Dorméus Béralus and to Mrs. Méséide Jaccaint, in the first section of the habitation, Sapour.

Sir and Madam:

"We have the honor of taking up the pen to wish success to your worthy family, with the purpose, Sir and Madam, according to our Christian nature and with the intelligence of honorable people, of fulfilling a courteous obligation. We approach you with affection, joy, prudence, respect, and satisfaction to request the hand of your daughter, Miss Zabéla Dorméus, with whom our young son called Joseph Duverna is deeply in love, and with whom, he has told us, he wishes to form a family, for it is the obligation of civilized people to humbly avow our consent. Therefore, Sir and Madam, as his governors, we testify for him wholeheartedly and we assure you that we will be responsible for whatever happens and we assure you that our son is a very prudent, gentle, and respectful son, dutiful to the old as well as the young, and in seeking to discharge our obligation honorably and faithfully, by virtue of this general testimony, Sir and Madam, we recommend to you, as we ask God to protect them for us, a day witnessing such satisfaction, requesting glory, respect and knowledge, union and steadfastness. In the hope of a favorable response upon receiving our request.

"And assuring you of our deep and sincere friendship

le bonjour ainsi que
votre respectable famille,
dans le But Mr. et Madanne
que d'après notre humanité
Chrétien et en intelligeance
des honnettes gens, tout en rem
plissant un devoir d'honne
té, Nous venons au devant de
vous, avec tendresse joie, sa
guié respect, et satisfaction
tout en vous demandant la
main de votre fille, Madémoi
selle Isabéla Dorméus que
notre jeune garçon nommé Jouph
Doverma aimait tendrement
dont il nous a lu ses pensées
tout en voulant Créer une famille
avec la tienne, car Ce devoir
est l'humble avec des gens
civilisés. Alors monsieur, et Mme
Nous Comme ses gouverneurs, nous
lui témoignons avec courage
et nous vous assurons que nous
serons responsable de tout
Ce qui arrivra. et nous vous
assurons que notre gar
çon est un enfant

très sage, docile, et rempli de respect,
obéissant envers les grands ainsi que
les petits et prétendent d'acquitter avec
honnêteté avec fidélité, notre devoir, en
vertu Monsieur et madame de ce grand
témoignage que nous vous proposons tout
en demandant à Dieu de leurs protégés
pour nous que divine providence leur
leurs donne la santé pour nous afin qu'un
jour de témoigner cette pareille satisfaction, demandant la gloire, le respect, la science, l'union, et la persévérance, En attendant
de nous une bonne réponse afin de sa-
voir notre diligence.

Et vous saluent d'un profond et
d'une sublime amitié
        Vos serviteurs.   Duverna St Louis,

            Lamère   Cléodica Noël.

son grand père et son parrain,
            Louis jeune Noël

sa grande mère,   Madame Louis jeune noël

Your servants:
    DUVERNA ST. LOUIS,
    His mother: CLEODICE NOEL.
    His grandfather and his godfather: LOUIS JEUNE NOEL.
    His grandmother: Mrs. LOUIS JEUNE NOEL."

Ladies and Gentlemen,

Since our young peasants are officially engaged they can henceforth see each other and talk freely with one another. The father of the fiancée points out to his future son-in-law the plot of land upon which their house will be built. From this house will develop the homes of those who will cluster together within this limited space held jointly by them, the whole of which constitutes *"la cour"* [court, courtyard], the inviolable heritage of the family. Among these little houses one is conspicuous for its somewhat special architecture — its rectangular form bearing a vague resemblance to a temple. This is the one which contains the altar of the god honored by the family . . .

Having completed the formality of the choice of the terrain, only the date of the marriage ceremony remains to be determined. But of what does this ceremony consist?

It rests primarily on the *conditional consent* of the parents and on the ritual celebration of union.

First, the future husband must *"pay for the good fortune of* [winning] *the young maiden."* To pay for the good fortune of the bride is a *sine qua non* [an essential act] and consists on the part of the fiancé of depositing with his parents-in-law a sum determined in advance as the price of their agreement. This dowry — for that is what it is — varies according to the social importance of the family with which one wishes to make the alliance. It can be fifty gourdes, one hundred gourdes, and beyond.[165] The money will be counted in public on the day of the nuptial celebration. Then, before the spectators who bring the finacée gifts, such as money, printed cloth, kerchiefs, and other presents, the father solemnly takes the hand of his daughter and places it in that of the young man; then, leading the couple into the *rétiro* [the place of refuge] before the altar upon which rest *plats de marassa, calebasses*, and *coquilles sacrées* [red clay pots or dishes of The Twins, gourdes, and sacred shells], and where are kept the special symbols of the gods honored by the family

---

[165] The Haitian gourde is worth twenty cents in American money.

— the drums and sacred rattles — the old man lights the white candle, throws some water and liqueur on the ground, then, while drawing the mysterious signs [vèvès] with a handful of flour and finally extending his hands toward the rising sun, beseeches the gods *Ogon, Damballa Legba, Sibi nan d'leau, all the dead and the good spirits to protect the couple and to bless the union which has just been formed according to the faith of their fathers and ancestors.*

It is finished.

And it is at this point that the second ceremony takes place — the least interesting. The whole gamut of pleasurable entertainment unfolds at the second ceremony — drinking, feasting, laughter and dancing, jokes and riddles. From now on the young married couple will live as they choose. Often they will remain separated from each other for a certain period while the husband hurries to cut or buy wood, to solicit advice from the architect of the area, to cut, raise, and frame his house, to cover it over with a thatched roof, to wicker its sides and wall them with mud, and to blanch them white with lime. He furnishes it very simply: a table, some metal and glass cups, one or two straw mats, a trunk, some chairs. This pretty much represents the furnishings of a newly set-up household of modest means. The family is established. Henceforth the husband and wife will help one another in the daily work, bound to each other in good and bad times. Thus many years may slip away in the monotony of days without excitement and novelty. If there is misfortune, or quite simply if prosperity comes to the ambitious household, they will, having consulted the Hougan, find it proper to ask the Church for a new consecration of this long life in common.

So this is, ladies and gentlemen, broadly speaking, a peasant family in the regions where the conditions of contemporary life and the proximity of large cities have not altered traditional authority.

Doubtlessly these traditions fall into disuse, are modified and transformed more or less rapidly and distinctly here and there. Doubtlessly some of them have not even left any appreciable trace in certain parts of the country and yet resist any disturbance in some other place. Doubtlessly . . . but as one can well see, they dominate the peasant conception of life because they are tied to time-honored beliefs that are difficult to uproot in these unsophisticated milieus. Need I point out that more than one philosopher regrets the disintegration of certain of these customs whose antiquated and obsolete symbolism possesses an inexpressible charm and poesy? Will you permit me to recall the sunny days of my adolescence when I heard the old men — laudator temporis acti [praiser of time past] — regretting the disappearance of traditions in the region of Grande Rivière du Nord? At that time, even a peasant marriage celebrated in the Church of the village called for a grand procession on horse, on one condition however: the married couple were to have the best horses and be preceded by a standard bearer and the standard itself was to be immaculately white.

At the gateway of the premises where the reception for guests was to take place, a temporary altar of green leaves dotted with purple laurel pointed the way to the courtyard. When the husband arrived there he quickly leaped from the saddle and ran to lock himself in the nuptial house. Then the bride, in front of the audience, very meekly knocked on the main door, repeating in a loud voice: "My husband, my husband, open the door for me." The husband immediately assented to the entreaty of his wife, handed over to her the keys of the household along with a blue handkerchief and some bread . . .

A pleasing symbol is it not and its significance for the bride may be translated thus: "I am the master here, I give you a place in this dwelling where henceforth I will see to your sustenance and clothing . . ."

And how could I forget another custom, dear to my native country some thirty years ago, and which consisted of celebrating sumptuous wedding feasts at nightfall? The nuptial procession, on coming back from the religious ceremony, passed through the village preceded by torchbearers . . .

Was this simply because the municipality, oblivious of the need for public illumination, left the streets in darkness, or rather was this a dim survival of the torch race, the beautiful ancient festival in which the runners passed the torch to each other in order to symbolize the transmission of life from generation to generation? What is my belief? I would be apt to choose the second hypothesis which would link our torchbearers to their parallels on the shores of the Mediterranean if I did not fear that I would be reproached for my penchant to bind the present and recent past to a more distant past blurred perhaps by the remoteness of the ages. The municipalities are no more lavishly lit today than yesterday and the old practices have disappeared forever . . .

And do other recollections full of restless ghosts haunt my imagination? How can I prevent myself from discovering in the gestures of our campagnards [country people] when they show civility to their hosts by bowing graciously, a testimony reminiscent of the elegant habits of the colonial society of the eighteenth century? You are aware that the great Seigneurs of Saint Domingue were passionate imitators of the usages of Versailles and trained their livery in "l'art exquis des poses." The peasant reverence is some kind of survival of the usages of the period.

Whatever it may be, some of the customs that I have tried to make come alive again are marked with the most transparent symbolism and since all human life is enveloped in symbols which mask the brutality of life, is it not deplorable that we permit some of the most suggestive of these symbols guarding the existence of people of the past to disappear?

We are ashamed of them because we have been told that they were superstitions and prejudices. Do you think so? "When you are shocked by some old absurd prejudice, bear in mind that it has been the fellow traveler of mankind for perhaps some ten million years, that it has sustained us when things were going wrong, that it has been the occasion for much happiness, that it has, so to speak, supported human life. Does this not tell us that there is something fraternal about the thought of man?"

*

*   *

But, in fact, what is the origin of most of the customs about which we have just spoken? Are they daughters of our soil or rather do they come to us from across the seas?

We are skeptical of either explanation. None of them are entirely local creations, yet none have reached us without alteration. They exist as our personality itself, the whole charged with reminiscences and stamped by successive mutations which mark the complexity of our ethnic origins, and since the evolution of our people operates in such a divergent manner that a small number among us acquires a social and intellectual culture that puts them in a separate world, very proud and very haughty from living in an ivory tower with only a distant and formal contact with the remainder lost in misery and ignorance, it is among the multitude that we will have the chance to discover the thread of traditions that came from across the seas. If we submit these traditions to a comparative examination they will reveal immediately that Africa is the country of origin for most of them.

But just as the beliefs from which they proceed, as we have asserted elsewhere, divide Africa into distinct zones, so will the distribution of the mores and customs in question extend over the large western half of the ancient Continent.

Shall we go back together to those times to compare the establishment of a family somewhere in the Congo, in the Sudan, and in Dahomey?

Ah! I understand full well the repugnance with which I am confronted in daring to speak of Africa and of African things! The subject seems vulgar to you and entirely devoid of interest, am I not right?

Beware, my friends, are not such sentiments resting on the groundwork of scandalous ignorance? We subsist on ideas rancid from the stupendous stupidity of an ill-balanced culture and our puerile vanity is not satisfied until we mumble phrases written to please others in which we glorify *the Gauls our ancestors.*

Well, our only chance to be ourselves is by not repudiating any part of our ancestral heritage. And! as for this heritage, eight-tenths of it is a gift from Africa. Moreover, on this small planet which is but an infinitesimal point in space, men have intermingled for milleniums to the point that there is no longer a single authentic savant, not even in the United States of America, who seriously supports the theory of pure races. And if I accept the scientific position of Sir Harry Johnston there is not a single Negro, as black as he may be, in the center of Africa who does not have some drops of Caucasoid blood in his veins, and perhaps not a single white in the United Kingdom of England, France, Spain, and elsewhere among the most haughty, who has not some drops of Negro or yellow blood in their veins. So it is true according to the verse of the poet:

All men are man. [Victor Hugo][19]

Our ancestors? Just how can I be humiliated by knowing from whence they came, if I bear, myself, my mark of human nobility boldly like a radiant star and if in my rise towards more enlightenment I am assuaged by the inviolable pangs of perfection.

Our ancestors? First, they are the dead whose worldly suffering, courage, intelligence, and feelings intermingled in olden times in the crucible of Saint Domingue to make of us what we are: free beings. Our ancestors? They are the dead whose combined vices and virtues speak silently in our evil hearts or in our heroic and proud conscience.

Our ancestors? They are all those who rose slowly from primitive animality to become the transitory being that we are, still faltering before the unknown which besets us but heirs of the unfading glory of being men. It is because our ancestors were men who suffered, who loved,

[19] Jean Price-Mars, *Lettre ouverte au Dr. René Piquion*, Port-au-Prince, 1967, p. 6.

and who hoped, that we can, we also, aspire to the full dignity of being men despite the brutal insolence of imperialisms of any nature.

Whites, blacks, mulattoes, griffes, octoroons, quadroons, marabouts, sacatras, of what importance are these empty labels from the cast-off colonial period if we perceive ourselves as men resolved to play our role properly in this miniscule part of the world scene which is our Haitian society.

So accept the ancestral inheritance as a whole. Take a good look at it, weigh it, examine it with intelligence and with circumspection, and you will see as in a broken mirror that it reflects the reduced image of human nature completely. Ah yes! the same causes have produced the same effects everywhere on the planet. Love, Hunger, and Fear have given rise to the same fables in the ardent imagination of men — whether they live in the tangled brushwood of the Sudan, whether they appeared in olden times on the hills where the Acropolis arose or on the shores of the Tiber where the City of the Seven Hills was built. And this is why the modern-day African [early 1900's] furnishes the sociologist with the elements which allow him to ascertain the psychology of primitive man. The constitution of the family is for him, above all, an act of faith, a religious initiation ceremony. So it was in ancient Greece and Rome, so it is in certain tribes of the Sudan, of Dahomey, of the Congo save for the inevitable variants engendered by the circumstances and necessities of the physical milieu. If you care to accept my word about this, shall we make a comparative study of the establishment of the family in these early stages of civilization by referring to the most instructive example of wisdom and meditation. Let us listen to Fustel de Coulanges describe the marriage ceremony among the Greeks and the Romans:

"Among the Greeks," he says, "the marriage ceremony was composed so to speak of three acts: the first took place before the hearth of the father, the third at the hearth of the husband, the second was the passage from one to the other.

"First, in the paternal home in the presence of the future bridegroom a sacrifice is offered by the father who is usually surrounded by his family. The sacrifice completed, he declares by uttering a sacramental expression that he gives his daughter to the young man. This declaration is completely indispensable to the marriage. For the young woman could not go immediately to worship at the hearth of the bridegroom if her father did not first detach her from the paternal hearth. In order that she may be admitted into the new religion she must be freed from every link and every attachment to her first religion.

"Secondly, the young woman is carried to the husband's home. Sometimes it is the husband himself who conducts her. In certain cities, the responsibility of bringing the young woman belongs to one of those men invested with a priestly character by the Greeks and who were known as heralds. The young woman is usually placed in a chariot, she has her face covered with a veil and wears a wreath on her head. The wreath was used in all ceremonies of worship. Her dress is white. White was the color of clothing in all religious proceedings. A person carrying a torch goes before her. This is the nuptial flame. Along the way everyone around her sings a religious hymn with this refrain:

ὦ ὑμεν, ὦ ὑμεναιε,   [O Hymen, O Hymenaie].

"This hymn is called the hymeneal [nuptial song] and the importance of this song was so great that its name was applied to the entire ceremony.

"The young woman does not enter by herself into her new dwelling place. Her husband must seize her, must simulate an abduction, and she must cry out and the women accompanying her pretend to defend her . . .

"After a sham struggle the bridegroom lifts her up in his arms and takes her through the doorway, taking great care that her feet do not touch the threshold.

"What has taken place is only the preparation and the prelude to the ceremony. The holy act is about to begin in the house.

"Thirdly, they approach the hearth, the bride is brought into the presence of the family divinity. She is sprinkled with lustral water; she touches the sacred fire. Some prayers are said. Then the married couple divide cake, bread, and some fruit between them. This kind of light meal which begins and ends with a libation and prayer, this sharing of the food vis-à-vis at the hearth places the married couple in communion with the household gods.

*

*   *

"The Roman marriage was much the same as the Greek marriage and also included three acts:

"1. The young woman leaves the paternal hearth. As she is not attached to this hearth by her own right, but only through the father of the family, only the authority of the father can detach her from it . . .

"2. The young woman is led to the home of the bridegroom. As in Greece, she is veiled, she wears a crown, and a nuptial torch precedes the procession. Those about her sing an old religious hymn . . .

"The procession stops before the husband's home. There the fire and water are presented to the young woman. The fire is the symbol of the household divinity, the water is the lustral water used by the family for all religious proceedings. In order that the young woman may enter the house it is necessary, as in Greece, to simulate abduction. The bridegroom must raise her in his arms and carry her over the threshold without letting her feet touch it.

"3. The bride is then led before the hearth where there are Penates [Roman tutelary gods], where all the household gods and the images of ancestors are grouped around the sacred fire. The married couple, as in Greece, offer a sacrifice, pour the libation, utter some prayers, and together eat from a cake of pure wheaten flour.

"This cake eaten during the recitation of prayers, in the presence and under the eyes of the familial divinities is what constitutes the sacred union of husband and wife . . ."[166]

This was marriage in the ancient Greco-Roman civilization.

And now let us see how it is among certain Negroes of Africa, and first in the Congo.

There, although young men and women are considered completely fitted for marriage, they must submit first to an initiation ceremony which makes it proper for them to share the full life of the tribe. We borrow the description of this curious rite from *La religion des primitifs* of Mgr. Le Roy [pp. 233-234]:

"The initiation which is applied to both sexes," he says, "varies widely in its ceremonial from tribe to tribe, but we find it everywhere, at least in a state of partial survival, here quite simple, there more complicated, symbolic, and solemn.

"Naturally it differs for boys and for girls, but one waits until there are a certain number of young people or young persons from the same village or neighboring villages of an admissible age. When that day comes the boys, who may then be from fifteen to eighteen and twenty years of age, are brought together under the leadership of a specialist and subjected, in costumes suited to the occasion, to various ordeals that they must undergo manfully. They are making sort of a retreat, living, eating,

---

[166] [Numa Denis] Fustel de Coulanges, *La cité antique*, [Paris]. [I continued to put quotation marks at beginning of each paragraph even though this pattern was not followed in the French text to the end of the quotation at this footnote.]

sleeping apart, generally in the near-by forest, devoting themselves to different exercises, repeating certain songs and certain dances, instructed mysteriously in what is permitted or forbidden, in the interests and traditions of the tribe, and so on . . .

"It is also the occasion to renew the alliance with the totem by symbolic ceremonies, a sacrifice, a communion. All of this lasts several days, often several weeks and even several months. Their black skin is wholly or partly covered by a white paint made of watered chalk or of flour: this is the color of the spirits. The ornaments of their costume are oftentimes very complicated. The dances follow one another. Often a new name is given: it is a second birth . . . The whole ceremony is generally terminated by a great feast calling for a solemn procession, a dinner, dances, and presents, let alone drinking which must receive special attention . . ."

The girls are subjected to an identical ceremony which likewise varies according to the country and R. E. Dennett describes this for us as it is in the Congo:

"When a girl becomes nubile, a little hut outside the village is built for her. Her head is shaved and her entire little body is covered with *takula*, or a powdered redwood mixed with water. Thus painted, the girl retires with friends of hers who have already passed through a similar ceremony, into her little hut; there she is offered a chicken or if her family cannot afford it, an egg. She remains here confined for six days, surrounded by her companions who watch over, amuse, and feed her during the day, serving her as if she were a princess and, at night, singing and dancing to the sounds of the *misunga* [the great dried pod of the Baobab tree].

"Meanwhile a nice hut [*shimbec*] is built for her in the village and two beds placed in it. She sleeps on one with two of her older friends, the second is at the disposal of her other and younger friends. Twice each day she submits to the painting process and for four or five months she is not permitted to work in any way.

"When the time comes for her to be brought to her husband, one of her parents enters her hut at sunrise and pulls her bed out by one leg. If she is not yet spoken for in marriage, then it is her father who pulls the bed into the court. After that the women of her family, bearing parasols, clean clothes, and ornaments, take her to the seashore and beat the paint off her with small supple switches; then they go to the nearest source of fresh water to dress and wash her. Her ankles are loaded with big copper rings, her wrists with bracelets, her neck and waist with all the necklaces of the family, across her breast a colored cloth hangs loosely and the rest of her costume is red: a parasol completes her dress. Then the procession is organized and all her friends, twirling their parasols, sing as they head through the villages toward her house. All along the way the young men of the countryside come to dance before her and present her with some little offering. Then she is taken to her husband and the dancing continues throughout the night."[167]

This is a strange ceremony, is it not, but one with a symbolism so transparent that it is unnecessary to emphasize it. In any case the union of man and woman among the Congolese signifies something other than complaisance to a carnal act. It implies on the contrary the rebirth of the couple to a new life in which the couple is supposed to lose the very memory of their former existence. Even the name of the married couple is changed, so important is it in their new state to be worthy to participate in the mysteries of their tribal religion. Since in this example there seems to be less analogy in form than in essence with the Greco-Roman ceremony, we will advance to a more comparable situation by attending a marriage ceremony in the Sudan among the *Ndogom Habbés* on the plateau of *Bandiagara*. Let us listen to Lieutenant Desplagnes:

"The young men inhabiting the villages on the plateau of *Bandiagara* live apart from their family, forming an association with their comrades of the same age. In turn, with the help of their Clan companions they build a home for themselves and prepare to set up housekeeping. All have a few girl friends of the same age who come to pass the evening with them, exchanging gifts. It is from among these young maidens that they choose their fiancée. In general, the young boys always wait for marriage until their older brothers have established a household so that they need not get their permission to precede them in marriage.

"When the young man has obtained the consent of his fiancée, he goes, accompanied by a friend, to the home of the young girl's father and announces his intention to become his son-in-law. If the future father-in-law accepts, a small gift is given to him, a bundle of wood, game, or fish. Then the day of the ceremony is set, as much as possible on a favorable day of the month that follows the end of the January harvests. Until this time the fiancé, aided by the comrades of his clan, goes to work in the field of his future father-in-law and prepares foods and drinks for the festival. On the eve of the marriage the young man sends 500 cowries

[167] R.E. Dennett, *At the Back of the Black Man's Mind*, [London, 1906], p. 69.

to the young maiden to dress her hair and for perfume, then buys some rice, a sheep, and a lot of millet beer with the help of his association. On the day named, the young men give a great feast in which the whole village takes part except for the future parents-in-law.

"In the middle of the dancing the friends of the husband carry off the fiancée from the companions who were defending her and conduct her to the sound of the tom-tom to the bridegroom's residence. The following morning, the newly married wife takes her jug and goes down to the spring or to the well to show that she is married and has taken charge of the household.

"On the first favorable day which follows the carrying off and the marriage, the new couple bring together all the friends of the husband's clan, then request the oldest man of the village, the Hanna Gara, to come and consecrate the new mansion of the family so as to gain celestial protection for the new couple. This elderly *Hanna Gara* (who, among the tribes living further to the south, takes the title of Hogon), high priest of the village, comes and seats himself dressed in his sacerdotal garb beside the new familial altar on which has been placed the object chosen by the husband as the sign of alliance between his new family and the divinity.

"The husband himself sacrifices the victims, white chickens and sheep; he sprinkles the altar and the sign of alliance with their blood while the old man beseeches Ammo to accord them numerous children, riches, and good fortune. The young wife immediately prepares a meal with the meat of the victims, from which the priest offers the first fruits to the divinity and to the ancestral spirits who will reside around the altar, and all feast in honor of the ancestors and the continuation of the family.

"By this ceremony the married couple are bound together before their ancestors and must be faithful to one another. If the husband should die the wife must mourn for one or two years before remarrying, furthermore if she wished to obtain a divorce she could not do so without a new sacrifice favorably received by the divinity.

"After the banquet all the young men go to greet the father of the husband's family and to proclaim the acceptance of a daughter-in-law into his family. This old man generally offers a gift to the young establishment. Thereafter the new husband goes alone to the home of his father-in-law and brings him an offering for having bestowed his daughter upon him; if he accepts, the father of the young wife must also send a gift to his daughter."[168]

Thus the tribal traditions are perpetuated by marriage according to the ancestral faith in Sudanese populations and, if you wish to have a clearer perception of the dual religious and traditional meaning that the Negro places in the marriage ceremony, we will take as an example a third type of nuptial ceremony among the people of Dahomey whose customs and beliefs have left such a strong imprint on the customs and beliefs of the Haitian people. But in Dahomey the ritual of weddings varies in splendor as to whether the weddings concern private persons or those of royal blood. Although it might be interesting to show you the difference between them I fear it would strain your patience and this is why we shall choose the example of a union of the nobility so that you may see its picturesqueness and deep beauty.

I will borrow from a colonial administrator, from A. Le Hérissé, who witnessed the following festivities of a princely wedding in the kingdom of Dahomey.

"I have preserved a delightful recollection of these festivities," writes Le Hérissé.

"It was evening, in the ancient dwelling place of the kings of Dahomey with the straight lines of their ruins profiled in the light of the moon. On all sides rose shadowy figures; their silence added anew to the melancholy of the premises. The bridegroom Mèvo was a chief of the city of Abomey. So he had invited all of his peers.

"When I arrived these people advanced to greet me. They had their loincloth tied around the waist and bare torso as a sign of respect. We were joined shortly by the bridegroom. He was draped in a white loincloth. Some of his attendants bore calabashes which they deposited at my feet. 'Minister,' he says, 'You are our chief. Deign to accept these liqueurs and offer them to my brothers and my friends. They will taste them only if you authorize them to do so.' The liqueurs are poured: each guest offers his glass to me, saying: 'Here is water! Sin dié!' To each I reply: 'Drink, bô nou.' So is the custom.

"All the princes align themselves according to their age and form a double line before one of the great doors of the palace; the ordinary people gather behind them.

"The bride emerges from the residence of her fathers. She is dressed in a long white loincloth leaving the arms free and attached above her breasts by a white shoulder scarf, her shoulders are covered with *Atiké*,

[168] Lieutenant Desplagnes, *Le plateau central nigérien*, [pp. 215-218].

a white powder smelling like incense, a necklace of pearls encircles her neck, silver rings, from which hang tiny bells, clash as they rustle on her wrists and ankles. She wears a tall conical headdress of white cloth. A white loincloth is spread on the ground; she kneels down and holds up her hands somewhat in front of her. She bows her head and lowers her eyes.

"At her side kneel two women, to her right a representative of the mother of the king Glélé (the grandmother of the chief prince of the dynasty), to the left the oldest daughter of the same king.

"The Méhou, master of ceremonies, calls for the bridegroom three times. The latter moves through the path formed by his guests. He lies down on the ground, covers himself with dust. He rises, takes a few steps, stops, and humiliates himself again. Then he lays on his stomach and, with the aid of his forearms and knees, crawls to within a few yards of his fiancée.

" 'What do you want?' the Méhou asks him.

" 'I wish to take a daughter of "our kings" as spouse.'

" 'Here she is! Approach!'

"The finacé crawls again.

" 'Mèvo,' the Méhou continues; 'we are pleased this has happened, you are the friend of Béhanzin; your father was the friend of Glélé; you are the grandson of Ghèzo. We are pleased that you marry a daughter of our kings.'

" 'Rest assured,' replies Mèvo, 'that your daughter will have an easy life in my hut. She shall not lack anything that a princess should have. If she does wrong, I alone will reproach her!'

"Here Mèvo is interrupted by the Méhounon, the old woman who has authority over the princesses.

" 'If your wife acts badly,' she says, 'it is your right to correct her. However do not strike her too strongly.'

" 'I understand, I will follow your advice. No harm will come to her in my home. In memory of her father, I will call her "Tokenha" (one who counts the pebbles in the river), because "Béhanzin, in the eye of the fish, counts river pebbles." ' [The allusion is probably to the fish that bore her father Béhanzin.]

"The discourse is finished. Mèvo crawls very near and opposite his fiancée.

"The representative of the king's mother takes a calabash filled with water, pours some of the contents on the ground in favor of the ancestors, and presents it to the fiancée then to Mèvo. Both wet their lips. After the same ceremony with a glass of liqueur, the married princess rises and begins to walk, accompanied by her two acolytes and other women in great numbers, her sisters, parents, friends.

"Mèvo precedes her, he clears the way. The cortege emerges into the square before the palace. Immediately guns and an ancient carronade [old cannon] proclaim the new marriage. The tom-toms boom, there are shouts of joy as the young boys give rhythm to their songs with *asan* [musical instrument made of a gourd with a long neck, half-filled with little stones striking the inner surface in cadence].

"The princess, daughter of the panther, walks slowly. (This is an indirect reference to the totem of the royal family.)

"The princess, daughter of the panther, marches slowly.

" 'Come on! Do it!'

"She walks slowly, gracefully as the panther in the forest.

" 'Come on! Do it!'

"The chameleon [allusion to the name of one of the kings, "Akaba" the chameleon] climbs the side of the fromager [silkcotton tree].

" 'Come on! Do it!'

"And in fact, lissome and graceful, the married princess walks staidly, followed by her companions.

"From time to time she calls to her husband: 'My husband,' she recommends, 'throw some cowries to those who accompany me, they are tired.'

"Mèvo then takes handfuls of cowries from some sacks within his reach and throws them into the air, and the gamins pounce upon them.

"The cortege disperses; for a long time into the night I hear shrill cries and the dull sounds of the tom-toms."[169]

I shall add to the various descriptions just given to you that in no part of Africa is marriage performed without the man paying a dowry to the family of the young woman. This dowry varies from tribe to tribe, but it is indispensable insofar as symbolizing the social and economic value of the family with whom one wishes to contract an alliance. For you must understand fully that the woman in Africa is above all the one who perpetuates the race and increases the number of workers in a family. Because of this twofold title she is wealth herself which a family cannot give up without compensation. What if, as [Friedrich] Ratzel says,[170] the

[169] A. Le Hérissé, *L'ancien royaume du Dahomey*, [pp. 218-221].
[170] Cited by [Jerome] Dowd, *The Negro* [*Races*, Vol. II, New York, 1914], p. 131.

king of Ouganda [Uganda] had 7000 wives as proof of his glory and magnificence, the simple mortal who cannot display so much pomp has to be more modest in his tastes. Thus the Bantus of the banana zone near the continental coast, according to [Robert H.] Milligan pay for the dowry of their wives according to the following tariff: 10 goats, 5 sheep, 5 guns, 20 trade-chests, 100 heads of tobacco, 10 hats, 10 mirrors, 5 blankets, 5 pairs of trousers, 2 dozen plates, a certain quantity of cloth and alcohol equivalent to $100, one chair, and one cat.

*

*　　*

Ladies and Gentlemen,

By way of conclusion, there remains nothing left but to draw profitable lessons of ethnological comparisons from those just delivered. First, there are startling analogies that exist between the ancient Greek and Roman customs and those which are still honored today in certain parts of Africa. In addition, our peasant populations on this side of the Atlantic are all imbued with these customs. We recognize on all sides almost the same symbolism which makes the union of man and woman an eminently religious act. We meet again almost the same ritual and the same propitiatory sacrifice which bind young married couples to the gods of the family, the city, or the tribe, almost the same symbolism in choosing white veil and wreath, white loincloth, powder and mask as the exterior signs of initiation to the new life. So today in our world the white veil, the wreath of orange blossoms, the white dress are the emblems of the purity and innocence of the virgin that love initiates into the life of the home. May I say, Gentlemen, that your white tie and your white gloves are perhaps also the exterior signs of purity . . . of intentions that you bring to the home?

In every case, in Greece, in Rome, as everywhere in Africa, the man is the master consecrated by the antiquity of the custom.

As head of the family bearing the responsibility of the group before the gods and ancestors, it is he alone who can authorize the male or female recipient to approach the altar where he sacrifices to the tutelary divinity. Though the thought may be more formal here or there, it is present everywhere, even where it is only in a partial state of survival. Well, now! then it seems to me that a fact of high social importance emerges: if the marriage ceremony assumes such a character of religious solemnity here and there, it also implies at the same time that a note of gravity is being attached to it, it implies that the constitution of the family is closely related to the continuity of divine worship and the well-being of the city or of the tribe. From this mystical character issues the solidity of the familial bonds. It [the family] is, in certain cases of the African regions of which we have spoken, a little community protected by the oldest male who is its natural head. He is the elder. The coming together of these communities in a given space forms the village, obedient to a chief chosen among the elders known for their appreciation of wisdom and experience. Under these conditions can one imagine the power of familial ties formed by such a combination of circumstances? This is what the Africologists never fail to point out. They all say how much the young Negro is attached to his village, to his family group, and particularly to the one who is the living incarnation of it, to his mother.

"Although the Black takes pleasure in traveling," Mgr. Le Roy [pp. 98-99] confirms for us, "he never forgets *his home*, his mother, his brothers. The name of his mother is remembered often faraway, in the gentle songs he repeats to himself in the evening in the caravan encampments, along the small footpaths he travels, and on the great rivers where his canoe glides noiselessly . . .

"Sick, abandoned, wounded, dying, from one end of Africa to the other, in all ranks and at all ages, he persists always in the same strongly touching appeal: 'My mother, my mother!'

"And likewise there is for him no insult more grave, and shall we say more vulgar, than that aimed at the woman who bore him . . ."

Another observer writes, "Whatever may be the opinion that one has of the African, we cannot doubt his love for his mother. Her name, whether she is dead or living, is always on his lips and in his heart. His first thought when he awakens is of his mother, his last thought at night is of her which lulls him to sleep. He confides secrets to her that he will reveal to no one else in the world. He will ask no other human to care for him when he is sick: she prepares his food, his remedies, his ablutions, and she also arranges the matting on which he rests. He takes refuge in her in every distress, knowing well that if the rest of the world turns against him she will remain constant in her love whether he be worthy of it or not.

"And if there is any cause justifying a man for resorting to violence against his fellowman it would be the insult he has heard directed against his mother.

"Among young boys it is the most frequent cause of quarrels and battles. And there is a saying among them that if one sees his mother and his wife in danger of perishing, he must first save his mother because the man who has lost his wife can take another, but he will never again have his mother."[171]

"The benediction of the parents is a sign of happiness, and their malediction the worst of calamities since it pursues the guilty son everywhere, poisoning his life and sowing misfortune around him. I have witnessed such a scene: with her clothes in shreds, features contorted like those of a fury, her thin body trembling uncontrollably, uttering almost inhuman cries, an old woman scraped handfuls of dust from the ground and with her long emaciated arms threw them in the direction of a young man fleeing desperately. And this spectacle was as impressive as the one in the first pages of the Bible, that of Cain being cursed by his mother and by God after the murder of Abel."[172]

The most ferocious Negrophobes will readily admit that such customs reveal the natural benevolence of a race and render the greatest honor to the general morality of the human species. We learn from Moreau de Saint Méry that these splendid virtues were carried to this country by the Negroes brought to populate Saint Domingue through the slave trade when he speaks with compassion of the devotion of the black women for their children.

"We cannot commend sufficiently," he writes, "the sentiments that maternal love has placed in the heart of black women. Never have little children, these frail creatures, had more assiduous care, and this slave who finds the time to bathe her child on every occasion and to clothe him is a respectable being." [Moreau de Saint-Méry, 1797-98, Vol. I, p.41].

But curious thing, in the country the filial devotion changes sharply and is addressed only to another creature: "la marraine" [the godmother]. The colonial historian informs us that, "To blaspheme the godmother of a Negro is to offer him a deadly insult, and often after long quarreling Negroes are heard shouting at each other: he has insulted me, but he has not blasphemed my godmother." [Moreau de Saint-Méry, Vol. I, p.35]. Moreover the godchildren of the same godmother call themselves brothers and sisters and consider themselves as such.

Ah! do you know why in Saint Domingue the godmother has almost replaced the mother in the affection of her child; it is because most often

---

[171] L[eighton] Wilson, *Western Africa* [cited] in Miss M[ary] H. Kingsley. [*West African Studies*, p. 374. Also cited in Le Roy, pp. 99-100.]

[172] Mgr. Le Roy, *La religion des primitifs*, [p. 100].

the child, hardly nubile, is torn from his mother whose service is required for exploitation and that henceforth he only knows his godmother while waiting to become, he too, one among the rest in the world of work. The profound reason for such a cruel disruption lies in the destructive action exercised by slavery on the social economy of the black, just as this monstrous system has been perpetuated for four hundred years by the white race on the black race. Ah! my friends, my heart is not large enough to contain all the love that I experience for all men. I do not thus have any place for hate. But I cannot keep from shuddering with horror at the thought of the carnage and destruction which have been pursued so implacably in this country and on the old continent by those who boast of themselves as being a superior humanity and who now dare to reproach the black race for its savagery and the instability of its institutions.

Yes, for four hundred years the white race, without pity or mercy, has kindled internal warfare in Africa, turning Negro against Negro, pursuing him like game without truce or mercy in order to satisfy its unspeakable traffic in human flesh, destroying all indigenous civilization and culture. For two centuries moreover it urged its boats loaded with human cattle toward the shores of this island already bloodied by the extermination of the Indian, and during two centures of outrageous promiscuity, of corruption, and of degeneration it sullied the age-old chastity of the black woman imposing upon her the brutal rule of concubinage. And so the status of the Negro family has been denigrated, destroyed, annihilated by the most wretched abomination that has ever maculated [stained] the face of the earth, so truly that shortly after 1804 our forefathers, by unflinchingly adopting a legal and religious statute which was so different from their ancient social conception, committed themselves without fear to the most formidable experiment that has been attempted among men.

What has been the result of the last one hundred years? It is visible in the new social form which is slowly emerging from the confusion of mores, beliefs, and customs. It is perhaps at the moment only a chrysalis of which the impatient, the myopic, and the ignorant are indignant, make fun, and are ashamed, but to which philosophers and brave men pay heed, moved and concerned. What will it be in one, two, five hundred years? I do not know. But then what were these nations and peoples who today are corrupted by ostentation, prejudices, and hate, during the nineteen hundred years that a magnificent civilization flourished on the shores of the Nile? What were they? Miserable barbarians, answers history.

"Men pass and it would not be good if they were eternal."

This is why those among us who make a profession of studying the historical and ethnic origins of these people are captivated by the fascinating intuition that its past vouches for its future. But, for mercy's sake, my friends, let us no longer scorn our ancestral heritage. Let us love it, let us consider it as an intangible whole. Let us repeat rather the proud reprimand that the old bard put into the mouth of an inhabitant of Olympus: "There is nothing ugly in the house of my father."

For myself, if I were to thank these young women of Primavera who have been so generous in their hospitality to me today, I would above all express my gratitude to them for having given me the opportunity of interpreting the meaning of our folk-lore and at the same time of benefiting from an hour of social ethics.

To you [the readers] as to them I have nothing more to say and from the depths of my heart I say: Thank you.

Bibliographie

Atlanta (The). — Publications. The Negro Church. A social study, 1903.
Aubin (Eugène). — En Haïti. Paris, 1910.
Audain (D' Léon). — Le mal d'Haïti. Port-au-Prince. 1908.
Bagheot [Bagehot]. — Lois scientifiques du développement des nations. (Paris, 1885).
Boissier. — La fin du paganisme. 2 volumes, Paris.
Boule (Marcellin). — Les hommes fossiles. Paris, 1923.
Bricourt [Bricout] J. — Où en est l'histoire des religions. Paris, 1912.
Bruhnes [Brunhes] (Jean). — Géographie humaine. Paris, 1912.
Cureau (D' A.). — Les sociétés primitives de l'Afrique équatoriale. Paris, 1912.
Delmas et Boll. — La personnalité humaine. Paris, 1922.
Delacroix (H). — La religion et la foi. Paris, 1922. — Le langage et la pensée. Paris, 1924.
Delafosse (Maurice). — Haut-Sénégal-Niger. 3 vol. Paris, 1911. — Les noirs de l'Afrique, 1922. — L'âme nègre, 1922. — Les nègres, 1927.
Deniker. — Les races et les peuples de la terre. Paris, 1926.
Desplagnes (Lieutenant L.). — Le plateau central nigérien. Paris, 1907.
Dodds [Dowd, Jerome]. — The negro races. New-York, 1914.
Dorsainville (D' J.C.). — Vaudou et névroses. Série d'articles publiés dans « Haïti médicale » en 1912 et 1913. Port-au-Prince. — Une explication philologique du Vaudou. Port-au-Prince, 1924.
Dubois (W.E.B.). — The negro. New-York, 1915.
Dubois (Félix). — Tombouctou la mystérieuse. Paris.
Dumas (Georges). — Traité de psychologie. 2 vol. Paris, 1923
Durkheim (Emile). — Les formes élémentaires de la vie religieuse. Paris, 1912.
Dwelshauvers. — L'inconscient. Paris, 1916.
Fleury (D' Maurice de). — L'angoisse humaine. Paris. 1924.

Frazer (Sir James). — Le Rameau d'or. Edition nouvelle abrégée. Traduction de Lady Frazer. Paris, 1923.

Funck-Brentano. — La civilisation et ses lois. Paris, 1876.

Fustel de Coulanges. — La cité antique. Paris.

Guignebert. — Le Christianisme antique. Paris, 1922.

Guilleminot. — Les nouveaux horizons de la science. Paris, 1926.

Hardy. — Vue générale de l'histoire d'Afrique. Paris, 1926.

Janet (Pierre). — L'automatisme psychologique (9ᵉ édition), Paris, 1925. — Les médications psychologiques (3 vol.). Paris, 1919-1925. — Article dans le « Traité de psychologie » de Dumas. — Les Névroses. Paris.

Johnstone [Johnston] (Sir Harry). — Liberia (2 vol.) London, 1906. — The negro in the new world. London, 1900. — The opening up of Africa (publié dans la collection *Home University Library*, 18 vol., sans date d'édition).

Lebon (Dʳ Gustave). — Lois psychologiques du développement des peuples. Paris, 1900. — Les opinions et les croyances. Paris, 1916.

Levy-Bruhl. — Les fonctions mentales dans les sociétés inférieures (2ᵉ éd.). Paris, 1912. — La mentalité primitive. — Paris, 1925.

Leroy (Mgr). — La religion des primitifs. Paris, 1911.

Le Hérissé (A). — L'ancien royaume du Dahomey. Paris, 1911.

Lhérisson (Dʳ Elie). — Etudes sur le Vaudou publiées dans « La Lanterne médicale ». Port-au-Prince.

Leuba (James H.). — Psychologie du mysticisme religieux. Traduction de M. Lucien Herr. Paris, 1920.

Loisy (A.). — La religion d'Israël. Paris, 1908. — Les livres du nouveau Testament. Paris, 1922. — Essai historique sur le sacrifice. Paris, 1920.

Moreau de St-Méry. — Description topographique, physique, civile, politique et historique de Saint-Domingue. Philadelphie, 1797. — La danse. Parme, 1803.

Mauris. — Article du « Mercure de France », nᵒ 531.

Nau (Emile). — Histoire des Caciques d'Haïti. Port-au-Prince, 1894.

Petit. — Histoire Universelle illustrée des peuples. Paris, 1913.

Peytraud. — L'esclavage dans les Antilles françaises avant 1789. Paris, 1897.

Pinard de la Boulaye (S.J.). — Etude comparée des religions. Paris, 1922.

Price (Hannibal). — La réhabilitation de la race noire. Port-au-Prince, 1900.

Reinach (Salomon). — Orpheus. Paris, 1900.

Sebillot. — Le folk-lore. Paris, 1913.

Semple. — Influences of geographic environment on the basis of Ratzel's system of anthropo-geography. New York and London, 1911.

Sergent (Emile). — Traité de pathologie médicale. Tome V, VI, VII, VIII. Neurologie et Psychiatrie.

Stanley. — A travers le continent mystérieux. Paris, 1879. — Dans les ténèbres de l'Afrique.

Söderblom. — Manuel d'histoire des religions. Paris, 1925.

Tauxier. — Le noir du Soudan. Paris, 1911.

Toutée (Colonel). — Du Dahomey au Sahara. Paris, 1907.

Trouillot (D). — Esquisse ethnographique de Vaudou. Port-au-Prince, 1885.

Vallaux (Camille). — Le sol et l'Etat. Paris, 1911.

Woodring. — Géologie de la République d'Haïti. Port-au-Prince, 1925.

Annotated Bibliography

In his bibliography Dr. Jean Price-Mars did not list all of the many sources mentioned in the text of *Ainsi parla l'Oncle*. The following alphabetical arrangement includes those cited in the original bibliography and are marked with an asterisk. The reader will quickly grasp the breadth of thought portraying the diffusion of ever-changing cultures within and between different milieus throughout time and space. These sources serve as the fundamental base of the innovative philosophical argumentation of Price-Mars. There are references to noted classical and early religious and scientific authors as well as to those recognized at the turn of history into the twentieth century, especially in France, England, Germany, the United States, and Haiti.

Some orthographical changes may occur in accordance with established contemporary usage. To aid the modern scholar I have followed, in most cases, the *National Union Catalog Pre-1956 Imprints*. The title of the additional sources will generally appear in the original language of the author and will bear the date of the earliest edition cited by the NUC. Those listed by Price-Mars will usually appear as he noted them, unless additional clarification is needed. Footnote and page numbers in parentheses serve to locate the author in the English text.

*Achille-Delmas, François, and Marcel Boll, *La personnalité humaine*, Paris, E. Flammarion, 1922. (Footnotes 120, 123; also see page 133)

*Atlanta University Publications, No. 8, Du Bois, W.E.B., ed., *The Negro Church*, Atlanta, Georgia, Atlanta University Press, 1903.
A social study. At one point the author traces *Obeah* from its African roots to Voodoo (or Hoodoo) and its degenerative facets in the United States. (Footnote 26)

*Aubin, Eugène, *pseud.* See Descos, Léon Eugène Audin Coullard, *En*

Haiti; planteurs d'autrefois, nègres d'aujourd'hui, Paris, A. Colin, 1910.

Some critics feel he is superficial. He has, however, received awards from the Académie Français. (Footnote 90)

*Audain, Léon, *Le mal d'Haiti:* ses causes et son traitement, Port-au-Prince, J. Verrollot, 1908. Also wrote: *Choses d'Haiti;* explications et conseils par le docteur Léon Audain, Port-au-Prince, L'Abeille, 1916. (Footnote 91)

Avienus, Rufius Festus, *Ora maritima.*

Roman poet and geographer, second half of the 4th century A.D. Though the *Ora maritima* (703 extant iambics), seems compiled mostly from Greek treatises of the 4th and 2nd centuries B.C., it preserves data concerning Greek geographical knowledge and early Greek and Carthaginian voyages in the Atlantic, c. 500 B.C. (See footnote 53 and text, page 78)

Babinski, Joseph François Felix (1857-1932), *Hystérie pithiatisme et troubles nerveux d'ordre réflèxe en neurologie de guerre* par J. Babinski et J. Froment, Paris, Masson, 1917 and *Ma conception de l'hystérie et de l'hypnotisme (pithiatisme)*, Chartres, Durand, 1906.

He is known especially for his work on the maladies of the nervous system; he transformed conceptions on hysteria, limiting it to phenomena that could be provoked or suppressed by suggestion (pithiatisme). He was assistant to Charcot at the Salpêtrière and chief of the neurological clinic at Hôpital de la Pitié, 1890-1927. (See text, pages 119-120)

*Bagehot, Walter, *Lois scientifiques du developpement des nations dans leurs rapports avec les principes de la selection naturelle et de l'héredité*, Paris, G. Balliere, 1885, 5th edition, translation of *Physics and Politics: or, Thoughts on the Application of the Principles of "Natural Selection" and "Inheritance" to Political Society*, London, H.S. King, 1872. (Footnote 44)

Al-Bakrī, Abū 'Ubayd 'Abd Allāh ibn Abd al-'Agēz (1040-1094)

Arabian geographer. *Description de l'Afrique Septentrionale*, Texte arabe revu sur quatre manuscrits . . . et publié . . . par le Baron de Slane, Alger, Imprimerie du gouvernement, 1857. (See text, page 68)

Barth, Auguste, *Les religions de l'Inde*, Paris, G. Fischbacker, 1879. (Quotation, page 36)

The Bible, or, The History of the Old and New Testaments.
    Letter to the Hebrews, Chap. I. (Footnote 61)
    II Samuel, Chap. VI, 12-16. (Footnote 97)
    II Kings, Chap. III, 15-16. (Footnote 97)
    St. Paul, First Epistle to the Corinthians, Chap. XIV. (Footnote 114)
    Exodus XXII, 28, 29. (Footnote 128)
    Leviticus XVIII, 6, 7, and following. (Footnote 138)
    Numbers XXVIII. (Footnote 139)
    I Kings, XVI, 34. (Footnote 142)

Bleek, Wilhelm Heinrich Immanuel, *Comparative Grammar of South African Languages*, 1867. (Footnote 23)
    There are different issues published 1862-69, London, Trübner & Co.; Cape Town, J.C. Juta.

Boissier, Gaston, La fin du paganisme, 2 vol., Paris, Hachette, 1891. Seven editions or more. (Footnote 149)

Boll, Marcel. See Achille-Delmas, François.

*Boule, Marcellin, *Les hommes fossiles;* éléments de paleontologie humaine, Paris, Masson et cie., 1923. (Footnotes 36, 37, 38)
    There is an English translation by Jessie Elliot Ritchie and James Ritchie, Edinburgh, 2nd edition, Oliver and Boyd, 1923.

Bovet, _____, "La Glossolalie," *Revue d'Histoire des Religions*, 1901. (See text, quotation, page 129)
    Unable to locate article in source indicated above as mentioned in Delacroix, (Footnote 118). The author is probably Pierre Bovet, who wrote on such subjects as bilingualism, religious education in the schools, and on the psychology of William James.

*Bricout, Joseph, *Ou en est l'histoire des religions?*, 2 vol., Paris, 1912. (Footnotes, 17, 67)

Brosse, Charles de, *De culte des dieux fétiches ou Parallèle de l'ancienne religion de l'Egypte avec la religion actuelle de Nigritie*, Paris, 1760. (Footnote 59)

Presented to *Académie des Inscriptions* in 1757, judged too incautious and published anonymously three years later.

Brown, John Porter, *The Dervishes*, or, Oriental spiritualism, Philadephia, J.P. Lippincott, 1868. (Footnote 117)

Brown, John Stafford. See Woodring, Wendell P.

*Brunhes, Jean, *La géographie humaine*, Paris, 1912. First edition, Paris, F. Alcan, 1910. (Footnote 50)
There are many English translations.

Burbank, Wilbur S. See Woodring, Wendell P.

Burnouf, Eugène, *Introduction à l'histoire de buddhisme indien*, Paris, Imprimerie royalle, 1844. (See text, page 36)

Burr-Reynaud, F., Haitian poet, 1866-1946. (See text, pages 178, 180-181)
Author of such poems as *Ascensions, Au fil de l'heure tendre*, and the *Poèmes quisqueyens*. He collaborated with D.V. Hippolyte in *Anacaona*, a dramatic poem in three acts, presented in 1927, and published Port-au-Prince, N. Telhomme, 1941.

Camus, Paul. See Deny, Gaston Georges.

Cassius Dio Cocceianus. Ordinarily known as Dio Cassius or Dion Cassius, Greek historian, c. 155-235 A.D., *Historia romana* (80 books, many editions, also in English). (See text, page 150)

Charcot, Jean Martin (1825-1893). His most important work is *Leçons sur les maladies du système nerveux faites à la Salpêtrière*, Paris, A. Delahaye, 1872, translated into English by George Sigerson, London, 1877.
Father of clinical neurology. Developed in 1880 the world's greatest center for clinical neurological research. Classified and gave first accurate descriptions of such diseases as multiple sclerosis. Studies undertaken in later life on hysteria and hypnotism were widely criticized and observations later discredited. But his description and method of diagnosis proved to be a scientific background for development of modern psychiatry. Sigmund Freud, his pupil, credited him with contributions to early psychoanalytic formulations on hysteria. (See text, pages 119, 163)

Charlevoix, Pierre François Xavier de (1682-1761), *Histoire de l'Isle espagnole ou de Saint-Domingue*, 2 volumes, Paris, F. Barois, 1730-31. (Text, page 52)
A standard work on early San Domingo (entire island). There is controversy as to manuscripts used. See Le Pers, Jean Baptiste.

Chesnutt, Charles Waddell. See text, page 175, and footnote [17].

*Cureau, Adolphe Louis, *Les sociétés primitives de l'Afrique équatoriale*, Paris, A. Colin, 1912. (Footnotes, 32, 33, 47, 63)

*Delacroix, Henri Joachim. *Les operations intellectuels* in Georges Dumas, *Traité de psychologie*, Vol. II, Paris, F. Alcan, 1923-24, (Footnote 66); *La religion et la foi*, Paris, F. Alcan, 1922, (Footnotes 115, 118, 119); *Le langage et la pensée*, Paris, F. Alcan, 1924, (Footnote 113 and quotations, pages 124-125).

*Delafosse, Maurice. *Haut-Sénégal-Niger:* le pays, les peuples, les langues, l'histoire, les civilizations, 3 vol., Paris, 1911, (Footnotes 25, 42, 43, 69, 141); *Les Noirs de l'Afrique*, Paris, Payot, 1922, (Footnotes 35, 54, 56, 63, 70); *L'âme nègre*, Paris, Payot, 1922; *Les nègres*, Paris, Editions Rieder, 1927.
Negroes of Africa, translation by F. Fligelman, Washington, D.C., Associated Publishers, 1931, is from *Les Noirs de l'Afrique* (historical) and *Civilizations Négro-Africaines* (ethnological), 1925.

Delorme, Demesvar (1831-1901). Haitian author. Wrote such works as *La misère au sein des richesses*; Reflèxions diverses sur Haiti, Paris, E. Dentu, 1873; *Les Théoriciens au pouvoir*; Causeries historiques, Paris, H. Plon, 1870. (Text, pages 176-178)

*Deniker, Joseph, *Les races et les peuples de la terre*; elements d'anthropologie et d'ethnographie, Paris, 1926, (Footnotes 39, 40); English translation: *The Races of Man*; an outline of anthropology and ethnography, New York, Charles Scribner's Sons, 1900, from the original French edition, 1900.

Dennett, Richard Edward, *At the Back of the Black Man's Mind*, or Notes on the kingly office in West Africa, London, Macmillan, 1906. (Footnote 167)

Deny, Gaston Georges, and Paul Camus, *Les folies intermittentes: la psychose maniaque-dépressive,* Paris, Baillière, 1907. (Footnote 112)

*Desplagnes, Lieutenant Augustin Marie Louis, *Le plateau central nigérien,* Paris, Emile Larose, 1907. (Footnotes 35, 40, 53, 71, 72, 73, 75, 76, 136, 168)

Doret, Frédéric, Haitian author. *Pour amuser nos tout petits, initiation aux fables de la Fontaine, avec une introduction sur la prononciation Créole,* Port-au-Prince, Haiti, 1924; *Le petit syllabaire haitien, basé sur la langue populaire d'Haiti,* Port-au-Prince, Chez l'auteur, 1905, H. Deschamps, 1945.

    The author emphasizes the use of Creole in schools, rather than just French. He endorses the precept of Pestalozzi — to proceed from the known to the unknown, (text, pages 178-180). *Le petit syllabaire haitien* was adopted by the Department of Public Instruction in the primary schools. Doret was also founder and editor of the weekly *Petit Revue,* usually 14-15 pages in length.

*Dorsainvil, Justin Chrysostome (1880-1942), a prominent Haitian physician and philosopher, interested in Haitian historical, political, and social problems. His most important works are: *Vodou et névrose,* Port-au-Prince, La Presse, 1931, which is a series of articles, some of which appeared in *Haiti Médicale,* 1912-1913, and also included *Une explication philologique du Vodou,* 1924; *Manuel d'histoire d'Haiti,* Port-au-Prince, Henri Deschamps, 1934; *Psychologie haitienne; vodou et magie,* Port-au-Prince, Telhomme, 1937.

    Dorsainvil attempts a scientific explanation of Vodou which is psychological and based on the authority of race. He attaches Vodou to primitive religions, believes that man has both a physical and psychological nature, and stresses that each race has its own talents. It is perfectly possible, he says, that certain individuals in certain races are better endowed for abstract thought than in other races. Therefore a people, four-fifths of whom have a Voudou mentality, cannot hope to become a people of purely French culture. (Footnotes 78,88, 99 and text, pages 117-119)

*Dowd, Jerome, *The Negro Races*, Vol. I, New York, Macmillan, 1907, Vol. II, 1914. (Footnote 170)
A sociological study of the African peoples.

Drouin de Bercy, *De Saint Domingue, de ses guerres, de ses révolutions, de ses ressources, et des moyens à prendre pour y établir la paix et l'industrie*, Paris, Hocquet, 1814. Also in J. Grouvel, *Faites historiques sur St.-Domingue depuis 1786 jusqu'en 1805*, Paris, Renard, 1814. (Footnote 85)

*Dubois, Felix, *Tombouctou la mystérieuse*, Paris, 1898. English translation by Diana White, New York, Longmans, Green, 1896. (Footnote 41)

*Du Bois, W.E.B., *The Negro*, N.Y., Oxford University Press, 1915; *The Negro Church, A Social Study*, Atlanta Publications, No. 8, W.E.B. Du Bois, ed., Atlanta, Atlanta University Press, 1903. (Footnotes 26, 58; also text, page 175 and footnote [17])

Dubois de Berne. Most probably Paul Charles Dubois (1848-1918), Swiss neuropathologist in the city of Bern. Wrote such works as *Les psychonéuroses et leur traitement moral*, 1904. Founder of Schweitzer Archiv für Neurologie und Psychiatrie. (Footnote 100)
Did research on neuroses and their treatment, electrotherapy; defined persuasion as distinct from hypnosis and suggestion; created and defined the term,psychoneurosis.

*Dumas, Georges, *Traité de Psychologie*, 2 vol., Paris, F. Alcan, 1923-24, (Footnote 66); "La pathologie mentale," *Traité de psychologie* II, 1923, (Footnote 105).

Dupré, _____ (Text page 133). Probably Ernest Pierre Dupré (1862-1921), French physician who identified several pathological conditions including mythomania, puerilism. Wrote *La mythomanie: études psychologique et médico-légale au mensonge et la fabulation morbide*, Paris, Impr. typographique, J. Gainche, 1905; *Pathologie de l'imagination et de l'émotivité*, Paris, Payot, 1925.

*Durkheim, Emile, *Les formes élémentaires de la vie religieuse*, Paris, F. Alcan, 1912; translated into English by Joseph Ward Swain,

N.Y., Macmillan, 1915. (Footnote 16, [9], and text pages 36-38; footnotes 21, 116)

*Dwelshauvers, Georges, *L'inconscient*, Paris, E. Flammarion, 1916. (Footnote 116)

Essai sur l'esclavage et observations sur l'état présent des colonies des Européens en Amérique in Moreau de Méry collection (Arch. col. F, Paris). Attributed to Lafond de Ladébat, Barbé de Marbois, or Billaud Varennes. (Footnote 84)

*Fleury, Paul Louis Edouard Maurice de, *L'angoisse humaine*, Paris, Les Editions de France, 1924. (Footnote 122)

*Frazer, Sir James George, *Le rameau d'or, édition abrégée, nouvelle traduction* par Lady Frazer, Paris, P. Geuthner, 1923, or the *Golden Bough*, a study in magic and religion, originally published 1890, London, Macmillan, 2 vol. (Footnotes 94, 129); *Adonis*, étude de religions orientales comparées, traduction par Lady Frazer, Paris, P. Geuthner, 1921, (Footnote 146).

Frobenius, Leo, *The Voice of Africa*, being an account of the travels of the German inner African exploration expedition in the years 1910-1912, 2 vol., translation by Rudolf Blind, London, Hutchinson, 1913, of *Und Afrika Sprach*, Berlin, Vita, 1912-1919, 4 vol.

German ethnologist (1873-1938) who helped establish scientific approach to ethnology; developed concept of culture circles; specialist on primitive tribes of Africa. (Footnote 58)

*Funck-Brentano, Théophile, *La civilisation et ses lois; morale sociale*, Paris, E. Plon, 1876. (Footnote 44)

*Fustel de Coulanges, Numa Denis, *La cité antique*, Paris, 1864. English translation by Willard Small, *The Ancient City:* a study on religious laws and institutions of Greece and Rome, Boston, Lee and Shepard, 1874. There are at least 27 editions of this work, by 1948. (Footnote 166)

Gaultier, Jules de, *Le Bovarysme;* la psychologie dans l'oeuvre de Flaubert, Paris, Société du Mercure de France, 1902; "René Quinton," *Mercure de France*, 181 (August 1, 1925), 695-702. (See Preface, page 8)

The term "collective bovaryism" was first coined by the

French philosopher Jules de Gaultier (1858-1942). The article on René Quinton is relevant because Price-Mars cited the scientist's theory of the origin of cellular life and the law of intellectual constancy to refute the racial theories of Gustave Le Bon.

*Guignebert, Charles Alfred Honoré, *Le Christianisme antique*, Paris, E. Flammarion, 1922. (Footnote 148)

*Guilleminot, Hyacinthe, *Les nouveaux horizons de la science;* sa vie, ses fonctions, ses origines, sa fin, Paris, 1926, 4 vol. (Footnote 121)

Halévy, Elie, *Histoire du peuple anglais au XIXe siècle*, Paris, Hachette, 1913, 4 vol. Also translated into English, 1949. *Le peuple anglais*, Vol. I, appeared in 1912. (Footnote 119)

*Hardy, Georges, *Vue générale de l'histoire d'Afrique*, Paris, 1926. (Footnote 55)

Hearn, Lafcadia, *Esquisses Martiniquaises*, Paris, *Mercure de France*, 1924. This is a translation by Marc Logé of "Martinique sketches" which appeared in the author's *Two years in the French West Indies*, New York, Harper, 1890. (Text, page 172)

Herodotus (c. 485-425 B.C.), Greek historian, born in Halicarnassus. One of best English translations of the histories of Herodotus is by John Enoch Powell, Oxford, 1949 (one of many). (Text, pages 63, 78-79)

Hislop, Alexander, *The Two Babylons*, or the papal worship proved to be the worship of Nimrod and his wife, 2nd edition, Edinburgh, 1858. In Footnote 93 Prince-Mars gives the French translation: *Les deux Babylones*, Paul Monnerat, ed., Paris. According to the *Catalogue général de la bibliotheque nationale*, it was translated by J.E. Cerisier, 1886.

Houdas, Octave Victor. See al-Sadi, 'Abd al-Rahman iban 'Abd Allah.

Ibn-Batuta, *pseud.* See el-Ouazzani, M.A. el-Mehdi (1304-1377), Arabian geographer who left description of customs and ceremonies in the court of the Malis. There are many translations in different languages, such as *Voyages d'Ibn Batoutah*, 4 vol., Paris, Impr. impériale, 1853-1858, or *Travels in Asia and Africa — 1325-1354*, translated and selected by H.A.R.

Gibb, London, G. Routledge and sons 1929. (Text, page 71)

al-Idrisi (1100-1166), Arabian geographer. *Description de l'Afrique et de l'Espagne*. Texte arabe pub. pour la premiere fois d'après les man. de Paris et d'Oxford avec une traduction, de notes et un glossaire, par R. Dozy et M.J. de Goeje, Leyden, E.J. Brill, 1866. (Text, page 68)

Innocent, Antoine, *Mimola*, ou, L'histoire d'une cassette; petit tableau de moeurs locales, Port-au-Prince, E. Malvál, 1906. (Footnote 89, 131, 137)

James, William, *Principles of Psychology*, New York, H. Holt, 1890, 2 vol; *The Varieties of Religious Experience*, New York, Longmans, Green, 1902; *Pragmatism — A New Name for Some Old Ways of Thinking*, 1907.
　　American psychologist and philosopher; considered to be America's most influential psychologist; established psychology on a physiological basis; initiated first psychological laboratory in America, 1876; in the James-Lange theory of emotion, he anticipates behavioral psychology; one of the originators of pragmatism. (Quotation and text, page 126; see *Varieties of Religious Experience*, particularly Lecture XX)

*Janet, Pierre, *L'automatisme psychologique*, Paris, F. Alcan, 1925 (many editions); *Les médications psychologiques*, 3 vol., Paris, F. Alcan, 1919, 1925; *Les Nevroses*, Paris, E. Flammarion, 1909.
　　French physician and psychologist (1859-1947), student of Charcot; founder of automatic psychology; extensive research on mental pathology hysteria; first to describe psychasthenia. (Footnotes 105, 147)

Johnson, James Weldon. See text, page 175 and footnote [17].

*Johnston, Sir Harry Hamilton, *Liberia*, 2 vol., London, Hutchinson, 1906; *The Negro in the New World*, London, Methuen, 1910; *The Opening up of Africa*, London, Williams and Norgate, 1911 (Home University Library of Modern Knowledge, No. 18).
　　British explorer; also vice or acting consul in Cameroons, Niger Coast Protectorate, and Mozambique. (Footnotes 5, 35, 38, 43 49, 51, 57, 95; also text, page 204)

Kingsley, Mary Henrietta, *West African Studies*, London, Macmillan, 1899. (Footnote 171; the quotation is by Leighton Wilson, *Western Africa*, 1856)

Koelle, Sigismund Wilhelm, *Narrative of Expedition into the Vy country of West Africa, and the Discovery of a System of Syllabic Writing, recently invented by the Natives of the Vy tribe*, London, Seeleys, 1849; *Outlines of a Grammar of the Vei language, together with a Vei-English Vocabulary*, London Church Missionary House, 1953. (See text page 81)

Labat, Jean Baptiste (1663-1738), *Nouveau voyage aux isles de l'Amérique*, six vol., Paris, P.F. Giffart, 1722. (Text, page 148)

Lasègue, _____. See Ernest Charles Lasègue (1816-1883), French physician; author of many books and articles on dyspepsia, mental and nervous disorders, diabetes. Described persecution mania (Lasègue's disease), 1852; sign of Lasègue (nervous disorder); syndrome of Lasègue (syndrome in hysteria). (Quotation, page 119)

*Le Bon, Gustave, *Les lois psychologiques de l'évolution des peuples*, Paris, Alcan, 1894, or in English, *The Psychology of Peoples*, London Edition, 1898; *Les opinions et les croyances; genèse-évolution*, 1916, (12th edition, original 1911); *La psychologie des foules*, 1895. (Footnote 82)
    French social psychologist, physician; formulated a collective and racist social psychology which emphasized the inferiority of the black man and condemned any hybridization with the superior white. From the moment that Price-Mars read *Les Lois* . . . in 1900 while attending medical school in Paris, he did not desist from attacking these theories. When Price-Mars revealed his objections to Le Bon in a private conversation the latter asked him why he did not write about his country. This became the vocation of Price-Mars.

*Le Hérissé, A., *L'ancien royaume du Dahomey: moeurs, religion, histoire*, Paris, Larose, 1911. (Footnote 28, 77, 130, 169).

Leibnitz, Gottfried Wilhelm, Baron von (1646-1716), German mathematician, physicist, philosopher. Often regarded as forerunner of modern symbolic logic, as he endeavored to develop a universal

symbolism and attendant algebra so that one might calculate
the truth of any proposition. Claims to have invented calculus
and conservation of vis viva (Kinetic energy) independently
of Newton. Adopted rationalistic approach to science. (Text,
page 13)

Leo Africanus, Joannes (1494?-1552). Wrote about Africa in Arabic;
published in French, in 1556. The English translation is: *The
History and Description of Africa*, written by Al-Hassan ibn-
Mohammed al-Wezaz al-Fasi, a Moor, baptized as Giovanni
Leone, but better known as Leo Africanus. Done into English
in year 1600 by John Pory and now edited, London, for the
Hakluyt Society, 1896, 3 vol., (Text, page 70)

Le Pers, Jean Baptiste (1675-1735), *La tragique histoire des filibustiers;*
histoire de Saint Domingue et de l'île de la Tortue, repaires
des filibustiers, écrite vers 1715 par le Rev. P. Lepers, recueillie
et adaptée par Pierre Barnard Berthelot, Paris, 1921 (6th
edition).

See Charlevoix, who wrote his work from the manuscripts
of Le Pers, Jesuit missionary to St. Domingue; parts of original
manuscript in la Bibliothèque nationale de Paris. (Text, page
52)

*Le Roy, Alexandre, *La religion des primitifs*, Paris, 1911 (many editions), English translation, *The Religion of the Primitives* by
Rev. Newton Thompson, 1922. (Footnotes 18, 23, 61, 62, 63,
172; text, pages 207, 215)

*Leuba, James H., *Psychologie du mysticism religieux*, French translation by Lucien Herr, Paris, Alcan, 1925, of *The Psychology
of Religious Mysticism*, London, New York, 1925.

Leuba, a psychologist, was born in Switzerland, 1868,
came to U.S. in 1887; professor of psychology, Bryn Mawr
College, 1889-1933, and emeritus since 1933. (Footnotes 116,
117)

*Lévy-Bruhl, Lucien, *Les fonctions mentales dans les sociétés inférieures*,
Paris, F. Alcan, 1912 (2nd edition, original 1910), or *How
Natives Think*, translated by Lilian A. Clare, New York, Alfred
A. Knopf, 1925; *La mentalité primitive*, Paris F. Alcan, 1925
(original 1922), translation into English by Lilian A. Clare,

Boston, Beacon Press, 1923 as *Primitive Mentality*. (Footnotes 19, 64, 65, 68)

Levy-Bruhl, French philosopher, psychologist and sociologist, and professor at the Sorbonne, is best known for his pioneering efforts in the psychology of primitive peoples. As a follower of Durkheim he sought to apply the theory of collective representations to an interpretation of primitive mentality, coining the expressions — pre-logical, law of participation, mystical. Price-Mars disagrees with him (pages 90-91), as would many others, and Levy-Bruhl himself later rejects the term *pre-logical*. In research methods he tried to demonstrate the unity of the human mind in space and time, thus taking, in anthropology, the comparative rather than the evolutionary or the philosophical approach.

*Lherisson, Elie, Haitian author publishing studies in *La Lanterne Médicale*, Port-au-Prince, Haiti. (Footnote 92)

Logre, Benjamin Joseph, "Etat mental des hystériques," in *Psychiatrie*, Vol. I, *Traité de pathologie médicale et de thérapeutique appliquée*, editors, Emile Sergent, L. Ribadeau-Dumas, L. Babonneix, Paris, Maloine et Fils, 1921 --, (Footnotes 104, 111)

*Loisy, Alfred Firmin, *La religion d'Israël*, Paris, Letousey, 1908, English translation, 1910; *Les livres du nouveau Testament*, Paris, 1922; *Essai historique sur le sacrifice*, Paris, E. Nourry, 1920. (Footnotes 61, 96, 125, 127, 128, 140, 143, 146)

Lucretius Carus, Titus, (c. 98 B.C. — 55 B.C.), *De Rerum Natura* (On the Nature of Things). There are many translations.

As a disciple of Epicurus he presents a mechanical view of the universe, i.e., that all things are composed of atoms and that the world had emerged from chaos by chance. He advocated reason over superstition. (Footnote 18)

Machault, _____ de, French colonial administrator. Papers probably in eighteenth century French colonial archives. (Quotation, pages 53-54)

Marc, Lucien François, *Le pays Mossi*, Paris, E. Larose, 1909. (Footnote 42)

Marcelin, Frederic, *Thémistocle Epaminondas Labasterre*, petit récit haitien, Paris, P. Ollendorff, 1901; *La vengeance de Mama, roman haitien,* Paris, P. Ollendorff, 1902; *Marilisse, roman haitien,* Paris, P. Ollendorff, 1903; *Questions haitiennes,* Paris, J. Kugelman, 1891, and many others.

A Haitian author of considerable talent especially in his novels in which he depicts local customs successfully and particularly in the realm of political life. (See text, pages 178, 181-182)

Matthew, William Diller, "Climate and Evolution," *Annals of the New York Academy of Science,* XXIV, February 18, 1915, pp. 171-318. (Footnote 36)

*Mauris,.Jules, "Le Procès de la Vierge qui pleure," *Mercure de France,* August 1, 1920, No. 531, pp. 673-714. (Footnote 145)

There is also a second article by Mauris: "Le second Procès de la Vierge qui pleure," *Mercure de France,* July 15, 1927, No. 698, pp. 277-318.

Milligan, Robert H., *The Fetish Folk of West Africa,* New York, Fleming H. Revell, 1912. (Quotation, page 214)

Monteil, Charles Victor, *Soudan français: monographic de Djénné, cercle et ville,* Tulle, Impr. de J. Mazeyrie, 1903. (Text, page 96)

*Moreau de Saint-Méry, Médéric Louis de, *Description topographique, physique, civile, politique et historique de la partie française de l'isle Saint-Domingue,* Philadelphia, Chez l'auteur; Paris, Chez Dupont, 1797-98, two volumes.

Dr. Price-Mars made many references to Saint-Méry. The Creole version and the French translation of *Lisette* on pages 29, 31 are from Vol. I, 65-66; footnote 24, page 51 is from vol, I, 32; reference to Saint-Méry on page 52, footnote 84 on page 108, and the quotations on pages 109 through 112 are from Vol. I, 46-50; reference, page 134 from Vol. I, 50; reference, page 137 from Vol. I, 50; reference, page 153 from Vol. I, 28; quotation, page 216 from Vol. I, 41; quotation, page 216 from Vol. I, 35.

*Nau, Emile, *Histoire des caciques d'Haiti,* Port-au-Prince, T. Bouchereau, 1855.

Baron Nau is listed only in the bibliography of Price-Mars.

Oldenberg, Herrmann, *Le Bouddha, sa vie, sa doctrine, sa communauté,* translated from the German, 1934. Original German publication, *Buddha, Sein leben, seine lehre, seine gemeinde,* was published in Berlin, W. Hertz, 1881. (Quotation, page 36)

Ovidius Naso, Publius (43 B.C.-c. A.D. 18), *Metamorphoses,* 15 books. Latin poet born near Rome who has had an enormous influence on European poety from the Augustan period to modern times. (Footnote 93)

Pechuël — Loesche, Eduard, *Die Loango-Expedition* ausgesandt von der Deutschen gesellschaft zur erforschung aequatorial-Africas, 1873-1876, Leipzig, P. Frohberg, 1879-1907. (Footnote 68)

Pestalozzi, Johann Heinrich (1746-1827). Most of his works, written in German, have been translated into many languages, as *How Gertrude Teaches her Children* (1801) and *The Swan Song* (1826). (See text, page 179)

Pestalozzi was a Swiss theorist and reformer widely acclaimed in his days as "the teacher of the young." He probably succeeded more than any other man, even Rousseau, in definitively changing the old pattern of teaching primary education. He particularly attacked neglect of education for the poorest children, "superficial verbosity" in recitation, and flogging for poor recitation. Pestalozzi believed that personality or the "inner dignity" of every individual was sacred, that love and kindness were the basic foundation on which to develop physical and intellectual powers, that education naturally began in the home, and that "life shapes us and the life that shapes us is not a matter of words but action." His fundamental doctrine of *Anschauung* (direct concrete observation) is often inadequately expressed by "sense perception" or "object lessons." It is from this doctrine that his followers have developed the well-known principles as from the known to the unknown, from the simple to the complex, from the concrete to the abstract.

*Petit, Maxime, *Histoire de France illustrée,* Paris, Larousse, 1909, 2 vol., and other editions; *Histoire générale des peuples de l'antiquité à nos jours,* publié sous la direction de Maxime Petit, Paris, Larousse, 1925-1926, 3 vol. (Footnote 27)

Pierre de Vaux or Valdo (1140?-1217), a rich Lyonese merchant gave up his wealth to his heirs and the poor and traveled throughout the surrounding area recommending penitence and poverty. He translated the Bible into the vernacular and created a sect called the *Poor Men of Lyons* or *Vaudois*. Its doctrine accepted Holy Scripture as the only source of belief and advised that the laity had the same rights as priests and the duty to instruct and evangelize their brothers. Although banned by the Council of Verona in 1184, this dogma spread through France, German states, Bohemia, and Poland.

While most historians agree that the name of *Vaudois* or *Waldenses* is derived from Pierre de Vaux or Valdo, actually the Provençal *vaux, vaudois* simply means valleys or inhabitants of valleys and quite often is a referent to the Protestant valleys in the Piedmont and Dauphiné regions of France, and therefore could include groups known as Josephists, Henricians, Petrobruisians. *Vaudois* is also the name given to sorcerers in some French provinces.

Eon de Lestoile, a fanatic and heretic Breton, lived during this same period. He imagined himself to be the Son of God, the one who must judge the living and the dead.

*Peytraud, Lucien Pierre, *L'esclavage aux Antilles françaises avant 1789* d'après des documents inédits des archives coloniales, Paris, Hachette, 1897.

Peytraud contains references, pp. xvi, 187, and 447, to *Essai sur l'esclavage et observations sur l'état présent des colonies des Européens en Amérique*, without the name of an author. The paper is in the collection of Moreau de Saint-Mery, Arch. Col, F, 129, Paris. (Footnote 84)

*Pinard de la Boullaye, Henry, *L'étude comparée des religions;* essai critique, 2 vol., Paris, G. Beauchesne, 1922. See Charles de Brosse. (Footnote 59)

Powell, John Wesley, *Fourteenth Annual Report of the Bureau of American Ethnology,* 1892/93, Vol. 2, pages 948-952, Washington, Government Printing Office, 1896. See also John Porter Brown or James H. Leuba. (Footnote 117)

Preville, Louis Armand Barbier de, *Les sociétés africains;* leur origine, leur évolution, leur avenir, Paris, Firmin-Didot, 1894. (Text, page 57)

*Price, Hannibal, *De la réhabilitation de la race noire par la république d'Haiti*, Port-au-Prince, J. Verrollot, 1900 (posthumous). Also wrote, *The Haitian Question*, or *La question haitienne* (par Verax, a pseudonym), New York, L. Weiss, 1891.

Price (1841-1893), essayist, historian, diplomat was appointed Minister of Haiti to Washington, D.C. in 1890; he was previously a member of the Haitian legislative assembly. He was one of the earlier Haitian writers who emphasized pride in being a Haitian and a Negro. The name "Price" was given to Dr. Jean Price-Mars at his birth by his father, also a Haitian congressman, in honor of his colleague. (Footnote 87)

Price-Mars, Dr. Jean, *La vocation de l'élite*, Port-au-Prince, Edmund Chenet, 1919; "Le phénomène et le sentiment religieux chez les nègres de Saint-Domingue," *Bulletin de la Société d' histoire*, Vol. II (*Revue de la Société d'Histoire et de Géographie d'Haiti*), 1925. (Footnote 81)

La vocation de l'élite, containing lectures delivered in 1906, 1907, and 1917, focuses on awakening the morale of the elites who were immobilized by the American Occupation. He chastized them for conceiving of themselves as "colored Frenchmen" instead of acting "as Haitians." As Haitian elites they should be leading and guiding their countrymen in preserving their historical traditions and social heritage as well as being proud of their indigenous culture.

Puymaigre, Théodore Joseph Boudet, Comte de, *Folk-lore*, Paris, E. Perrin, 1885. (Quotation, page 12)

Quatrefages de Bréau, Jean Louis Armand de (1810-1892), *L'espèce humaine*, Paris, G. Baillière, 1877, English translation, 1879; *Crania ethnica*, Paris, G. Baillière et fils, 1872-1882; *Les Pygmées* J.B. Baillière, 1887, translated by Frederick Starr, London, Macmillan, 1895. There are many other works. (Text, page 60)

Quatrefages de Bréau, French naturalist, ethnologist, physician, and biologist, did extensive work in human anthropology. He described the parietal angle known as

Quatrefages's angle; made accurate observations and descriptions of zoological phenomena; refuted the view that pygmies represented a reversal to an earlier and inferior Negro type.

Quinton, René. See Jules de Gaultier.

Ratzel, Friedrich (1844-1904), *Völkerkunde*, Leipzig, Bibliographisches Institut, 1855-88, 3 vol. The English translation, *History of Mankind* is from the second German edition and by A.J. Butler, New York, Macmillan, 1896-98. (Footnote 170 and text, page 213)

Réclus, Jean Jacques Elisée (1830-1905), *Nouvelle géographie universelle*, Paris, Hachette, 1876-94, 20 vol., or *The Universal Geography*, ed. by E.G. Rowenstein, London, S.J. Virtue, 1878-94. This work won the Gold Medal, Paris Geography Society, 1892. There are other works as *La terre; description des phénomènes de la vie du globe*, Paris, L. Hachette, 1868-69, 2 vol., also translated into English. (Text, page 57)

Réclus is one of the outstanding French geographers of the 19th century. In 1871 he was sentenced to imprisonment in a penal colony for life because of his connection with the Paris Commune, but because of the intercession of many reputable scientists he was merely banished and was granted amnesty in 1879.

*Reinach, Salomon (1858-1932). One of his most famous works is *Orpheus; histoire générale des religions*, Paris, A. Picard, 1900. There are over 40 French editions as well as the various English translations by Florence Simmonds.

Reinach was a French archaeologist and anthropologist who had made important archaeological discoveries in the Mediterranean areas, especially in Greece and the Greek islands. He was well known for his lectures on art and his interpretation of the history of religion. (Footnotes 15, 20, and 146)

al-Sadi,'Abd al-Rahman iban 'Abd Allah (1596-1656?), author of Arabian documents relative to the history of the Sudan: *Tarikh-es-Soudan*, edited by O. Houdas with the collaboration of Edm. Benoist, or *La Chronique du Soudan*, translated by Octave Victor Houdas, Paris, E. Leroux, 1898-1900. (Footnote 41)

St. John, Sir Spenser Buckingham, *Hayti or The Black Republic*, London, Smith, Elder, 1884, or *Haïti ou la république noire*, translated by J. West, Paris, E. Plon, Nourret, 1886. (Footnote 144)

St. John represented Great Britain as minister and consul-general in Haiti from 1863 intermittently to 1884. When the book appeared it was heavily criticized by the Haitians. St. John not only considered Haitians incapable of self-government but more importantly he called their religion, the traditional *Vodun*, merely fetish worship which included cannibalistic practices. Like many nineteenth century observers St. John had little understanding of this religion. The book was reprinted by Frank Cass, London, 1971; this is a reprint of the second edition (1889) which has additional information on *Vodun* and a "spirited defence of his objectivity and lack of prejudice." It is his chronicle of the different regimes of Emperor Faustin I, General Fabre Nicolas Geffrard, Major Sylvain Salnave, General Nissage Saget, General Michel Domingue, and General Boisrond Canal which makes the book historically significant.

Seabrook, William Buehler, *The Magic Island*, London, Harrap, 1929 and New York, Blue Ribbon Books, 1929. The articles to which Price-Mars referred were: "An Ecstasy of Whirling," (How the Dervishes of Tripoli seek Religious Exaltation through Rhythm), *Asia*, XXVII, January, 1927, pp. 21-27 and "In the Rufai Hall of Torture," (How the Syrian Howling Dervishes seek Religious Exaltation through Pain), *Asia*, XXVII, February, 1927, pp. 130-134, 151.

The Magic Island, referring to Haiti, was popularly received by at least a half million readers. Seabrook writes of his experiences in the Haitian mountains as he lived with the family of Maman Célie, a voodoo priestess who initiated him into the cult herself. He also describes various barbaric rites and repeats stories of sorcery and witchcraft gathered from the most primitive to the most cultured members of Haitian society. Only a few American scholars questioned his psychological approach and first-hand interpretations. Price-Mars wrote a lengthy, critical review (in French), including the historical origins of *Vaudou* and its relationship to Haitian life. While Seabrook, he said, undoubtedly had first-hand knowledge of various world wide religious practices, he had not chosen to write an objective analysis but instead had embellished facts with fantasy. (Text, page 128)

*Sébillot, Paul, *Le folk-lore:* littérature orale et ethnographicque traditionnelle, Paris, O. Doin et fils, 1913, one volume, (Footnotes 1, 2, and 3)

Söderblom, Nathan, *Manuel d'histoire des religions,* édition français by W. Corsevant, Paris, E. Leroux, 1925. (Footnote 146)
    Söderblom was primate of the Lutheran Church of Sweden (cathedral in Uppsala). He was an ecumenical world church leader, theologian, and historian of religions. In 1930 he was given the Nobel Peace Prize in recognition of an ecumenical spirit that sought "universal peace through Christian unity."

*Semple, Ellen Churchill, *Influences of Geographic Environment on the Basis of Ratzel's System of Anthropo-geography,* New York, H. Holt, 1911. (Footnote 45)

Sergent, Émile, Louis Ribadeau-Dumas, Léon Babonneix, editors of *Traité de pathologie médicale et de thérapeutique appliquée,* Paris A. Maloine et fils, 1920--, *Neurologie* et *Psychiatrie,* Volumes V, VI, VII, VIII. (Footnote 104)

de Sézellan (du Cap), _____, Lettre de M. de Sézellan du Cap, le 7 juin 1763, *Papiers de Saint-Domingue, Carton XV,* Paris. (Footnote 31)
    Sézellan is probably an Intendant or minor official of this type in Le Cap.

Shakespeare, William, *Hamlet,* Act I, Scene 5, Line 166: "There are more things in heaven and earth, Horatio, Than are dreamt of in your philosophy." (Quotation, see text, page 174)

Spieth, Jakob (1856-1914), *Die religion der Eweer in Süd-Togo,* Leipzig, J.C. Hinrichs, 1911. (Footnote 127)

*Stanley, Sir Henry Morton (1841-1904), *Through the Dark Continent,* 2 vol., London, S. Low, Marston, Searle and Rivington, 1878, or, *A travers le continent mystérieux,* 2 vol., translation by Mme., H. Loreau, Paris, Hachette, 1879; *In Darkest Africa,* 2 vol., London, S. Low, Marston, Searle and Rivington, 1890, or, *Dans les ténèbres de l'Afrique*, 2 vol., 1890. (Footnotes 34, 40)

Statius, Publius Papinius (c. A.D. 40-94).
    Statius was a Latin poet who wrote *The Thebais*, an epic in twelve books, about the expedition of seven kings to restore Polynices to the throne of Thebes. He was a great admirer of Virgil and tried to be an authentic follower of this tradition. (Footnote 18 and quotation, page 38)

Sylvain, Georges (1866-1925), *Cric? Crac?*, a translation of La Fontaine's *Fables* in a Creole version, Paris, Ateliers Haitiens, 1901, *Dix années de lutte pour la liberté (1915-1925)*, 2 vols., Port-au-Prince, Impr. H. Deschamps, 1959.
    Sylvain was a leading member of the Haitian literary school, *La Ronde*. He was Minister Plenipotentiary to Paris (1909-1911) and a leader of intellectual protest and resistance to the American Occupation until his death. He was president of l'Union Patriotique and founded *La Patrie* to voice his nationalistic sentiments. He believed that Haitian poetry justified itself and he often used the expressive Creole in preference to the French language. (Text, pages 178-179)

Taine, Hippolyte Adolphe, *Philosophie de l'art*, Paris, 1865, English translation by John Durand, New York, Henry Holt, 1865, contains lectures given to students of Art by this French historian during the winter of 1864 in Paris at the *Ecole des Beaux Arts* as Professeur d'Esthètique et d'Histoire de l'Art in this institution. (Footnote 60)

*Tauxier, Louis, *Le noir du Soudan*; pays Mossi et Gourounsi; documents et analyses, Paris, E. Larose, 1912. (Footnotes 42 and 141)

Thoms, William J. (1803-1885), English antiquarian, esp., on folklore of early England.
    Sébillot in *Le Folk-lore*, pages 1-3, tells us that Thoms was the author of the term *folk-lore*. Thoms, charged with writing the preface of the first publication of the Folk-Lore Society (*Folk-Lore Record* I, 1878, xiii-) used the pseudonym Ambrose Merton as he was too modest to reveal himself as the author of this term. This is rectified in *Folk-Lore Record* II, "First Report of the Council of Folk-Lore Society," p. 1-3, May 29,

1879. (Footnote 1 and text, pages 11-12)

*Toutée, Georges Joseph, *Du Dahomé au Sahara;* la nature et l'homme, Paris, A. Colin, 1907 (original 1899). (Footnote 126)

*Trouillot, Duverneau, *Esquisse ethnographique: Le Vaudoun; aperçu historique et évolutions,* Port-au-Prince, Impr. R. Ethéart, 1885. (Footnote 86)

Vaissière, Pierre de, *Sainte-Domingue,* Paris, Perrin et cie, 1909.
This is an excellent study, based on archival material, both French and English, and on rare publications. If one reads Leabeau, Peytraud, and Vaissière, one has an invaluable background for an understanding of conditions in Saint Domingue before the Revolution. (Footnote 29)

*Vallaux, Camille, *Géographie sociale: Le sol et l'état,* Paris, O. Doin et fils, 1911. (Footnote 46)

Verneau, René (1852-1938). Verneau is the author of *Anthropologie, Vol. II,* Section I, in *Les Grottes de Grimaldi* (Baousse-Rousse). . . , Monaco,Impr. de Monaco, 1906-1919, 2 vol. See also "Les Grottes de Grimaldi: Resumé et conclusions des études anthropologiques," *L'Anthropologie,* XVII, 1906, pp. 292-320. (Footnote 37 and text, page 61)

Washington, Booker T. See text page 175 and footnote [17].

Wilson, Leighton, *Western Africa: Its History, Condition, and Prospects,* New York, Harper and Brothers, 1856, (Reprint, Negro University Press, 1970).
Wilson was a missionary in Africa for eighteen years; later he was secetary of the Presbyterian Board of Foreign Missions. (Footnote 171)

*Woodring, Wendell P., John Stafford Brown, and Wilbur S. Burbank, *Geology of the Republic of Haiti,* Port-au-Prince, [Baltimore, The Lord Baltimore Press], 1924; in French, *Géologie de la République d'Haiti,* Port-au-Prince, 1924.

Zupanic, _____, "Les premiers habitants des pays Yougo-Slaves," *Revue Anthropologique,* 1919, p. 32. (Footnote 38)

Bibliography of the Translator

Antoine, Jacques C., *Jean Price-Mars and Haiti*, Washington, D.C., Three Continents Press, 1981.

Bastide, Roger, "Le Dr. J. Price-Mars et le Voudou," *Témoignages sur la vie et l'oeuvre du Dr. Jean Price Mars, 1876-1956*, Port-au-Prince, Imprimerie de l'Etat, 1956, pp. 196-202.

_____,"Price-Mars et le Vaudou haitien," *Présence Africaine*, 71, 3rd Quarterly 1969, pp. 19-23.

_____, *African Civilizations in the New World*, Translation from the French by Peter Green, New York, Harper and Row, 1971, (original, 1967).

Bastien, Rémy, "The Role of the Intellectual in Haitian Plural Society," *Annals of the New York Academy of Sciences*, 83, January 1960, pp. 843-849.

_____, "Vodoun and Politics in Haiti," in Harold Courlander and Rémy Bastien, *Religion and Politics in Haiti*, Washington, D.C., Institute for Cross-Cultural Research, 1966.

_____, "Idéologie, recherche et développement," in Emerson Douyon, ed., *Culture et développement en Haiti*, Montreal, Lémeac, 1972, pp. 121-130.

_____, "Social Anthropology: Recent Research and Recent Needs," in Vera Rubin and Richard P. Schaedel, eds., *The Haitian Potential*, New York, Teachers College Press, 1975, pp. 11-16.

Bellegarde, Dantes, *Pour une Haiti heureuse*, 2 vols., Port-au-Prince, Cheraquit, 1927-29.

_____, *La résistance haitienne*, Montreal, Editions Beauchemin, 1937.

_____ , "Hommage à Price-Mars," *Témoignages sur la vie et l'oeuvre du Dr. Jean Price Mars, 1876-1956*, Port-au-Prince, Imprimerie de l'Etat, 1956, pp. 6-10.

Berrian, Albert H. and Richard A. Long, eds., *Negritude: Essays and Studies*, Hampton, Virginia, Hampton Institute Press, 1967.

Bissainthe, Max, *Dictionnaire de bibliographie haitienne*, Washington, D.C., The Scarecrow Press, 1951, Supplement, I, 1973.

Bohannan, Paul, *Social Anthropology*, New York, Holt Rinehart Winston, 1963.

Bonhomme, Arthur. See Denis, Lorimer.

Bourguignon, Erika, *Religion, Altered States of Consciousness, and Social Change*, Columbus, Ohio State University Press, 1973.

_____, *Possession*, San Francisco, Chandler & Sharp, 1976.

Bulletin de l'Académie des Sciences Humaines et Sociales d'Haiti, No. 4, or *Revue de la Faculté d'Ethnologie*, No. 29, Port-au-Prince, Imprimerie Rodriguez, 1977.

The Cambridge History of Africa, III, Roland Oliver, ed., London, Cambridge University Press, 1977.

Catalogue général de la librairie française, Otto Lorenz and D. Jordell, eds., Paris, Librairie Nielsson, 1892-1934.

Chesnutt, Charles Waddell, *The House behind the Cedars*, Boston, Houghton Mifflin, 1900.

_____, *The Colonel's Dream*, New York, Doubleday, 1905.

Cornevin, Robert, "Le Docteur Jean Price-Mars premier laureat du prix des Caraibes," *Conjonction*, 103, 1966, pp. 11-13.

_____, "Jean Price-Mars (1876-1969)," *Introduction, Ainsi parla l'Oncle*, Third Edition, Montreal, Editions Lémeac, 1973.

Coulthard, G.R., *Race and Colour in Caribbean Literature*, London, Oxford University Press, 1962.

Courlander, Harold, *The Drum and the Hoe*, Berkeley, University of California Press, 1960.

_____, "Voudoun in Haitian Culture," in Harold Courlander and Rémy Bastien, *Religion and Politics in Haiti*, Washington, D.C., Institute for Cross-Cultural Research, 1966.

Damas, Leon G., "Price-Mars: The Father of Haitianism," in Albert H. Berrian and Richard A. Long, eds., *Negritude: Essays and Studies*, Hampton, Virginia, Hampton Institute Press, 1967, pp. 24-38.

Denis, Lorimer and François Duvalier, "La civilisation haitienne (Notre mentalité est-elle africaine ou gallo-latine?)," *Revue Anthropologique*, (Paris), 46, October-December 1936, pp. 353-373.

Denis, Lorimer, François Duvalier, and Arthur Bonhomme, *Les tendances d'une génération*, Port-au-Prince, 1934.

Dewey, Loring D., ed., *Correspondence Relative to the Emigration to Hayti of the Free People of Colour in the United States together with the Instructions to the Agent Sent out by President Boyer*, New York, 1824.

Dorland's Illustrated Medical Dictionary, Philadelphia, W.B. Saunders, 1974.

Douyon, Emerson, ed., *Culture et développement en Haiti*, Montreal, Lémeac, 1972.

Du Bois, William Edward Burghardt, *The Souls of Black Folk*, Chicago, A.C. McClurg, 1903.

————————————————, *The Negro*, New York, Henry Holt, 1915.

Durkheim, Emile, *Les formes élémentaires de la vie religieuse*, Paris, F. Alcan, 1912.

Duvalier, François. See Denis, Lorimer.

Evans-Pritchard, Edward Evan, "Levy-Bruhl's Theory of Primitive Mentality," *Bulletin of the Faculty of Arts*, 2: part 1 (Cairo), 1933.

————————————————, *The Nuer*, Oxford, Clarendon Press, 1940.

Foisset, R.P., "Ainsi parla l'Oncle," *La Phalange*, May 26-30, 1945.

——————————, "Le folklore," *La Phalange*, December 30, 1948.

Fouchard, Jean, *Les marrons du syllabaire*, Port-au-Prince, Henri Deschamps, 1953.

————————, "L'école nationaliste Price-Mars," *Témoignages sur la vie et l'oeuvre du Dr. Jean Price Mars, 1876-1956*, Port-au-Prince, Imprimerie de l'Etat, 1956, pp. 177-181.

——————————, *Le marrons de la liberté*, Paris, Editions de l'Ecole, 1972.

Frères de l'Instruction Chrétienne and Pradel Pompilus, *Manuel illustré d'histoire de la littérature haitienne*, Port-au-Prince, Henri Deschamps, 1961.

Gennep, Arnold van, *Religions, moeurs et légendes: essais d'ethnographie et de linguistique*, Paris, Mercure de France, 1908.

————————————, *Les rites de passage*, Paris, E. Nourry, 1909, translation in English, *The Rites of Passage* by Monika B. Visedom and Gabrielle L. Caffee, Chicago, University of Chicago Press, 1960.

Herdeck, Donald E., Maurice A. Lubin, et al, eds., *Caribbean Writers*, Washington, D.C., Three Continents Press, 1979.

Herskovits, Melville J., *Life in a Haitian Valley*, New York, Alfred A. Knopf, 1937.

_____, *Cultural Anthropology*, New York, Alfred A. Knopf, 1955.

Holly, Arthur (pseud., Her-Ra-Ma-ël), *Les daimens du culte Voudo*, Port-au-Prince, E. Chenet, 1918.

Holly, James Theodore, *A Vindication of the Capacity of the Negro Race for Self-Government, and Civilised Progress . . .*, New Haven, 1857.

Irele, Abiola, "Negritude or Black Cultural Nationalism," *Journal of Modern African Studies*, 3, October 1965, pp. 321-348.

Jahn, Janheinz, *Muntu*, translation from the German by Marjorie Grene, New York, Grove Press, 1961, (original, 1958).

_____, *Neo-African Literature*, translation by Oliver Coburn and Ursula Lehrburger, New York, Grove Press, 1969, (original, 1966).

Johnson, James Weldon, "Self-Determining Haiti," *The Nation*, III, 1920, Nos. 2878-2880, and 2882.

_____, *Black Manhattan*, New York, Alfred A. Knopf, 1930.

_____, *Along This Way*, New York, Viking Press, 1933.

Laguerre, Michel S., "The Place of Voodoo in the Social Structure of Haiti," *Caribbean Quarterly*, 19, September 1973, pp. 36-50.

_____, "Voodoo as Religious and Political Ideology," *Freeing the Spirit*, III, (1) 1974, pp. 23-28.

_____, *The Black Ghetto as an Internal Colony*, Ann Arbor, Michigan, University Microfilm International, 1980.

Laleau, Léon, "Ainsi parle un neveau . . .," *Témoignages sur la vie et l'oeuvre du Dr. Jean Price Mars, 1876-1956*, Port-au-Prince, Imprimerie de l'Etat, 1956, pp. 14-16.

Le Bon, Gustave, *The Psychology of Peoples*, 1924 edition, reprint of London edition, 1898, translated from Le Bon, *Les lois psychologiques de l'évolution des peuples*, Paris, Alcan, 1894.

Levy-Bruhl, Lucien, *How Natives Think*, New York, Alfred A. Knopf, 1926, translation into English by Lilian A. Clare of *Les fonctions mentales dans les sociétés inférieurs*, Paris, Alcan, 1910.

Lewis, Ioan M., *Ecstatic Religion: An Anthropological Study of Spirit Possession and Shamanism*, Harmondworth, Middlesex, England, Penguin Books, 1971.

Logan, Rayford W., "Education in Haiti," *Journal of Negro History*, XV, October 1930, pp. 401-460.

_____, *The Diplomatic Relations of the United States with Haiti, 1776-1891*, Chapel Hill, University of North Carolina Press, 1941.

Long, Richard. See Berrian, Albert H.

Lubin, Maurice A., "A Giant Dies — Leader of the Haitian Thought," *Negro History Bulletin*, 32, October 1969, pp. 16-18.

_____, *Haiti et Culture*, Paris, Louis Soulanges, 1974.

_____, See Herdeck, Donald E.

Mars, Louis, *The Crisis of Possession in Voodoo*, New York, Reed, Cannon & Johnson, 1977, translated from *La crise de possession*, Port-au-Prince, Imprimerie de l'Etat, 1946.

_____, "Phenomenon of 'Possession,' " *Tomorrow*, III, Autumn 1954, pp. 61-74.

_____, "Une nouvelle étape dans la réflexion sur les théolepsies en Haiti," *Cahiers des Religions Africaines*, 10, July 1976, pp. 203-210.

Murphy, Gardner, *Personality: A Biosocial Approach to Origins and Structure*, New York, Harper & Brothers, 1947.

The National Union Catalog Pre-1956 Imprints, The American Library Association, Chicago, Mansell Publishing, 1968-1979.

The New Century Cyclopedia of Names, Clarence Barnhart, ed., New York, Appleton-Century-Crofts, 1954.

The Oxford Classical Dictionary, London, Oxford University Press, 1970.

Paul, Emmanuel C., "Taches et responsabilités de l'ethnologie," *Revue de la Faculté d'Ethnologie*, Series III, December 1958-Jan/Mar 1959, pp. 11-19.

Paultre, Emile, *Essai sur M. Price-Mars*, Port-au-Prince, Editions des Antilles, 1966, Second edition, (including the first essay on Price-Mars, 1932).

Pestalozzi, Johann Heinrich, *Wie Gertrud ihre Kinder lehrt*, Bern, H. Gessner, 1801.

_____, *Schwanengesang*, 1826.

Pompilus, Pradel. See Frères de l'Instruction Chrétienne.

Pressoir, Catts, "Ainsi parla l'Oncle," *Le Nouvelliste,* October 20,22,23, 1928.

Price-Mars, Jean, *La vocation de l'élite,* Port-au-Prince, Edmond Chenet, 1919.

_____, *Ainsi parla l'Oncle,* Imprimerie de Compiegne (France), 1928.

_____, *Une étape de l'évolution haitienne,* Port-au-Prince, La Presse, 1929.

_____, *La renaissance nègre aux Etats-Unis de l'Amérique du nord,* Port-au-Prince, La Presse, 1929.

_____, *Préface* to *La montagne ensorcelée* by Jacques Roumain, Port-au-Prince, Imprimerie du S.N.P.E., 1931.

_____, *Préface* to Lorimer Denis, François Duvalier, and Arthur Bonhomme, *Les tendances d'une génération,* Port-au-Prince, Impr. du Collège Vertières, 1934.

_____, "Classe ou Caste," a study of *The Haitian People,* James G. Leyburn, 1941, *Revue de la Société d'Histoire et de Géographie d'Haiti,* XIII, July 1942, pp. 1-50.

_____, "Ma réponse à l'attaque de M. l'Abbé Foisset," *Haiti Journal,* June 18-21, 1945.

_____, "Sociologie religieuse, Essai critique," *Revue de la Société Haitienne d'Histoire et de Géographie,* 19, October 1948, pp. 1-21.

_____, *La République d'Haiti et la République Dominicaine,* 2 Vol., Port-au-Prince, 1953. Also in Spanish.

_____, *Lettre ouverte au Dr. René Piquion: le préjugé de couleur est-il la question sociale?,* Port-au-Prince, Editions des Antilles, 1967.

_____, *Antenor Firmin,* Port-au-Prince, Imp. Seminaire Adventiste, 1978 (posthumous).

Price-Mars, Marie Madeleine, *Notice Biographique et Bibliographique du Dr. Jean Price-Mars.*

Redpath, James, *A Guide to Hayti,* Boston, Haytian Bureau of Emigration, 1861, Reprint, Westport, Conn., Negro Universities Press, 1970.

Romain, Jean Baptiste, "Jean Price-Mars ethnologue," *Conjonction,* 110, 1969, pp. 3-7.

_____, *Quelques moeurs et coutumes des paysans haitiens,* Port-au-Prince, Imprimerie de l'Etat, 1959.

—————————, "Introduction au Vodou haitien," *Conjonction*, 112, 1970, pp. 3-17.

—————————, *L'anthropologie physique des Haitiens*, Port-au-Prince, Imp. Seminaire Adventiste, 1971.

Rubin, Vera and Richard P. Schaedel, eds., *The Haitian Potential*, New York, Teachers College Press, Columbia University, 1975.

Schaedel, Richard P. See Rubin, Vera.

Shannon, Magdaline W., "President's Commission for the Study and Review of Conditions in Haiti and its Relationship to Hoover's Foreign Policy," *Caribbean Studies*, XV, January 1976.

Simpson, George E., "The Belief System of Haitian Vodun," *American Anthropologist*, 47, January 1945, pp. 35-39.

—————————, "Au Dr. Price-Mars," *Témoignages sur la vie et l'oeuvre du Dr. Jean Price Mars, 1876-1956*, Port-au-Prince, Imprimerie de l'Etat, 1956, p. 48.

—————————, *Religious Cults of the Caribbean: Trinidad, Jamaica, and Haiti*, Rio Piedras, Puerto Rico, Institute of Caribbean Studies, University of Puerto Rico, 1970.

—————————, *Black Religions in the New World*, New York, Columbia University Press, 1978.

Smith, Michael G., *Dark Puritan*, Kingston, University of the West Indies, 1963.

Témoignages sur la vie et l'oeuvre du Dr. Jean Price Mars, 1876-1956, Port-au-Prince, Imprimerie de l'Etat, 1956.

Trouillot, Henock, "La pensée du Docteur Jean Price-Mars," *Revue de la Société Haitienne d'Histoire, de Gèographie et de Géologie*, 29, July-October 1956, entire issue.

—————————, "Le Jubilé du Dr. Jean Price-Mars," Part I, and "La signification d'un Congres," Part II, *Revue de la Société Haitienne d'Histoire, de Géographie et de Géologie*, III, January-April 1957, pp. 55-82.

Tylor, Sir Edward Burnett, *Primitive Culture*, London, Murray, 1871.

United States Department of the Interior, *Report of the Secretary of the Interior, 1863*, Washington, D.C., U.S. Government Printing Office, 1864.

Verschueren, J. (psued. for Op-Hey, Henri), *La République d'Haiti*, 3 vol., Weltren, Belgium, 1948, (especially Vol. III, *Le culte du Vaudoux en Haiti: ophiolâtrie et animisme*).

Viatte, Auguste, "L'oeuvre de Price-Mars dans son cadre mondial,"

Témoignages sur la vie et l'oeuvre du Dr. Jean Price Mars, 1876-1956, Port-au-Prince, Imprimerie de l'Etat, 1956.

——————————, *L'anthologie littéraire de l'Amérique francophone*, Sherbrooke, Québec, CELEF, 1971.

Washington, Booker T., *Up From Slavery*, New York, Doubleday, Page & Co., 1901.

Wesley, Charles H., "Lincoln's Plan for Colonizing the Emancipated Negroes," *Journal of Negro History*, IV, January 1919, pp. 7-21.

World Who's Who in Science (from antiquity to the present), The Marquis Biographical Library, Chicago, Marquis Who's Who, 1968.

Yinger, J. Milton, *Toward a Field Theory of Behavior*, New York, Macmillan, 1970.

——————————, *The Scientific Study of Religion*, New York, Macmillan, 1970.